MENTAL FILES

Mental Files

———

FRANÇOIS RECANATI

OXFORD
UNIVERSITY PRESS

OXFORD
UNIVERSITY PRESS

Great Clarendon Street, Oxford, OX2 6DP,
United Kingdom

Oxford University Press is a department of the University of Oxford.
It furthers the University's objective of excellence in research, scholarship,
and education by publishing worldwide. Oxford is a registered trade mark of
Oxford University Press in the UK and in certain other countries

First Edition published in 2012

Impression: 1

British Library Cataloguing in Publication Data
Data available

Library of Congress Cataloging in Publication Data
Data available

ISBN 978–0–19–965998–2 (hbk)
978–0–19–965999–9 (pbk)

Printed in Great Britain by
MPG Books Group, Bodmin and Kings's Lynn

I really do think that this file story helps (a bit) with empirical theorizing about the cognitive mind.

(Fodor 2008: 96)

PREFACE

The idea of a mental file or 'dossier' was introduced by several philosophers in the late 1960s or early 1970s, in connection with the referential use of definite descriptions (Grice 1969: 140–4) or with identity statements (Lockwood 1971: 208–11; Strawson 1974: 54–6). It was subsequently exploited by several authors, including Evans (1973: 199 ff., 1982: 276), Bach (1987: 34–7), Devitt (1989: 227–31), Forbes (1989, 1990: 538–45), Crimmins (1992: 87–92), and myself (Recanati 1993: chapters 7, 10, and 15), but the most influential elaboration is due to John Perry, to whom I am heavily indebted. (Perry's first sustained appeal to mental files occurs in his 1980 paper 'A Problem about Continued Belief'. He has written extensively about the topic ever since.) At about the same time, similar notions were introduced into linguistics to deal with definiteness, anaphora, and information structure (Karttunen 1976; Du Bois 1980; Reinhart 1981; Heim 1983, 1988; Vallduví 1992, 1994; Erteschik-Shir 1997), and into cognitive science in connection with memory, perception, and attention (Anderson and Hastie 1974; Anderson 1977; Treisman and Schmidt 1982; Kahneman and Treisman 1984; Treisman 1988, 1992; Kahneman, Treisman, and Gibbs 1992).[1,2] The theory of mental files presented in this book has connections to these various uses of the

---

[1] Given this chronology, it is not quite right to say that 'the provenance of the file idea is…unphilosophical' (Fodor 2008: 124 n.).

[2] I have mentioned some of the works in which the file notion explicitly occurs, but it also occurs implicitly in Strawson's early work, e.g. in 'Singular Terms and Predication' (1961) or 'Identifying Reference and Truth-Values' (1964) when he talks about 'stretches of identifying knowledge' (Strawson 1971: 63, 79). In the same vein as Strawson, Chafe talks of human knowledge as consisting of 'a large number of cognitive units which are our knowledge of particular individuals and events' (Chafe 1976: 43). (I haven't searched

notion of file. These connections are well worth exploring, since they are what ultimately gives the theory its empirical bite. In this book, however, I am only concerned with the conceptual foundations. My focus, like that of the other philosophers writing on the topic, is on how mental files can shed light on singular reference in language and thought.

According to the theory I present here (a sequel to that in *Direct Reference*), we refer through mental files, which play the role of so-called 'modes of presentation'.[3] The reference of linguistic expressions is inherited from that of the files we associate with them. The reference of a file is determined relationally, not satisfactionally; so a file is not to be equated to the body of (mis-)information it contains. Files are like singular terms in the language of thought, with a non-descriptivist semantics. In contrast to other authors, I offer an *indexical model* according to which files are typed by their function, which is to store information derived through certain types of relation to objects in the environment. The type of the file corresponds to the type of contextual relation it exploits. Even detached files or 'encyclopedia entries' (as I call them in *Direct Reference*) are based on epistemically rewarding relations to their referent, on my account.

The file metaphor has been extremely popular lately and I am indebted to many of those whose investigations converge with mine. I am grateful, in particular, to the participants in two workshops I organized in Paris on the themes of this book: the Mental Files workshop in November 2010 (with Imogen Dickie, Graeme Forbes, Robin Jeshion, Krista Lawlor, Christopher Peacocke, John Perry, Jim Pryor, Laura Schroeter) and the Perceptual Concepts and

---

earlier sources, but one might. Thus, according to Kevin Mulligan—referring to Beyer (2008)—the file notion occurs in Husserl's work.)

[3] That is actually a triple role: modes of presentation are supposed to account for 'cognitive significance', for clustering/coordination of information, and for reference determination.

Demonstrative Thought workshop in February 2011 (with Joseph Levine, Christopher Mole, and David Papineau).

I learnt a lot from the questions and responses of the audience on several occasions on which I presented materials from the book, especially the Barcelona workshop on Singular Thought in January 2009, several seminars (or workhops) at the University of St Andrews and at Institut Jean-Nicod in 2010 and 2011, my Gareth Evans Memorial Lecture at the University of Oxford in January 2011, the BPPA Masterclass in philosophy I gave in London in April 2011, the second and third PETAF workshops (Cerisy-la-Salle, June 2011, and Budapest, September 2011), the Philosophy of linguistics/Mental phenomena workshop in Dubrovnik in September 2011, and the first meeting of the PLM network in Stockholm also in September. After finishing a draft of the book, I used it as basis for a series of six talks on language and thought at Ruhr-Universität Bochum from November 2011 to January 2012, at the invitation of Albert Newen, and I benefited from the discussions that followed each of the talks (as well as from those that followed the talks I gave in Cologne and Düsseldorf shortly afterwards). I also benefited from the discussions that took place in my EHESS seminar on mental files in 2011–12.

I am much indebted to my graduate students, particularly Gregory Bochner, Marie Guillot, Michael Murez, Andrea Onofri, and Felipe Nogueira de Carvalho, for insightful discussions of the topics dealt with in the book. Michael Murez deserves special thanks. He provided a wealth of comments and challenges at every step in the elaboration of this work and I am most grateful to him. I owe a good deal also to Daniel Morgan and Thea Goodsell, and to Peter Momtchiloff's anonymous advisers, for written comments which helped me to improve the final version of the book.

I have re-used materials from a few published or forthcoming papers in the book, namely: 'The Communication of First-Person Thoughts' (1995), 'Singular Thought: In Defence of Acquaintance' (2010a), 'Mental Files and Identity' (2011), 'Empty Singular Terms in the Mental-File Framework' (2012*b*), 'Reference through Mental Files' (forthcoming *a*), and 'Perceptual Concepts: In Defence of the Indexical Model' (forthcoming *b*). I thank the editors and publishers of the relevant journals or volumes for the permission to re-use the materials in question.

Finally, I gratefully acknowledge support from the European Community's Seventh Framework Programme FP7/2007–2013 under grant agreement n° FP7-238128 and especially ERC grant agreement n° 229441–CCC.

CONTENTS

Part I

Singular Thought and Acquaintance:
Rejecting Descriptivism

1

Singularism vs Descriptivism

1

Descriptivism is the view that our mental relation to individual objects goes through properties of those objects. What are given to us are, first and foremost, properties whose worldly instantiation we are able to detect, and only indirectly objects. That is so because (according to the view) our knowledge of objects is mediated by our knowledge of their properties.[1] Objects are given to us only qua instantiators of whatever properties we take them to have. On this view, my friend John is only given to me as the x who has all (or perhaps most of) the properties I take him to have: being my friend, being called 'John', having a certain appearance, having a certain history (e.g. having been my classmate in such and such years), and so on and so forth. Whoever has the relevant properties—assuming a single individual does—is John. Likewise, the computer I am typing on is the x that has the properties of being (or looking like) a computer, being in front of me, having been bought by me at such and such a place at such and such a time, being currently used by me for typing,

---

[1] 'The descriptivist strategy is to explain the capacity to refer to concrete individuals in terms of a capacity to refer to the properties and relations that are exemplified by such individuals, things that might more plausibly be thought of as internal to the mind, or at least as things that the mind could grasp from the inside' (Stalnaker 2008: 12).

and so on and so forth.[2] On the descriptivist picture, 'we get at physical objects only by a semantic shot in the dark: we specify properties or relations and hope that they are uniquely exemplified' (Chastain 1975: 254).

Since, according to Descriptivism, we live in a qualitative world of properties—a world where objects only have secondary or derivative status, from an epistemic point of view—it would be philosophically revealing if we purged our language of its singular terms, as Quine recommended (Quine 1960: 181–6). Thus regimented, our language would be able to express only so-called 'general propositions', i.e. propositions about properties, such as the proposition that every F is G, or the proposition that nothing is both F and G. Translated into such a descriptivist language, statements allegedly about individual objects turn out to express general propositions: 'a is G' translates as 'The F is G', and, as Russell pointed out, 'The F is G' expresses a general proposition just like 'An F is G', 'Every F is G' or 'No F is G'.

In contrast to Descriptivism, Singularism holds that our thought is about individual objects as much as it is about properties. Objects are given to us directly, in experience, and we do not necessarily think of them as the bearers of such and such properties (even though the properties of objects are revealed to us when we encounter them in experience). On this view the Quinean 'elimination of singular terms' is a bad idea. We can think of individual objects in two ways, according to Singularism. We can think of them directly, if we are acquainted with them in experience; or we can think of them indirectly, qua bearers of such and such properties. It can be maintained that the content of a 'descriptive' thought—a thought that is only indirectly about individual objects—is a general proposition, i.e. a proposition that involves only properties; but Singularism differs

[2] The last two sentences sound like metaphysical claims, but Descriptivism is a semantic/epistemological thesis, not a metaphysical thesis. As Jackson puts it, to argue for Descriptivism 'is not to advance the controversial view that objects are bundles of properties; it is to insist that we access objects via their properties' (Jackson 1998a: 216).

from Descriptivism in holding that, in addition to such thoughts, there are also *singular thoughts*: thoughts that are directly about individual objects, and whose content is a singular proposition—a proposition involving individual objects as well as properties.[3]

To a large extent, the history of the philosophy of language and mind in the twentieth century centres around the debate between Singularism and Descriptivism. Analytic philosophy in England started with Russell's and Moore's advocacy of 'direct realism', a doctrine according to which we are directly acquainted with objects and properties in the world. Over the years, despite radical changes in his doctrines, Russell kept opposing knowledge by acquaintance to knowledge by description. Russell's insistence on acquaintance and direct reference led him to reject Frege's sense/reference distinction, on the grounds that, if reference is mediated by sense, we lose the idea of direct acquaintance and succumb to Descriptivism (Hylton 2005). As I am about to argue (§2), this was Russell's major mistake. First, contrary to what Russell thought, Frege's distinction is not incompatible with Singularism (even though Frege himself had clear descriptivist tendencies); that we have learnt from the work of Gareth Evans, another major twentieth-century advocate of Singularism (Evans 1982, 1985; see also McDowell 1977 and 1984). Second, and more important, once you give up Frege's sense/reference distinction in favour of a monostratal semantics à la Russell, you are bound to embrace some form of Descriptivism: that is exactly what happened to Russell. After Russell himself became a descriptivist, Descriptivism became the orthodoxy. It took decades before the community of analytic philosophers as a whole rediscovered Singularism and rejected Descriptivism.

---

[3] Again, Descriptivism and Singularism as I am describing them are semantic/epistemological theses, not metaphysical theses. Thus to say, with Quine, that singular terms can be dispensed with is not to say that *the world* does not consist of objects. As Pérez Otero (2006: 260–4) emphasizes, Quine was an ontological singularist (or 'particularist'), despite his Descriptivism, while Kripke is a singularist on both counts.

Today, in the twenty-first century, the situation is changing once again. Some philosophers attempt to revive Descriptivism by putting forward more sophisticated versions aimed at disarming some of the objections that made it fall into discredit in the 1970s. Others attack Singularism construed as a dogma we unquestioningly inherited from our elders. Acquaintance, they tell us, is a myth.[4] My aim in this book is to defend Singularism, and to provide a specific version: the mental file approach. I will argue that it is a better and more promising view than even the most sophisticated versions of Descriptivism.

2

For Russell, knowledge is, or rests on, a direct relation between the mind and things outside the mind. This relation Russell calls 'acquaintance'. Without a direct relation of acquaintance between the mind and its objects, no genuine 'knowledge of the external world' would be possible, Russell thought. That is the doctrine of *direct realism*, which Russell and Moore opposed to neo-Hegelian idealism. This non-negotiable principle—that knowledge is based on a direct relation of acquaintance between the mind and its objects—leaves it open what exactly acquaintance amounts to, and, in particular, which entities one can be acquainted with and which one cannot. But Russell thought that the principle of acquaintance itself had semantic consequences, and that it was incompatible with Frege's doctrine about sense and reference.

Besides knowing objects, the mind knows truths about objects. Let us assume, as both Frege and Russell did in their discussion involving that example, that we know that Mont Blanc is 4,000

---

[4] Thus the most recent book on the topic starts with the following declaration: 'None of the several reasons that have been offered for imposing an acquaintance constraint on singular thought can stand up to scrutiny. Acquaintance is an unnecessary artifact, an unwanted relic of a bygone era in the philosophy of language and mind' (Hawthorne and Manley forthcoming: chapter 1).

metres high. Knowledge here is a relation between the mind and a 'proposition', namely, the (true) proposition that Mont Blanc is 4,000 metres high. Frege and Russell agreed that the mind is related to propositions (in Frege's terminology: thoughts) which it 'grasps'; but they disagreed about the nature and constituency of such propositions. For Frege, a proposition about Mont Blanc does not involve Mont Blanc itself (the *reference* of the proper name 'Mont Blanc') but a mode of presentation of Mont Blanc (the *sense* of the proper name). For Russell, grasping and believing the proposition that Mont Blanc is 4,000 metres high gives us knowledge about Mont Blanc only if Mont Blanc itself is a constituent of the proposition. If the proposition contains some mediating entity rather than the object itself, it will not be about the object in the strong sense which is required for knowledge. So, unless 'Mont Blanc itself is a component part [of the proposition]...we get the conclusion that we know nothing at all about Mont Blanc' (Letter to Frege, 12 December 1904, in Frege 1980: 169). Russell therefore advocated a one-level semantics, in which the meaning or content of a representation (whether linguistic or mental) is its reference, and nothing else. The meaning of a singular term is an individual object; the meaning of a predicate is a property or a relation; the meaning of a sentence is a proposition, that is, an 'objective complex' involving objects (if the proposition is singular) and properties or relations.

But as I said, that departure from Frege was a major mistake. Like Frege, Russell accepts that propositions are the content of attitudes such as belief. In order to play that role, propositions must obey certain obvious constraints. For example, it must *not* be possible for a rational subject to believe and disbelieve one and the same proposition. But it is certainly possible for a rational subject looking at a particular mountain to believe that the mountain in question is less than 4,000 metres high even though (i) that mountain is Mont Blanc, and (ii) the subject in question believes that Mont Blanc is 4,000 metres high. Such a situation may obtain if the subject does not realize that the mountain she is seeing is Mont Blanc. In that sort of case Frege is safe, for he can appeal to senses or modes of presentation: what the subject is said simultaneously to believe and disbelieve is not one and the same proposition (namely the proposition that a given mountain is 4,000 metres high) but two distinct propositions, involving two distinct modes of presentation of what turns out to be the same mountain. The subject believes of that mountain under mode of presentation m_1 that it is less than 4,000 metres high, and of the same mountain under mode of presentation m_2 that it is 4,000 metres high. Since $m_1 \neq m_2$, there is no irrationality on the subject's part. Russell, however, is forced to say that the subject holds contradictory beliefs. Since, in his framework, no senses go into the proposition believed, but only the mountain itself (the same in both cases), he cannot avoid the conclusion that the subject simultaneously believes and disbelieves the proposition consisting of the mountain in question and the property of being 4,000 metres high.

At this point two rescue options are available but they are both deeply unattractive. The first option consists in denying that propositions understood à la Russell—R-propositions, for short—are the complete content of the attitudes, i.e. that in terms of which we should account for the subject's rationality. On this option, R-propositions are said to be believed or disbelieved only under guises. This option, which has been pursued by some philosophers in the so-called 'neo-Russellian' camp, amounts to a concession of defeat; for guises are nothing but modes of presentation, and modes of presentation are now allowed to enter into finer-grained propositions construed as the *complete* content of the attitudes. Far from conflicting with Frege's construal of propositions as involving senses, this view merely introduces a new, coarser-grained notion of 'proposition', namely R-propositions, playing a different role and corresponding roughly to an equivalence class of Fregean propositions. This is a variant of Frege's two-level approach rather than a genuine alternative of the sort Russell was after. In any case, Russell himself insisted that propositions in his sense—R-propositions—*are* the object of the attitudes and should therefore be answerable to considerations of cognitive significance. There is no difference between Russellian propositions and Fregean propositions on this score. This means that the option I have just sketched was not really available to Russell.

The other option is what Russell went for. It consists in maintaining the general principle of direct reference, while giving up its application to the case at hand (and to any case that raises the same sort of objection). So, in the Mont Blanc case, contrary to what Russell initially thought, the subject does *not* hold a belief that is about Mont Blanc in the strong and direct sense which he was interested in characterizing. The fact that the subject is disposed to ascribe contradictory predicates to the same mountain shows that she thinks of that mountain under distinct guises, hence that her beliefs are only indirectly about the mountain. What the subject really believes, in the above scenario, are the following propositions: that *the mountain she is seeing* (or, in Russell's framework, that *the object that is causing such and such visual sense-data*) is less than 4,000 metres high, and that *the mountain known as 'Mont Blanc'* is 4,000 metres high. These propositions contradict each other only given the extra premise that the mountain the subject is seeing is the mountain known as 'Mont Blanc'. In the case at hand, precisely, the subject does not believe the extra premise, so her rationality is preserved. As for Russell, his theoretical position is also preserved: he can maintain that, for the subject to entertain a singular belief about an object *a*, *a* must be a component part of the proposition which she believes. In our scenario the propositions believed by the subject only involve (possibly relational) properties such as the property of being currently seen by the subject or the property of being known as 'Mont Blanc'; they do not involve Mont Blanc itself. It follows that the subject does *not* hold a singular belief about Mont Blanc, appearances notwithstanding. She holds only general beliefs about whatever mountain she is seeing, or whatever mountain is called 'Mont Blanc'. The subject's thought concerns Mont Blanc only indirectly, via descriptions such as 'the mountain I see' or 'the mountain called *Mont Blanc*'; and the same thing is true whenever the subject is disposed to ascribe contradictory predicates to some object her thought is, in some loose sense, 'about'. Russell is thus led to hold that we are acquainted with, and can directly refer to, only a very limited number of individual objects: objects that are given to us *in such a transparent manner that no identity mistake can arise*. The list of such objects is rather short: the immediate data of the outer senses, the data of introspection, and possibly ourselves, are the candidates which Russell cites. The *other* things—ordinary objects like Mont Blanc, this chair, or my friend John—we know only 'by description', via properties which these objects possess and with which we *are* acquainted.[5]

---

[5] 'Among the objects with which we are acquainted are not included physical objects (as opposed to sense data), nor other people's minds. These things are known to us by what I call "knowledge by description"' (Russell 1912: 81). 'The sense-data which make up the appearance of my table are things with which I have acquaintance, things immediately known to me just as they are. My knowledge of the table as a physical object, on the contrary, is not direct knowledge. Such as it is, it is obtained through acquaintance with the sense-data that make up the appearance of the table…The table is "the physical object which causes such-and-such sense-data." This *describes* the table by means of the sense-data' (Russell 1912: 74). Note that, for Russell, sense-data themselves are 'particulars'; so it is not fully accurate to describe Russell's view as the view that we know objects only through their properties. The description is accurate only if we specify, as I did in the text, that the properties in question may be relational. Thus, for Russell, we know the table through 'its colour, shape, hardness, smoothness, etc.' (Russell 1912: 73), but these 'things of which I am immediately conscious when I am seeing and touching my table' (id.) are not, at a fundamental level, properties of the table but rather particulars bearing certain *relations* to the table. We know ordinary objects such as the table via their relations to these particulars with which we are directly and transparently acquainted. This brand of Descriptivism I call 'Relational Descriptivism'. David Lewis, whose position I will discuss in the concluding chapter, held such a view. According to Relational Descriptivism, ordinary objects are thought of descriptively, in terms of their relations to special objects which are given to us directly. For Russell, the special objects in question are the data of our senses (both outer and inner). For Lewis, the special object is the subject-at-the-time-of-thinking—the 'centre' in Lewis's centred-worlds framework. Relational Descriptivism is a partial form of Descriptivism in that not everything is thought of descriptively: the special objects are an exception (we are directly acquainted with them). But this is Descriptivism nonetheless because ordinary objects of reference, such as the objects we perceive around us (e.g. the table), *are* thought of descriptively.

For a singularist that option is a disaster. It enables Russell to maintain the contrast between the two kinds of knowledge—direct and indirect, by acquaintance or by description—only by so drastically limiting the first kind that Russell now appears as the champion of Descriptivism. On the resulting view, almost all of our knowledge of individual objects is knowledge by description. The most typical sort of knowledge of objects by acquaintance, namely perceptual knowledge (such as the knowledge one gains of Mont Blanc when one sees the peak), now counts as knowledge by description. Defeat has not been conceded, since the idea of acquaintance remains (and acquaintance still is the foundation for all our knowledge); but defeat has taken place nonetheless. In contrast to our knowledge of the internal world, our knowledge of the external world—our knowledge of the mountains and chairs around us—is indirect, descriptive knowledge based on properties. Descriptivism rules.

3

The disaster could have been avoided. For Frege's two-level semantics, far from entailing the indirectness of all our knowledge, was in fact the surest way of protecting Singularism from cognitive significance objections of the sort Russell's Singularism succumbed to. Let me spell this out.

First, Frege's two-level semantics does not entail the indirectness of all our knowledge, because it is possible to make room for *non-descriptive senses*, i.e. senses that are acquaintance-based. On the 'neo-Fregean' approach advocated by McDowell, Evans, Peacocke, and others, there is a basic distinction between knowledge by acquaintance and knowledge by description, as on Russell's approach. When I see the mountain, I get acquainted with it. But this does not mean that the mountain is not presented to me in a particular way, distinct from other ways it might be presented to me. In experience, we are acquainted with objects, but this is compatible with there being modes of presentation under which we are acquainted with them. What follows from the contrast between the two kinds of knowledge is not the lack of any mode of presentation in the acquaintance case, but only the lack of any *descriptive* mode of presentation. Russell's claim that a two-level semantics à la Frege is incompatible with Singularism therefore depends upon an overly narrow, descriptivist construal of 'sense', a construal that was encouraged by Frege himself but which was by no means mandatory.

Second, once we have acquaintance-based senses in addition to the objects of acquaintance (the referents), cognitive significance objections are powerless to threaten Singularism. It is no longer possible to claim that the subject is not in direct contact with the object, on the grounds that identity mistakes are possible. Identity mistakes admittedly reveal that the object is given to the subject under varying modes of presentation, but the object's being given under a mode of presentation no longer entails that it is not given 'directly'. Modes of presentation are now construed as *ways the object is given to the subject*, and an object may be given either directly, in experience, or indirectly, via descriptions. Non-descriptive modes of presentation are ways the object is (directly) given to the subject in experience, while descriptive modes of presentation are ways the object is (indirectly) given via properties which it uniquely instantiates. When, facing Mont Blanc, the subject thinks 'That mountain is less than 4,000 metres high', she thinks of Mont Blanc under a non-descriptive mode of presentation based on her perceptual relation to Mont Blanc. Such a mode of presentation presupposes acquaintance and can only be grasped by a subject who is suitably related to the object the thought is about. When the subject thinks 'The tallest mountain in Europe is 4,000 metres high', her thought is about Mont Blanc only in a weaker, indirect sense: she now thinks of Mont Blanc under a descriptive mode of presentation, and the resulting thought is one that can be grasped even if one is not acquainted with Mont Blanc. The neo-Fregean framework therefore enables us to maintain the basic contrast which Russell's one-level semantics forced him to give up: that between a demonstrative thought such as 'That mountain is less than 4,000 metres high', which is singular and can only be grasped if one is suitably acquainted with the mountain, and a descriptive thought like 'The tallest mountain in Europe is 4,000 metres high', which is general in nature and sets no such acquaintance requirement.

The idea of 'directness' turns out to be ambiguous. 'Direct reference' can mean that the only meaning or content of a representation is its reference, to the exclusion of any sense or mode of presentation, as in Russell's one-level semantics; or it can mean, as in singularist frameworks, that the subject is directly acquainted with the object in experience and does not think of it descriptively as the instantiator of such and such property. The two ideas are clearly independent, and it was a mistake on Russell's part to argue from Singularism to the rejection of Frege's two-level approach. I call it a major mistake because I think Russell's one-level semantics is what killed Singularism by letting it succumb to cognitive significance objections.

My aim in this book is to defend Singularism; so I will assume a two-level semantics with a sense-reference distinction.[6] In such a framework, the singularist distinction between knowledge by description and knowledge by acquaintance reduces to the distinction between two kinds of sense or mode of presentation: descriptive and non-descriptive.

Before presenting my version of the view, based on the idea of a mental file (Part II), I want to say something more about Descriptivism. If the Fregean, two-level framework can accommodate the basic distinction between knowledge by acquaintance and knowledge by description, as following Evans I have argued it can, why should it

---

[6] Since, in my framework, mental files are what plays the role of sense, and mental files are representational 'vehicles', it can be argued that the theory put forth in this book is *not* a two-level semantics à la Frege. For discussion of this issue (and remarks on the ambiguity of 'sense'), see Chapter 18, §1.

not be possible for Descriptivism itself to accommodate that distinction? Can we not make Descriptivism sophisticated enough to solve the problems it faces and account for whatever facts have to be accounted for? In Chapter 2, I will show that, indeed, some of the singularist objections can be met by moving to more sophisticated versions of Descriptivism. I will present what I take to be the best possible version, since the best possible versions of both theories should be used in assessing the relative merits of Descriptivism and Singularism.

2

Can Descriptivism Account
for Singularity?

1

The most obvious problem with Descriptivism is that it ascribes, or seems to ascribe, the wrong truth-conditions to prima facie singular thoughts—e.g. the thought that that peak [pointing to Mont Blanc] is less than 4,000 metres high. I assume that such thoughts have *singular truth-conditions* (Recanati 1988: 113, 1993: 16; see also Peacocke 1975: 110–12, Schiffer 1977: 30–1). Whenever a thought has singular truth-conditions, the following schema holds:

There is an object x such that the thought is true with respect to an arbitrary possible world w if and only if, in w,... x...

In our example, there is a certain object x, namely Mont Blanc, such that the thought 'That peak is less than 4,000 metres high' is true if and only if x is (a peak) less than 4,000 metres high. An individual object is irreducibly involved in the thought's truth-conditions, which cannot be stated without referring to it.[1] That fact is arguably what motivates Russellian talk of 'singular

[1] A descriptive thought such as the thought that the highest peak is 4,000 metres high does not have singular truth-conditions, for the following reason. *Any* object's being both the highest peak and 4,000 metres high would be sufficient to make the thought true (Peacocke 1975: 111), so there is no particular object x such that *only* x's

propositions' involving the object itself. But Descriptivism has trouble capturing that singularity: it construes such thoughts as (directly) only about properties. Thus Russell, in his descriptivist phase, would have analysed the proposition expressed by 'That peak is less than 4,000 metres high' as 'containing', in addition to the property of being less than 4,000 metres high, not an object (the peak) but *another property*, for instance the property of being a peak currently seen by the subject. As a result the thought only has general truth-conditions: it is true iff *some object or other* has a certain complex of properties. Any object will do: there is no specific object *x* such that the thought is true iff *x* has the relevant properties. The connection to the individual object which the subject is actually seeing is lost, as is the contrast between such thoughts and truly general thoughts (such as the thought that *some peak* is less than 4,000 metres high, or the thought that *the tallest peak in Europe* is 4,000 metres high).

There may still be philosophers who are sceptical of the 'intuition' that demonstrative judgements have singular truth-conditions that tie them to particular objects. Invoking that intuition, they may argue, simply begs the question against the descriptivist. I will not go into that debate, for denying our truth-conditional intuitions regarding rigidity and singular reference is not the dominant strategy to adopt if you are a descriptivist faced with the above objection. The dominant strategy consists in showing that Descriptivism has the resources for accounting for the singularity intuition.

having such and such properties would make the thought true. There is an implicit modal element here, as indicated by the phrase 'would make the thought true': the truth-conditions I am talking about are the 'possible-world truth-conditions' of the thought, not its 'actual truth-conditions' (see Kripke 1980: 6–7 for the relevant distinction). That is the reason why, in contrast to earlier versions (including that in Recanati 2000: 325–6), I have formulated the schema in terms of 'truth with respect to an arbitrary possible world'. I am indebted to Graeme Forbes and Jeff King, and also to Quine (2000: 429), for discussion of this issue.

To get the truth-conditions right, it is claimed, the descriptivist only has to go two-dimensional. On this view, what 'That peak is less than 4,000 metres high' expresses is the general proposition that *the peak actually seen by the subject* is less than 4,000 metres high. What the operator 'actually' does here is rigidify the description. The proposition is still general, but the rigidifier forces the description to pick out its referent in the 'context' rather than in the 'circumstance of evaluation'. In the context at hand, the description denotes an object (namely Mont Blanc—the peak which happens to be currently seen by the subject). That object is not a component of the proposition— the proposition only contains properties, to keep using Russell's metaphor—but the property through which it is determined, and which *is* a constituent of the proposition, only has a reference-fixing role in the singular case (as opposed to the descriptive case): it serves to determine, in context, which object is relevant for evaluating the thought as true or false. In the two-dimensional framework, what characterizes the singular case is the fact that truth-evaluation takes place at a later stage than reference determination: what is evaluated for truth at the second stage is only the claim that the referent (deter- mined at the first stage through the reference-fixing property) pos- sesses the predicated property—in our example, the property of being less than 4,000 metres high.[2] This two-stage approach makes it possible to capture the singularity intuition: there is an object *x*,

---

[2] What is evaluated thus turns out to be a 'singular proposition' containing an object (Mont Blanc) and the predicated property (being less than 4,000 metres high). But that proposition is not the primary content of the thought: the primary content is general, not singular. The primary content, together with the context of thought, determines the secondary content (the above-mentioned singular proposition), and the secondary content, together with the circumstance of evaluation, determines a truth-value. The two-dimensional move enables the theorist to achieve singularity at the level of secondary content while remaining faithful to Descriptivism in the analysis of primary content. (Note, however, that a two-dimensionalist *need not* be a descriptivist: one can retain the idea that there is a 'primary' layer of content with a reference-fixing role *without* analys- ing that primary content in descriptivist terms. See §3 below and Chapter 18 §1 for more on this issue.)

namely *whatever turns out in context to have the reference-fixing property*, such that the thought is true in an arbitrary circumstance *w* iff *x* satisfies the predicate in *w*. Still, that object *x* is not directly given as a component of the proposition: the proposition is *general*—it contains only properties—but the rigidifier restricts one of the properties to a reference-fixing role and makes the resulting truth-conditions suitably singular.

2

The two-dimensional move goes a long way towards accounting for the singularity intuition; but I do not think it suffices. One reason is that it is possible to rigidify a description in a sentence 'The *F* is *G*' without thereby making the sentence express a singular proposition that cannot be grasped unless one is acquainted with the reference of the description. I am not denying that a sentence 'The *F* is *G*' *can* be used to express a singular proposition: following Donnellan (1966), I hold that that happens whenever a description is used 'referentially' as opposed to 'attributively'.[3] Typically, when a description is used referentially, the speaker is acquainted with some object *a* he wants to talk about and he chooses the description 'the *F*' to refer to *a* because he believes, or pretends to believe, that *a* is the *F*. To understand such a use, the hearer herself must be acquainted with *a* and she must grasp the speaker's intention to refer to *a* by the use of the description 'the *F*'. The important point is that the speaker has a certain object in mind as being the *F*, and the hearer must know which individual that is. But a rigidified use of a definite description 'the *F*' can be fully understood even though the hearer does not know which object is referred to, in context, by that description. In other words, a rigid use need not be referential: it may be attributive. Thus I may say: 'The actual *F*, whoever he is, is *G*.' To understand this, one

---

[3] See Chapter 17 for an analysis of the distinction in the mental file framework.

must understand the utterance as ascribing the property of being G to whoever turns out in context to uniquely possess the property of being F; but there is no need to independently *identify* the object in question, and no acquaintance constraint applies. This difference between a description that is merely 'rigidified' and one that is referentially used shows that the 'singularity' which the two-dimensional move enables the descriptivist to capture is not the strong form of singularity which the singularist is after.

Of course, I have (still) not said what acquaintance is, and what counts as 'identifying' what the speaker is talking about. It is time to say a bit more. The crucial distinction we need at this stage is that between two modes of determination of the reference: what Kent Bach calls the *satisfactional* and the *relational* modes. Here is what Bach, inspired by Burge (1977), wrote about this twenty-five years ago:

> If *all* your thoughts about things could only be descriptive, your total conception of the world would be merely qualitative. You would never be related in thought to anything in particular. Thinking of something would never be a case of having it 'in mind', as we say colloquially, or as some philosophers have said, of being '*en rapport*', in 'cognitive contact', or 'epistemically intimate' with it. But picturesque phrases aside, just what is this special relation? Whatever it is, it is different from that involved in thinking of something under a description. If we can even speak of a relation in the latter case, it is surely not a real (or natural) relation. Since the object of a descriptive thought is determined SATIS- FACTIONALLY, the fact that the thought is of that object does not require any connection between thought and object. However, the object of a *de re* thought is determined RELATIONALLY. For something to be the object of a *de re* thought, it must stand in a certain kind of relation to that very thought. (Bach 1987: 12; see also Bach 1986: 188–9 and the references therein)[4]

---

[4] See also Levine: 'Let's distinguish two kinds of mode of presentation (where by a "mode of presentation" is meant the means by which a representation connects to its referent): ascriptive and non-ascriptive. An ascriptive mode is one that involves the ascription of properties to the referent, and it's (at least partly) by virtue of its instantiation of these

In perception, we are related to the object we perceive. The perceptual relation is what enables us to gain (perceptual) information from the object. In communication too we are related to the object we hear about, albeit in a more indirect manner (via communicative chains). In general there is acquaintance with an object whenever we are so related to that object that we can gain information from it, on the basis of that relation. Acquaintance relations are epistemically rewarding (ER) relations, on this view.[5] (Of course, which relations are epistemically rewarding depends upon one's cognitive equipment, since one must be capable of exploiting the relations to gain information.) To think of an object directly or non-descriptively is to think of it through some such relation. In such a case, what determines the reference—what one's thought is about—is the relation: the reference is the object to which we stand in the relevant relation, even if that object does not have the properties we take it to have. Donnellan gives the following example:

> One is at a party and, seeing an interesting-looking person holding a martini glass, one asks, 'Who is the man drinking a martini?' If it should turn out that there is only water in the glass, one has nevertheless asked a question about a particular person, a question that it is possible for someone to answer. (Donnellan 1966: 48)

Here the speaker uses the description 'the man drinking a martini'. Had the description been used attributively, its reference (if any) would be determined 'satisfactionally' as whoever uniquely possesses the property of being a man drinking a martini. But the description has been used referentially: the speaker has a certain

properties that the object (or property) is the referent. A non-ascriptive mode is one that reaches its target, establishes a referential relation, by some other method. The object isn't referred to by virtue of its satisfaction of any conditions explicitly represented in the mode of presentation, but rather by its standing in some particular relation to the representation' (Levine 1998: 457).

[5] See Chapter 3, §3.

object in mind, i.e. she stands in some ER relation to some object she wants to say something about. Despite the speaker's choice of the description to pick out the man in question, what determines her reference is the relevant ER relation: here, the perceptual relation singles out a man (the interesting-looking person the speaker is watching) who as a matter of fact drinks water, not martini.

Referential descriptions raise all sorts of theoretical problems, but when it comes to demonstratives of the sort illustrated by our earlier example ('That peak is less than 4,000 metres high'), it is pretty clear that what determines what the thought is about is the relevant relation. The thought is about what the speaker is looking at, namely Mont Blanc. The relational character of reference determination in such cases is what is arguably missing from the descriptivist picture, even after the two-dimensional move. It is that relational character that anchors the thought to a particular object and makes it singular in the strong sense. As Peirce insisted, singularity as such cannot be described, [6] it can only be given through actual world relations (1967a: §419). For Peirce, as for all the authors who made roughly the same point (e.g. Austin and Strawson), singularity and indexicality are closely related: for indexicals systematically exploit the contextual relations in which we stand to what we talk about. For that reason, Kent Bach calls non-descriptive modes of presentation *mental indexicals*; for they, too, systematically exploit the contextual relations in which we stand to what we think about. (More on this in Chapter 5.)

3

Can Descriptivism be further amended so as to capture the relational character of singular thought? At first sight, it cannot; for Descriptivism holds that, with a few notable exceptions (thoughts about oneself, or about one's mental occurrences), all thoughts about particular objects

---

[6] 'Describe and describe and describe, and you never can describe a date, a position, or any homaloidal quantity' (Peirce 1967a: 260).

are descriptive; and this entails that reference is (almost) always determined satisfactionally. However, a distinction can be drawn, *within* the
general category of descriptive thought, between two sub-categories, one
of which corresponds to that of prima facie singular thoughts. Such
thoughts, it may be argued, are descriptive, *but* the descriptive condition
or property that fixes the reference is distinguished by its relational or
token-reflexive character.[7] So, in the Mont Blanc example, the demonstrative 'that peak' can be analysed as a description involving a certain
relation of the thinker (or of the thought-occurrence) to the peak: e.g.
'the peak I am seeing', or perhaps, 'the peak that is causing this visual
experience' (Searle 1983). In the case of a 'descriptive thought' such as
'The tallest peak in Europe is 4,000 metres high', that token-reflexive
feature is missing. It is therefore possible to make the two-dimensional
version of Descriptivism even more sophisticated by letting it account
for prima facie singular thoughts in terms of the relational or token-
reflexive character of the properties that fix the reference. For example, a
singular thought such as 'That peak is less than 4,000 metres high' can
be analysed, in a two-dimensional elaboration of Russell's view, as a
proposition containing (i) the thinking subject (or, possibly, the mental
occurrence of the thought), with which the subject is directly acquainted,
(ii) a relation R between the subject (or the thought-token) and some
other object y, and (iii) a property P predicated of y. In the case of 'That
peak is less than 4,000 metres high', R might be the following relation:

$$\lambda x \lambda y \; (y \text{ is a peak} \; \& \; x \text{ is watching } y \; \& \text{ for all } z, \text{ if } z \text{ is a peak and } x \text{ is watching}$$
$$z, \text{ then } z = y)$$

Applied to the first component of the thought (the thinking subject),
this gives us a relational property, namely the property of *being the*

---

[7] Thus Jackson writes: 'There is an important distinction...between the kinds of
properties that do the picking-out job. Sometimes they are properties that do not
involve essentially a relation to a subject, and sometimes...they do' (Jackson 1998b: 66).
See n. 5, p. 10 on 'Relational Descriptivism'.

peak the subject is looking at. The role of that property, in the two-dimensional framework, is to fix the reference, that is, to determine the object *y* (namely Mont Blanc) whose possession or lack of possession of the predicated property (being less than 4,000 metres high) determines the thought's truth-value.

This analysis—2-D Relational Descriptivism, as we may call it—is the best version of Descriptivism I can think of, but it still raises two crucial objections. First, to grasp the singular thought expressed by an utterance such as 'That peak is less than 4,000 metres high', it is not sufficient for the hearer merely to understand that the speaker is looking at a (unique) peak and saying of it that it is less than 4,000 metres high: the hearer herself must come to occupy an epistemic position enabling her to entertain a singular thought about the same object. As we have seen, entertaining such a thought involves standing in a suitable ER relation to the object of the thought. (Typically, the hearer will have to look in the same direction as the speaker, in order to *see the peak for herself.*[8]) This constraint on what counts as understanding in the singular case is left unaccounted for by 2-D Relational Descriptivism. Second, 2-D Relational Descriptivism entails that acquaintance relations are always represented as part of the content of singular thoughts; but this is debatable, to say the least. Kripke and many others have argued that acquaintance relations themselves need not be represented. For example, what determines the reference of the name 'Aristotle' in language or thought is a communication chain leading back to Aristotle, but users of the name need not have any thought regarding the communication chain, nor do they need to have the very concept of a communication chain. There *being* an appropriate communication chain is sufficient.[9]

Of course, there still are philosophers who resist that conclusion. Thus David Lewis, the leading advocate of 2-D Relational Descriptivism,

---

[8] See Strawson 1971: 78.
[9] See the quotation from Geach pp. 31–2.

bites the bullet regarding the internalization of acquaintance relations. He holds that Aristotle is typically thought of under the description 'the one I have heard of under the name of *Aristotle*':[10] this *is* a way of referring to a communication chain that even the dumbest of us can presumably be credited with. So, perhaps, the jury is still out and we should remain neutral on the issue, whether or not the acquaintance relations are represented. But, precisely, 2-D Relational Descriptivism does not remain neutral: 2-D Relational Descriptivism is firmly committed to the internalization of acquaintance relations, and this, I take it, is a weak point that makes the position vulnerable.

Before proceeding, a caveat is in order. As I mentioned in n. 2, there are *non-descriptivist* forms of two-dimensionalism, and they do not fall prey to the objection I have just raised. Non-descriptivist forms of two-dimensionalism do not claim that the 'primary' content they posit for a given thought or thought constituent is something the subject of thought is able to articulate or to represent in thought. The primary content of a thought constituent is taken to be its *function* or *role*, which function or role contextually determines its referential or 'secondary' content; but there is no reason why the subject should (be able to) articulate or think about that function or role. My own account of singular thought in terms of mental files, to be presented in what follows, is arguably 'two-dimensional': something like the character/content distinction (or the distinction between primary and referential content) applies to mental files, on my account. That is the gist of the indexical model to be presented in Part III. My critique of 2-D Relational Descriptivism should therefore be properly understood: it is the descriptivist component that I reject, not the two-dimensional component.[11]

---

[10] Lewis 1983: 155; Lewis's own example involves Hume rather than Aristotle.

[11] See Chapter 18 for more on this issue.

Part II

Introducing Files

3

Non-Descriptive Modes of Presentation as Mental Files

1

A rational subject, S, may take different (and possibly conflicting) attitudes towards the judgement that a given individual is F—for example, she may reject it as false or accept it as true—depending on how that individual is presented. For one and the same individual x, say Cicero, S may accept the claim that x was a philosopher if that claim is made in a certain way ('Cicero was a philosopher'), while rejecting the claim that x was a philosopher if it is made in a different way ('Tully was a philosopher'). Both 'Cicero was a philosopher' and 'Tully was a philosopher' say of the individual to whom both 'Cicero' and 'Tully' refer that he was a philosopher, so they make the same claim (true iff the individual in question was a philosopher), but the subject's acceptance or rejection of the claim depends upon the mode of presentation of the referent the two names share. If the referent is presented as Cicero, the claim is accepted, but if he is presented as Tully, it is not. That, of course, is possible only if S does not realize that Cicero is Tully. I assume that S has both the names 'Cicero' and 'Tully' in her repertoire, and that both names, as she uses them, refer to one and the same individual. The problem is that S herself does not know that. For her, there are two distinct individuals, and two distinct claims are made (one with respect to each of them).

To account for that sort of situation, Frege posited modes of presentation, or 'senses', in addition to the reference of linguistic expressions. And he appealed to this idea to account for the informativeness of identity statements such as 'Cicero is Tully'. At the level of reference, the statement is trivial, since an individual (the common referent of 'Cicero' and 'Tully') is said to be identical to that very individual—hardly a contingent matter. At the level of sense, however, the statement is informative precisely because the senses associated with 'Cicero' and 'Tully' are distinct. Sense determines reference, but does so only contingently. Because of that element of contingency, it is not guaranteed that the referents determined by two distinct senses (e.g. the sense of 'Cicero' and the sense of 'Tully') will be the same, and indeed a subject like S, unaware of certain contingent facts, takes them not to be the same. If the *senses* of the names were themselves the same (as in 'Cicero is Cicero'), the statement would be trivial and recognized as such by whoever understands it.

Now what *are* senses or modes of presentation? Frege himself thought of them as essentially descriptive. The referent is presented as having certain properties or standing in certain relations to other entities. Since sense is supposed to determine reference, a unique object must have the relevant properties or stand in the relevant relations to other entities. So a sense can, in principle, be expressed by means of a *definite description* 'the F'. The unique object which satisfies the descriptive condition ('F') is the referent. In so-called 'Frege cases' such as 'Hesperus'/'Phosphorus', 'Cicero'/'Tully', etc., where the cognitive significance of two terms differs even though their reference is the same (in such a way that a rational subject may be led to ascribe contradictory properties to what is in fact the same object), the suggestion is that the subject, S, associates different descriptions with the two terms.

The problem with Frege's descriptive take on senses is that, if accepted, it forces the theorist to posit reference-determining descriptions in the head of the subject *whenever* a Frege case is possible. Now there are three types of case in which contemporary philosophers of language and mind have been reluctant to posit such descriptions in the head: the cases of reference through *perception*, the cases of reference through *communicative chains*, and the cases of reference through *indexicals*. Let me briefly consider the three cases in turn, and the anti-descriptivist arguments based on them.

2

As we saw in Chapter 1, Descriptivism conflicts with the widely held view, originating from Russell, that there are two types of reference (both in language and thought): descriptive reference, and direct reference. Descriptive reference is *conceptually mediated* reference: we think of some object qua possessor of (possibly relational) properties, or qua satisfier of certain conditions. That type of reference is possible even though we know the referent only 'by description', without being acquainted with it. But in experience, we *are* acquainted with objects: we perceive them, for example, and that enables us to refer to them directly, without having to think of them as bearers of such and such properties. Indeed, when we perceive an object and have a thought about it, *the object the thought is about is the object the perception is about*; and that, arguably, *is not determined by properties the subject takes the referent to have* (Pylyshyn 2003, 2007).

Note that, in some cases, we are simply unable to properly describe the object that is given to us in experience: we don't know what it is, yet that does not prevent us from referring to it directly (without conceptual mediation) and e.g. wondering what *it* can be (Dretske 1988: 73). As Campbell puts it,

> Your visual system is managing to bind together information from a single thing, and you are consequently able to attend consciously to it, even though you have not managed to apply the right sortal concept to it. (Campbell 2006: 205)

In such cases, even though we are unable to conceptually articulate what our thought is about, Frege cases are still possible. I may be perceptually related (through distinct sense modalities, say) to what I take to be two objects, which happen to be one and the same object. Faced with such cases, the Fregean is likely to say that the reference-fixing description in the mind of the subject must be something like 'what I am now seeing' or 'what I am now touching'.[1] But this supposes, on the part of the subject, reflective abilities the exercise of which does not seem to be required to suffer from identity confusions of the type which Frege cases illustrate. The subject need not reflect on her perceptual relation to objects in order to have thoughts about the objects she perceives; nor does she have to reflect on her perceptual relation to objects to be in a position to think of the object in different ways, corresponding to the various ways in which she perceives it. (As for the subject's disposition to treat the referents as distinct, it can be established, at a pre-reflective level, by testing her expectations the way infants' expectations are standardly tested in experimental psychology.[2])

In cases such as the 'Cicero'/'Tully' case, the subject is able to describe the referent, but the descriptions he or she can provide do not fill the Fregean bill. First, the descriptions the subject can provide

[1] Russell would say that, in such examples, the description in the mind of the perceiver is 'what is causing these sense data'.

[2] In 'Sortals and the Identification of Objects' (Lowe 2007: 525–30), Jonathan Lowe argues that one may perceive an object without (yet) being able to *single it out in thought*. To make something one perceives an object of thought, one must think of it under some 'category' or other (e.g. as a piece of matter, or as a living organism). Lowe acknowledges that sometimes we have no idea which category something we perceive falls under ('whether what we have just seen is, say, a wild animal or just a shadow in the undergrowth', Lowe 2007: 528), but argues that in such cases, even though we use a singular vehicle in thought ('I wonder what *that* was'), the thought we entertain is a descriptive thought about whatever we have just perceived. Such thoughts, he says, 'are not, in the relevant sense, "singular thoughts" at all' (Lowe 2007: 529). I need not take a stand on this issue because, even if Lowe is right that singular thought presupposes a minimal ability to categorize the object, the relevant categories are far too general to count as reference-fixing descriptions anyway. (For a related debate, see the discussion of Kelly 2001 in Abath 2008.)

are often indefinite ('a famous Roman orator') rather than definite. That does not prevent the term(s) from referring. Second, when the subject is able to provide a definite description, the descriptive condition often fails to be satisfied by a unique object. Again, that does not prevent the term with which the description is associated from referring. Thus, to use Kripke's biblical example, 'Jonah' would still refer to a certain historical figure even if no one did actually experience what that individual is mostly famous for having allegedly experienced (being swallowed by a whale): we might, without contradiction, say things like 'it turns out that Jonah was never swallowed by a whale', even if the description associated with 'Jonah' is 'the biblical figure who was swallowed by a whale'. Third, assuming the description the subject can provide is definite and uniquely satisfied, the satisfier need not be the referent of the term whose sense we are trying to characterize, as in Kripke's Gödel/Schmidt case.

This type of consideration led a number of theorists, in the late 1960s and early 1970s, to argue in favour of an 'externalist' approach to reference determination. According to Kripke, Donnellan, and others, what determines the reference of a name on a given use is not a description in the head of the users, but historical facts about that use and the communicative chain to which it belongs. The first published statement of the historical-chain view of reference-determination dates back to 1969 and is due to Peter Geach, who puts it as follows:

> For the use of a word as a proper name there must in the first instance be someone acquainted with the object named. But language is an institution, a tradition; and the use of a given name for a given object, like other features of language, can be handed on from one generation to another; the acquaintance required for the use of a proper name may be mediate, not immediate. Plato knew Socrates, and Aristotle knew Plato, and Theophrastus knew Aristotle, and so on in apostolic succession down to our own times; that is why we can legitimately use 'Socrates' as a name the way we do. *It is not our knowledge of this chain that validates our*

> *use, but the existence of such a chain*; just as according to Catholic doctrine
> a man is a true bishop if there is in fact a chain of consecrations going
> back to the Apostles, not if we know that there is. (Geach 1972: 155;
> emphasis mine)

The sentence in bold type is meant to rebut a possible Fregean response: that the description in the mind of the users in that sort of case is something like 'the person called *Socrates*', a description which (if the historical-chain picture is correct) would be satisfied by whoever stands at the other end of the communicative chain which eventuates in the current use of the name. Geach's point, that the *existence* of such a chain is sufficient to enable a name-user to successfully refer, parallels the point made earlier about the non-reflectiveness of perceptual reference: the communicative chain does not have to be represented, any more than the perceptual relation to the referent has to be represented in order for the subject to successfully refer to an object he is acquainted with.[3]

Besides names and definite descriptions, we refer by means of indexicals, e.g. personal pronouns ('I', 'you'), temporal and spatial adverbs ('here', 'now'), etc. There is no doubt that indexicals present their referent in quite specific ways, but indexical modes of presentation are essentially perspectival and cannot be captured by means of objective, non-indexical descriptions. As Castañeda and (following him) Perry forcefully pointed out, for any indexical α and non-indexical description 'the F', it is always possible for the subject to doubt, or to wonder, whether α is the F (Castañeda 1999, Perry 1993).

To be sure, it is not the same thing to say that we don't (always) refer through descriptions and to say that we don't (always) refer through *objective, non-indexical* descriptions. This suggests that, perhaps, Descriptivism can be rescued by letting the relevant descriptions be

---

[3] Kripke makes the same point in his 1970 *Naming and Necessity* lectures: 'It is not how the speaker thinks he got the reference, but the actual chain of communication, which is relevant' (Kripke 1980: 93).

indexical descriptions like 'the bright thing over there'. But I don't think Descriptivism can be saved this way. Indexical descriptions are descriptions that contain indexicals. Thus 'the bright thing over there' contains the indexical 'there'. The claim that indexical modes of presentation cannot be captured by means of objective, non-indexical descriptions is the claim that, to the extent that they can be captured by descriptions, the descriptions in question will *themselves* contain indexicals. The indexical component in them is therefore ineliminable or 'essential': any attempt to cash it out descriptively will produce an indexical residue, to which the same limitation applies. This shows that the indexical component in question is, at bottom, a *non-descriptive* component; and this (of course) argues against Descriptivism.[4]

Reichenbach has suggested that an indexical is equivalent to a token-reflexive description (Reichenbach 1947: §50). Thus a given token of 'I' presents its referent as the utterer of that token, a token of 'now' presents the time it refers to as including (or overlapping with) the time at which this token is uttered, etc. Insightful though it is, this move cannot support a descriptivist approach to indexical modes of presentation. What is needed to support such an approach is an objective, *non-indexical* description that provides the sense of the indexical. But for the token-reflexive description to count as non-indexical, the token in terms of which the referent is described must itself be described in objective/non-indexical terms, rather than referred to by means of a demonstrative like 'this token' (itself a

---

[4] Admittedly, the indexical residue can be accommodated in a theory like Russell's (or Lewis's) which makes room for special objects which are given non-descriptively (indexically) and in terms of which everything else is described (Chapter 1, n. 5 and Chapter 2, §3). Such theories advocate a *partial* form of Descriptivism (namely Relational Descriptivism). I have already said why I find that position unsatisfactory, even in its two-dimensional version, and why we should give up Descriptivism altogether. That is what the theory of mental files enables us to do. (See Chapter 18 for more on the contrast between the theory of mental files, which gives up Descriptivism, and Relational Descriptivism.)

variety of indexical). Now if the token is objectively described as, say, 'the F-token', the token-reflexive description will no longer be suitable for capturing the sense of the indexical. It is certainly possible for me to doubt that I am uttering the F-token, or to doubt that the F-token is being uttered now (or here), and that is sufficient to establish that the token-reflexive description ('the utterer of the F-token', 'the time/place at which the F-token is uttered'...) does not provide the sense of the corresponding indexical ('I', 'here' or 'now'). In any case, such token-reflexive descriptions can only be grasped by fairly sophisticated users of the language, able to reflect upon the relations between token-representations and objects in the context in which these representations occur. Indexical thinking indeed exploits these relations, but in no way presupposes the ability to reflect on them.

3

The three types of objection to descriptive senses are not unrelated. Demonstratives, which (I have just said) are a variety of indexicals, typically demand, or rely upon, perceptual acquaintance with the referent. As for communicative chains, Geach aptly describes them in terms of 'mediated acquaintance'. One of the aims of the theory of mental files is precisely to offer a unified approach to these varieties of reference (through perceptual acquaintance, through communicative chains, and through indexicals), and, within that framework, to overcome the difficulties which beset Frege's approach.

A non-descriptive mode of presentation, I claim, is nothing but a mental file. Mental files are based on what Lewis calls 'acquaintance relations'.[5] According to the account I develop in this book, different types of file correspond to different types of relation. The role of the

---

[5] The paradigm is, of course, perceptual acquaintance, but the notion of acquaintance can be generalized 'in virtue of the analogy between relations of perceptual acquaintance and other, more tenuous, relations of epistemic rapport. There are relations that someone bears to me when I get a letter from him, or I watch the swerving of

files is to store information about the objects we bear these acquaintance relations to. So mental files are 'about objects': like singular terms in the language, they refer, or are supposed to refer. They are, indeed, the mental counterparts of singular terms.[6] What they refer to is not determined by properties which the subject takes the referent to have (i.e. by information—or misinformation—*in* the file), but through the relations on which the files are based. The reference is the entity we are acquainted with (in the appropriate way), not the entity which best 'fits' information in the file.

The characteristic feature of the relations on which mental files are based, and which determine their reference, is that they are *epistemically rewarding* (hence my name for them: ER relations). They enable the subject to gain information from the objects to which he stands in these relations. In all the cases mentioned above as objecting to Frege's descriptivist approach, ER relations are involved. Relations of perceptual acquaintance are ER relations: they are the sort of relation to objects which makes the perceptual flow of information possible. Thus, by holding an object in my hand, I can get information about its weight; by looking at it I can get information about its visual appearance. Perceptual files are, to use Perry's analogy, 'buffers' in which we store the information gained on the basis of these short-term relations. The relations of 'mediated acquaintance' established through communicative chains are also ER relations, which enable the subject (through communication) to gain information from the object at the other end of the communicative chain.

a car he is driving, or I read his biography, or I hear him mentioned by name, or I investigate the clues he has left at the scene of his crime. In each case there are causal chains from him to me of a sort which would permit a flow of information. Perhaps I do get accurate information; perhaps I get misinformation, but still the channel is there. I call such relations as these *relations of acquaintance*' (Lewis 1999: 380–1).

[6] This makes them 'concepts' if, like Imogen Dickie, we use 'concept' to abbreviate 'representation deployable in thought' (Dickie 2011: 292). In Chapter 5 (§3) I will argue that, to count as representations deployable in *thought*, mental files must satisfy Evans's Generality Constraint; and I will distinguish mental files, which satisfy the constraint, from 'proto-files', which do not.

The corresponding files are more enduring than perceptual buffers because the ER relation established through a communicative chain lasts longer than a transient perceptual relation.

The contextual relations to objects which indexical reference exploits are also ER relations, and they are typically short-lived, but not always. According to Perry (2002), the SELF file (which provides the sense of the indexical 'I') is based upon a special relation which every individual (permanently) bears to himself or herself, namely identity.[7] In virtue of *being* a certain individual, I am in a position to gain information concerning that individual in all sorts of ways in which I can gain information about no one else, e.g. through proprioception and kinaesthesis. The mental file SELF serves as repository for information gained in this way.[8] In contrast, the files associated with the other indexicals ('here', 'now'...) are based on short-lived ER relations to the place we are in, or to the current time, which relations enable the subject to know (by using his senses) what is going on at the place or time in question. They are similar to perceptual buffers, which is to be expected given the link between indexicality and perception.

On the mental file picture, what distinguishes descriptive from non-descriptive senses is the mechanism of reference determination. To use Kent Bach's terminology, reference determination is 'satisfactional' in the descriptive case, and 'relational' in the non-descriptive or *de re* case (see the quotations from Bach and

[7] In token-reflexive format, the relation is that which holds between a token thought (or a file) and an individual iff the individual is the thinker of the thought (or the owner of the file). See Chapter 5, §1.

[8] As we shall see in due course, this is not the only sort of information about oneself that can go into the file. There is much information about myself that I cannot get in the first person way, e.g. through proprioception or introspection. Information about my date of birth is a case in point: when I was born is something I learn through communication, in the same way in which I learn my parents' birthdates. That information goes into my SELF file, however, because I take it to concern the same person about whom I also have direct first-person information, namely myself. So a file based on a certain ER relation contains two sorts of information: information gained in the special way that goes with that relation (first-person information, in the case of the SELF file), and information not gained in this way but concerning the same individual as information gained in that way.

Levine on pp. 19–20). Now, as we have seen (Chapter 2, §3), there is a variety of Descriptivism which accommodates the relational nature of *de re* thought: it does so by 'internalizing' the relations and incorporating them into the content of the associated descriptions. On this view, the sense of a singular term always is that of a definite description, but in the allegedly 'non-descriptive' cases the descriptive condition F is relational. Thus the descriptivist can say that in the perceptual case the mode of presentation is something like 'what I am seeing' or 'what I am touching';[9] and similarly for the other cases that raise prima facie difficulties for the descriptivist. As I stressed repeatedly, this view supposes reflective abilities the exercise of which is not actually required for having the relevant thoughts. The mental file picture avoids this intellectualist pitfall. Mental files are based on relations to objects. Their function is to store information gained in virtue of standing in that relation to objects, and to represent them in thought. By deploying the file (or its 'address' or 'label') in thought, the subject can think about the object in virtue of standing in the relevant relation to it. But to entertain the thought, the subject does not have to reflect upon the relation in which she stands to the object.

To sum up, the (Perry-inspired) picture I am offering is this. In his cognitive life the subject encounters various objects to which he stands in various contextual relations. Some of these relations—the acquaintance relations—are epistemically rewarding in that they enable the subject to gain information from the object. Among the acquaintance relations, some are distinguished by the fact that certain types of file specifically correspond to them. The role of a mental file based on a certain acquaintance relation is to store information acquired in virtue of that relation. The information in question need not be veridical; we can think of it in terms, simply, of a list of predicates

[9] Or, in token-reflexive form: 'what is causing this visual/tactile experience'. (See Searle 1983 for a token-reflexive analysis of the content of perceptual experience, and Russell 1912 for an early version of the view.)

which the subject takes the referent to satisfy. The referent need not actually satisfy the predicates in question, since the subject may be mistaken. Such mistakes are possible because what determines the reference is not the content of the file but the relevant relation to the object. The file corresponds to an information channel, and the reference is the object from which the information derives, whether that information is genuine information or misinformation.

4

In *Reference and the Rational Mind*, Taylor criticizes the authors like myself who analyse concepts in terms of mental files, on the grounds that this conflates 'concepts' and 'conceptions' (Taylor 2003: 75–82, 181–4). As defined by Taylor, conceptions seem to be mental files and he describes them as such:

> A conception...is a kind of mental particular, a labeled, perhaps highly structured, and updateable database of information about the extension of an associated concept. For example, each thinker who can deploy the concept <cat> in thought episodes is likely to have stored in his head a database of information (and misinformation) about cats. (Taylor 2003: 181)

Taylor's main objection to equating concepts and conceptions is that this entails that 'what concepts a cognizer has supervenes, more or less, on what beliefs the thinker has' (Taylor 2003: 77). But I deny that this unwelcome consequence holds if concepts are equated to mental files. The problem with Taylor's notion of a 'conception' is that, even though he describes a conception as a mental particular, it seems to correspond to the *content* of a mental file (at a time) rather than to the file itself. I draw a sharp distinction between the two things—the file itself, and its content.[10] That is the reason why I can

[10] By 'content' here I mean the information (or misinformation) in the file. This is distinct from the content in the *semantic* sense. (Actually there are two notions of

take mental files to be constituents of thoughts without falling prey to Fodor's objection that 'you don't think everything you believe about John when you think [a thought about John]' (Fodor 2008: 95 n.).[11] The file's deployment in thought gives access to the file's content but to deploy the file in thought is not the same thing as actually accessing all of its content.[12]

The distinction between the file and its content can also be invoked in response to Kit Fine's worry regarding the Fregean analysis of informative identity statements in terms of senses. Fine formulates the problem as follows:

> Surely one may learn something different upon being told 'Cicero = Tully' and upon being told 'Cicero = Cicero'.... It is hard to see how to

content in the semantic sense: the 'primary' content of a file—what corresponds to Kaplan's 'character'—is its function or role, namely the storing of information derived through the ER relation on which the file is based; while the 'secondary' or referential content of a file is the entity to which the subject stands in the relevant ER relation. Both of these notions are distinct from the 'content' in the sense of *information contained in the file*.)

[11] Fodor's objection is presented as the response to Jesse Prinz's question, 'why one shouldn't use the whole "John" file, rather than just its label, to represent John in thought'.

[12] Andrew Woodfield (1991) takes the same position as Taylor and Fodor. He characterizes a conception (or 'F-conception', where 'F' stands for 'file') as 'a unified package of representations of information about x stored in long term memory, the whole package being like a file in a filing system' (Woodfield 1991: 548). Thus understood, an F-conception is a complex entity: a 'bonded aggregate of entries' (Woodfield 191: 568 n.). On this view we get the unwelcome consequence emphasized by Taylor, but in addition we get what Woodfield describes as a 'mereological paradox': 'concepts are parts of beliefs, yet beliefs are parts of concepts' (Woodfield 1991: 549). Woodfield concludes that one must choose: if concepts are files, that is, if they contain information, they can't themselves occur as constituents in thought; and if they are thought constituents, they can't contain stuff (as files do). In other words: either they are like words, or they are like paragraphs. Woodfield mentions Crimmins (1989: 286) who tries to have it both ways (a concept is '*in one way* like a file folder in a filing system', and 'also *in one way* like a word in a language') but denies that this makes sense:

> an F-conception is in no way like a word in a language. If F-conceptions have headers, the *header* might be a word or a phrase. But the entries are like sets of sentences. And the F-conception itself is a complex particular containing the header and the entries as parts. (Woodfield 1991: 549 n.)

[continued overleaf]

account for this possible cognitive difference except in terms of a semantic difference. The main problem with the Fregean position is to say, in particular cases, what the difference in the meaning or sense of the names might plausibly be taken to be. Although there appear to be good theoretical reasons for thinking that there *must* be a difference, it seems hard to say in particular cases what it is. For as Kripke (1980) has pointed out, it seems possible for a speaker, or for speakers, to associate the same beliefs or information with two names, such as 'Cicero' and 'Tully.' And if the information or beliefs are the same, then how can the sense be different? (Fine 2007: 35)

To address this problem, we must realize that there are two options for modes of presentation. They may be descriptive, in which case the object is thought of as the possessor of a certain identifying property. (This is Frege's own construal of senses.) But there are also non-descriptive senses or modes of presentation, and these, I claim, are mental files. Even though files contain information

But I don't see what all the fuss is about. Mental files are like words, indeed. Words *have* meaning, but that does not make them complex entities. Similarly, mental files have content (in the informational sense) but that does not necessarily make them complex entities or 'aggregates'. As Crimmins puts it in his book,

> I do not assume that a notion [= mental file] has internal logical complexity in the way a description, a bundle of predicates, a cluster of beliefs or an image might. I assume that notions are constituents of beliefs, but I do not assume the reverse. (Crimmins 1992: 79)

Crimmins thinks this sets limits to the usefulness of the file metaphor:

> Though files have their information literally *inside* them, *containing* this information, it may be misleading to think of notions as *containing* information. Notions are *parts of* beliefs. The file analogy can lead one to get the issue of what-contains-what backwards. (Crimmins 1992: 87 n.).

But I think it suffices to say explicitly that for a file to 'contain' information just is for it to *have* a certain informational content. On this view a file may occur as a constituent in a thought, without the entries it 'contains' themselves occurring in that thought. (If you're not convinced that this move is sufficient, or if you want to take the file metaphor more literally, you can go along with Woodfield and Fodor and say that what occurs in thought is the 'label' or 'header' of the file rather than the file itself.)

(or misinformation), what plays the role of sense is not the information in the file, but the file itself. If there are two distinct files, one associated with 'Cicero' and the other with 'Tully', then there are two distinct senses, *even if the information in the two files is the same* ('a Roman orator'). On this view, to be spelled out in Chapter 4, to say that the two terms flanking the identity sign have different senses is to say that they are associated with two distinct files.

4

Mental Files and Identity

1

Identity statements are informative, Frege says, whenever the senses of the terms on each side of the identity sign are distinct. Thus 'A = B' is informative, in virtue of the distinctness of the relevant senses, while 'A = A' is not, since (presumably) the same sense is exercised twice. In mental file talk, this translates as follows: an identity statement 'A = B' is informative to the extent that the terms 'A' and 'B' are associated with distinct mental files. If the two terms are associated with the same file, the statement reduces to a (trivial) assertion of self-identity.

To say that there are two distinct mental files is to say that information in one file is insulated from information in the other file. Files are a matter of information clustering. Clustering takes place when all the information derives from the same source, through the same ER relation, and when it takes place, it licenses the integration and inferential exploitation of the information in question. The role of the file is precisely to treat all the information as if it concerned one and the same object, from which it derives.[1] But integration and

---

[1] This point has been emphasized by virtually every mental file theorist. Here are a few citations (selected more or less at random): 'File folders are stable physical mechanisms that serve to bind together a changing body of documents about a single putative topic, and to segregate that body from others that might concern different topics'

exploitation of information is blocked if the relevant information is distributed in distinct files, for then, there is no presumption that all the information derives from the same object. So, even if I know that Cicero is bald, and that Tully is well-read, I cannot conclude that some bald man is well-read, despite the fact that Cicero is Tully: the information 'is bald' is in the Cicero file, while the information 'is well-read' is in the Tully file. Informational integration and inferential exploitation of information only takes place within files, on this picture.

There is, however, an operation on files whose role is precisely to overcome that architectural limitation, by licensing the integration/exploitation of information distributed in distinct files. That operation, following Perry, I call *linking*. When two files are linked, information can flow freely from one file to the other, so informational integration/exploitation becomes possible.[2] Thus if I learn that Cicero is Tully, this allows me to put together the pieces of information in the two files, and to infer that some bald man is well-read.

(Schroeter 2007: 601); 'Updating one's files involves being disposed to collect information as if there is some one individual that one's file F has always been about. One's screening and pruning dispositions are responsive to this purported fact' (Lawlor 2001: 88); 'Cluster[ing] information about [an object] reflects the putative fact that it is all information about a single [object]' (Recanati 1993: 183); 'Each mental file is a repository of information that the agent takes to be about a single individual. That the system of files constitutes the agent's individuation of objects is partly captured by normatively governed file dynamics: the updating, merging, separation and initiation of mental files' (Jeshion 2010: 131); 'One reason for not allowing an individual concept [= a file] to change its referent is that the referent fixes a condition for the coherence of information within an individual concept: if 'is F' belongs in belief mode to a given individual concept, then "is not F" should not. The constraints on updating would not obtain if an individual concept might shift its referent' (Sainsbury 2005: 232); 'Each file is a cluster of information that the [subject] takes to be information about a single thing. Taking information in the file to be about a single thing consists in attempting … to keep the file free of contradiction, and to keep the file's contents consistent with the general beliefs about particulars that the system contains' (Dickie 2010: 222). See also Millikan 1997: 504–6, 2000: 141–4.

[2] This will be qualified in Part VII, with the introduction of 'vertical' linking.

From a cognitive point of view, linking is a quite fundamental operation. It is involved, for example, in the phenomenon of recognition (which involves linking a perceptual file and a file based on memory)—or at least, in *some* forms of recognition.[3] It is that operation which I think accounts for the cognitive effect of accepting an identity statement. To accept the identity 'A = B' *is* to link the two files corresponding to the terms on each side of the equals sign. It would be incoherent to accept the identity 'Cicero = Tully', and not let the information in the respective files get together and breed.

2

Lockwood and Strawson were the first to claim that identity judgements should be understood in terms of their effects on the management of files in the mind of the thinker (Lockwood 1971: 209; Strawson 1974: 51–6). Two 'segregated bundles or clusters of identifying knowledge', Strawson says, are 'brought together and tied up into one for a given audience of an identity statement' (Strawson 1974: 52). But the operation on files which, according to them, results from accepting an identity statement is the 'merge' operation through which the two files become one. 'The purpose of an identity statement', Lockwood says, is 'to get the hearer to merge these files or bodies of information into one' (Lockwood 1971: 209). As several authors noticed, however, the 'merge' model is not adequate to describe the cognitive effects of identity judgements.

Two linked files may end up being merged, after some time (especially as new information accumulates), but there are all sorts of reasons also for not automatically merging two files that are linked (Lawlor 2001: 62–5 and 92–3). For example, it would be very risky to merge two files on the basis of an identity judgement that one may accept

---

[3] On the distinction between different forms of recognition, see Chapter 7.

with less than 100 per cent subjective probability (Millikan 1997: 508). Linking is less risky, as it can easily be undone. So merge is an option for dealing with an identity, but it should not be automatic.[4] Second and most importantly, the 'merge' model is incompatible with the mode of presentation idea we are trying to explicate (Millikan 2000: 147–9). It is of the essence of modes of presentation that there can be a multiplicity of modes of presentation for the same object. On the picture I have presented, mental files qua non-descriptive modes of presentation correspond to various relations in which the subject stands to objects, and there is no doubt that a subject can and typically does stand in several relations simultaneously to the objects in his or her environment. Nor is this situation contrary to some normative ideal, as if the coexistence of several files for a single object was a defect to be avoided whenever possible. Imagine that I see a certain man cutting his grass and recognize him as Noam Chomsky. (Or imagine I learn he is Noam Chomsky, through an identity statement which I accept.) My perceptual file and my Chomsky file get linked, but there is no reason why either should disappear. Perry describes the perceptual buffer as being 'absorbed' into the more permanent file in such cases, but I think the buffer should only

---

[4] 'An agent can retain two notions [= files] of an individual, while linking them, in the way one does when one recognizes that "two" of one's acquaintances are actually a single individual. Why might two notions be retained when such a recognition takes place? One reason for this would be to allow the possibility of easy revision in case the "recognition" was in error' (Crimmins and Perry 1989: 256). 'Learning that Hesperus is Phosphorus does not require me to combine my information about them in a single undifferentiated bundle: the information may remain grouped into two parts within the bundle, so that I can still make sense of the possibility of changing my mind about the identity statement' (Millican 1990: 192 n.). 'If the identification [A = B] is tentative, the notions [= files] may retain their identity; if not, they may merge and become one' (Perry 2002: 196). See also Edelberg 1995: 330: 'When [Barsky] concludes that the two murderers are the same person [he may do one of two things. He may] take a new file folder and dump into it the contents of the two earlier folders: the result is a single file. [Or he may] take a new folder, and place carefully into it the two folders he has already constructed, so that he ends up with three files: a file containing two subfiles. (Notice that in the second system, it's easier for Barsky to sort things out if he changes his mind.)'

disappear when the ER relation on which it is based no longer holds.[5] Taking seriously the idea that mental files are modes of presentation based upon contextual relations to objects demands that we accept the existence of a multiplicity of files for the same object even when the files are linked and the subject is aware that they stand for a single object.

The Strawson–Lockwood idea that two linked files should be merged makes sense in the context of their own enquiry, however. Strawson was concerned with a very specific type of file, associated with proper names (his topic in the relevant passage of *Subject and Predicate in Logic and Grammar*). That type of file is what I call an 'encyclopedia entry' (Chapter 6, §3). Encyclopedia entries do obey the norm that there should be exactly one per object of interest. In *Reference and Reflexivity*, Perry describes files as 'little cards in the mind on which we jot down information about people, things and places. My picture is *a card for each person, place, or thing*' (Perry 2001b: 54; emphasis mine). Similarly, Lockwood writes that 'a given mental file is to be thought of as containing all and only such information as is known or believed by a person to hold true of a single individual. Usually, *a speaker will not expect his hearer to possess more than one such file on a given particular*' (Lockwood 1971: 209; emphasis mine).[6] These descriptions fit encyclopedia entries well, though I think it is a mistake to apply them to files in general. As we shall see, encyclopedia entries abstract from specific ER relations: they are based on a higher-order relation to the referent—a relation which holds if the subject bears *any* specific ER relation to it. Since encyclopedia entries abstract from specific ER relations, there is no point in entertaining

---

[5] For qualifications, see Chapter 7 on the 'conversion' of files. What I call 'incremental conversion' in that chapter can be described as a form of absorption (of one file by another). On the 'absorption' issue Perry himself shows some hesitation: see Perry 2012: 86–7.

[6] The Strawson–Lockwood constraint is similar to the so-called 'Mutual Exclusivity' constraint discussed by psychologists (Markman and Wachtel 1988; Markman 1989). According to that constraint, each object can only have one name.

distinct encyclopedia entries about the same object.[7] All such files would be based on the same relation to the object (the higher-order relation) so their multiplicity could only reflect the mistake of thinking that there are two objects where there is one. But encyclopedia entries are only one particular type of file, and the Strawson–Lockwood constraint 'one object, one file' only applies to that type of file. It does not apply to files in general, hence there is no reason to accept that, in general, linking does or should give rise to a merging of files.

3

Besides judgements of identity, the cognitive effect of which is to link two files, there are also *presumptions* of identity, whose status is quite different. While linking only operates on distinct files, presumptions of identity are operative within a single file. As I wrote above, to put various pieces of information in the same file means that they are supposed to concern the same object. Pieces of information in the same file can thus be inferentially integrated (whether or not they actually do concern the same object). This Campbell describes as 'trading on identity' (Campbell 1987, 1994, 2002; see also Millikan 1997, Fine 2007).

It is tempting to regard presumptions of identity as nothing but *implicit* judgements of identity. On this view the difference between Argument A and Argument B below is that, in Argument A, the judgement of identity is explicit, while it remains implicit in Argument B (which is therefore enthymematic). The reason why it can remain implicit in B is that the identity is obvious and trivial, so it 'goes without saying' and can be suppressed, in contrast to what happens in Argument A.

---

[7] For qualifications, see Chapters 14–15, on 'vicarious' files (files we use to track other people's perspective on things).

Argument A	Argument B
Cicero is bald	$Cicero_i$ is bald
Tully is well-read	$Cicero_j$ is well-read
Cicero = Tully	[implicit premise: $Cicero_i = Cicero_j$]
------------------------	---
Someone is bald and well-read	Someone is bald and well-read

The suppressed premise in Argument B is meant to ensure that the two occurrences of 'Cicero' in the explicit premises of the argument actually co-refer (if they did not co-refer, the argument would be invalid, indeed). As Campbell and many others have shown, however, this view of Argument B as enthymematic and resting on a suppressed premise is indefensible. In general, the attempt to reduce presumptions of identity to implicit identity judgements launches an infinite regress:

> If this view were correct, we would also need to make sure that the uses of ['Cicero'] in the suppressed premise are linked with the uses of ['Cicero'] in the explicit premises, and we would need further suppressed premises to secure these connections. The problem recurs, and we are embarked on a regress. (Campbell 1994: 75)[8]

---

[8] See also Fine (2007: 68): 'According to the [suggestion]… what it is to think that the individual Cicero is a Roman and then to have the coordinated thought that he is an orator is to think the additional thought that the one individual is the same as the other. But if the new thought is to have the desired effect, then it must be supposed that the individuals in the new thought are represented as the same as the respective individuals in the original thoughts; and so the account is circular.' And Schroeter (2008: 115 n.): 'To insist that the subject must make an explicit identity judgment before she can recognize that two thoughts are about the same thing would be to invite a vicious regress—for even the simplest inference from "P" to "P" would then require infinitely many explicit identity judgments to establish the co-reference of premise and conclusion. The moral here is much the same as the one Lewis Carroll drew in the case of modus ponens: we must have some basic way of taking two thoughts to be co-referential which does not require an explicit identity judgment.' Humberstone and Townsend (1994: 245) make essentially the same point: 'the mere presence of […] repeated terms does not indicate that the concept of identity is involved'.

This means that we cannot regard arguments like the one under consideration as enthymematic, needing but a further (object-language) sentence to be made completely valid; there is no evading unthinking reliance on sameness of reference. (Sainsbury 2002: 135)

Indeed I used subscripts in Argument B to distinguish the two occurrences of 'Cicero' in the explicit premises, but the use of the *same* subscripts in the implicit premise is illegitimate: what we have in the implicit premise are *two new occurrences* of 'Cicero'. If we give them new subscripts, as we should, it becomes apparent that the implicit premise does not help—it cannot bridge the alleged gap between the explicit premises and the conclusion:

Argument B

$Cicero_i$ is bald

$Cicero_j$ is well-read

[implicit premise: $Cicero_k = Cicero_l$]

Someone is bald and well-read

I conclude that identity presumptions are not (implicit) identity judgements. There are two distinct types of case, not one. Campbell describes them as follows:

In the first [type of case, corresponding to Argument B], we trade directly upon co-reference, moving directly to the conclusion....It seems to me that we can do this just when the two tokens have the same sense. In the second type of case, when the tokens do not have the same sense, it would not be legitimate to move directly to the conclusion. The inference depends upon a suppressed premise which assures us that the tokens s and s' refer to the same thing. (Campbell 1987: 275–6)

In the mental file framework, the two types of case Campbell describes correspond to the case in which the two pieces of information belong to a single file, and the case in which they belong to distinct files but can still be inferentially integrated provided the files in question are linked (by means or an implicit or explicit identity judgement). In the first type of case there is no identity judgement, implicit or explicit, but a mere presupposition of identity resulting from informational clustering.

4

I said that files contain predicates. All the predicates in a given file record information concerning the individual the file is about (the referent of the file). So far, I have only mentioned monadic predicates. But there are also relational predicates, which record relational information. Relational predicates, such as 'loves Mary', record information concerning the individual x the file is about (say, John), but that information also concerns the other individual (Mary) whose relation to x is recorded. That means that, in the mental file framework, such information is *shared* between two files.

Information sharing between files can be represented in various ways: by duplicating the information ('loves Mary' in the JOHN file, 'is loved by John' in the MARY file), or by storing the information in a single file and introducing into the other file a pointer to the first file so as to make the shared information accessible from the second file.[9] *How* the sharing of information between files is best implemented is an issue to be dealt with in the formal theory of relational data bases. Goodsell complains that 'the phenomena alone are compatible with several different versions of the file model', corresponding to different ways of representing information sharing, and that 'this prejudices our investigation of what explains the phenomena' (Goodsell 2011: 14). But I do not see why this is a problem. We investigate the phenomena by constructing models for them, and we follow the model where it leads to see, precisely, *where* it leads. In any case, we can also

---

[9] See Hendriks 2002: 7–8, referring to Vallduví's account.

abstract from the details of implementation, as I do here. The only thing that matters as far as I am concerned is that we construe relational information as information that is shared between files.

In *Subject and Predicate in Logic and Grammar*, Strawson summarizes the three operations on files which, according to him, respectively correspond to acceptance of monadic information, acceptance of relational information, and acceptance of identity information:

> Imagine a man as, in part, a machine for receiving and storing knowledge of all items of which he already has some identifying knowledge. The machine contains cards, one card for each cluster of identifying knowledge in his possession. On receipt of an ordinary predication invoking one such cluster, the appropriate card is withdrawn, the new information is entered on it and the card is returned to stock. On receipt of an ordinary relational predication invoking two such clusters, the two appropriate cards are withdrawn, cross-referring entries are made on both and both cards are returned to stock. On receipt of an identity-statement invoking two such clusters, the two appropriate cards are withdrawn and a new card is prepared, bearing *both* the names of which one heads one of the original cards and one the other, and incorporating the sum of the information contained in the original cards; the single new card is returned to stock and the original cards are thrown away. (Strawson 1974: 56)

Strawson talks about 'ordinary relational predication', presumably to distinguish such relational information from the relational information conveyed by identity statements. Identity is a relation, but, according to Strawson, when we accept an identity statement we do not record a new piece of information in either of the two files; what happens, rather, is that existing information is reorganized through the merging of the files. Strawson concludes that identity information works differently from ordinary predicative information, whether monadic or relational.

Michael Murez (2011) complains that this 'dynamic' approach to identity introduces an unjustified asymmetry between identity and the other relations. Still, the essentials of Strawson's description of the three types of case can be retained. What is common to the case of ordinary relational predication and to the case of identity is what is lacking in the case of monadic predication: the sharing of information between files. When ordinary relational information is received, that information is shared between the files which the piece of information connects through the mechanism of cross-reference; when identity information is received, it is not only that piece of information (identity information) that is shared between the files, but *all* the information in the files. Information sharing is total in the case of identity statements, while it is partial in the case of ordinary relational information. (As we have seen, we need not think of the total sharing of information between files in terms of merging, as Lockwood and Strawson did; we can think of it in terms of linking. When two files are linked, information flows freely between them.)

The difference I have just pointed out between relational information, acceptance of which yields partial information sharing, and identity information, acceptance of which yields total information sharing, does not justify the asymmetry Strawson posits between ordinary cases of predication (whether monadic or relational), on the one hand, and identity statements on the other hand. Only in the former cases is new information recorded in the files, on Strawson's account. Identity is supposed to work differently, through reorganization of existing information in the files. But, as Murez argues, we are not compelled to accept that asymmetry. Nothing prevents us from using *the same representational format* for both ordinary relational information and for identity.

Acceptance of identity information yields linking, but linking itself can be represented by *storing the relevant identity information in the files*, e.g. the piece of information '= Mary' in the JOHN file and the piece of information '= John' in the MARY file (assuming the identity statement is 'John is Mary'). The effect of adding this piece of information is that all the information in the other file becomes accessible from the file where the identity information is stored.[10] We don't *have to* represent linking that way—there are different ways of implementing the idea—but the fact that we can use the identity predicate to store identity information in the files and thereby achieve linking shows that the Strawsonian asymmetry is not forced upon us simply in virtue of accepting the mental file framework.

[10] In Chapter 14 I will introduce a new form of linking: vertical linking. Vertical linking links a regular file in the thinker's mind with a vicarious file used to track someone else's perspective on some object. Vertical linking does not lead to information sharing between the linked files, and should not be represented by storing identity information *in* them, for one and the same reason: the information in a vicarious file is information available to the person whose perspective is tracked, and that person may be unaware of the identity. (See Chapter 15, §1, for more on this issue.)

Part III

The Indexical Model

5

Mental Indexicals

1

The critical feature of mental files, qua non-descriptive modes of presentation, is that their reference is determined relationally rather than satisfactionally. In natural language, there is a class of expressions, namely indexicals, which have that property as well: their reference is determined through contextual relations (between the token indexical and the entity it refers to). The linguistic phenomenon of indexicality is relatively well understood, so it is worth enquiring whether the indexical model applies in the mental realm. According to Kent Bach, it does: he refers to non-descriptive modes of presentation as 'mental indexicals'. In this book I too defend the applicability of the indexical model to singular thought, and to mental files qua vehicles of singular thought. Mental files, I will argue, possess the essential features of indexicals. (The main problem for this view comes from stable files—files whose reference does not seem to depend upon the occasion of tokening. We shall deal with them in Chapter 6.)

As expression types, indexicals do not refer. Only tokens of an indexical refer, because indexical reference is achieved through relations between tokens of the indexical and other entities in the context of tokening; entities which gain their status as referent in virtue of standing in these relations to the relevant token. For example, a token of 'I' refers to the person who stands in the appropriate relation to that token in the context of tokening, that of being its utterer or producer; a token of 'here' refers to the place where the token is produced; and so on and so forth. Correlatively, only a token of an indexical sentence expresses a proposition. A type indexical, and the type sentence in which it occurs, only possess a linguistic meaning (a 'character'), which Kaplan describes as a rule mapping tokens of the indexical expression/sentence to the 'contents' they carry in context. Thus the character of 'I' is the rule that (a token of) 'I' refers to the person who produces it, the character of 'here' is the rule that a token of 'here' refers to the place where it is tokened, and so on and so forth. Since the character of an indexical encodes the relation that must hold between a token of the indexical and an entity for that entity to be assigned to this token as its referent, indexicals are aptly called 'token-reflexives': their linguistic meaning reflects the relations which hold between their tokens and their referents.

Besides Kaplan (to whom we owe the character/content distinction) and Reichenbach (to whom we owe the idea of token-reflexivity), another theorist of indexicality who deserves credit is C. S. Peirce. Peirce introduced the type/token discussion into the philosophy of language, and he offered a tripartite classification of signs into icons, indices, and symbols. A symbol is a sign that signifies by convention, while an index signifies in virtue of 'existential relations' to entities in the context in which the sign is tokened. (Icons can be ignored in the context of the present discussion.) As a sign of fire, smoke is an index; it signifies in virtue of its causal relation to fire. The word 'fire' is a symbol: it is a sign of fire in virtue of the conventions of the English language. But there are also hybrid signs, that is, signs which belong to several categories simultaneously. Indexicals are a case in point. They are symbols, according to Peirce: like the word 'fire', they have meaning in virtue of the semantic conventions of English. That standing meaning corresponds to their Kaplanian 'character'. But in context, indexicals mean what they do in virtue of contextual relations holding between tokens of the indexical and their referent. Thus the relation between a token of 'I' and its referent is like the relation between smoke and fire. Since the reference of an indexical depends upon a contextual relation to other things in the context of tokening, indexicals are indices. Thus they are both symbols and indices, and belong to the hybrid category of 'indexical symbols'. Their most interesting feature actually is the connection between the standing meaning of the type and the relational meaning of the token: what the meaning of the type actually encodes *is* the relation which holds between the token and the referent. That connection is most neatly captured through the Reichenbachian notion of 'token-reflexivity'.

Figure 1 summarizes what I call the indexical model, inspired from the work of Peirce, Reichenbach, and Kaplan. The key features of the model are the following ingredients:

(i) There are *two semantic dimensions*, corresponding to character and content, or to standing meaning and reference, and they map onto the type/token distinction.

(ii) Reference is determined through *contextual relations* to the token (hence indexicals are context-sensitive).

(iii) The standing meaning is 'token-reflexive'—it reflects the relation between token and referent.

Does this model apply to thought? Obviously, the notion of conventional meaning does not apply in the mental realm. But at least the type/token distinction applies. As far as mental files are concerned, they are typed according to the type of ER relation they

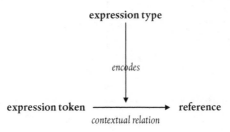

Figure 1. The Indexical Model for Language

exploit. Thus the SELF file exploits the relation in virtue of which one can gain information about oneself in a way in which one can gain information about no one else (as Frege puts it). My SELF file is not the same as yours, and they refer to different persons, of course, but they belong to the same type: they are both SELF files, unified by the common ER relation it is their function to exploit. We see that the *function* of files—namely, informational exploitation of the relevant ER relation—plays the same role as the conventional meaning of indexicals: through their functional role, mental file types map to types of ER relations, just as, through their linguistic meaning (their character), indexical types map to types of contextual relation between token and referent. The indexical model therefore applies to mental files, modulo the substitution of functional role for linguistic meaning (Figure 2).

At this point, the obvious question which arises is: What are the existence and individuation conditions for mental file tokens? To this issue I now turn.

2

Since the function of a (type of) file is to exploit a given (type of) ER relation, a token of that type should come into existence only if the subject stands in the appropriate contextual relation to some entity,

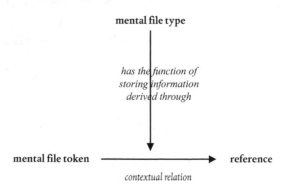

Figure 2. The Indexical Model for Thought

a relation in virtue of which it will be possible for him or her to gain information from it.[1] Unless there is an information channel of the appropriate type which the file can exploit, there should be no tokening of that type of file. Or, to put it in slightly different terms: opening a file of type α in a context c presupposes that there is, in c, a unique object x such that the subject stands in relation R_α to x and, in virtue of standing in that relation to x, is able to gain information from it which the role of the file is to store. So the very existence of mental files (qua tokens) appears to be contingent upon the existence of certain contextual relations to entities in the environment. (This will be qualified shortly.)

On this view, a file (token) exists, or should exist, only as long as the subject is in the right acquaintance relation to some entity; a relation which makes it possible for him or her to gain information concerning that entity. Thus in virtue of being a certain person, I am in a position to gain information concerning that person through e.g. proprioception. The mental file SELF serves as repository for information gained in this way. The mode of presentation HERE which occurs in my current thoughts concerning this place is a temporary mental file dependent upon my present relation to the place in question. I occupy this place, and this enables me to gain information concerning it simply by looking and listening. The perceptual information thus gained goes into the temporary file, and, when the contextual relation on which the information link depends no longer exists, the file is suppressed. When I leave this room, I can no longer think of this room as HERE; I have to think of it under a different mode of presentation. I can still think HERE-thoughts, but the HERE-modes of presentation occurring in those thoughts will be modes of presentation of different places, hence different modes of presentation (though modes of presentation of the same *type* as my present HERE-mode of presentation).

---

[1] I say 'should' because the claim is normative (see below).

Likewise, demonstrative files, such as the files THAT MAN or THAT THING, are based on certain contextual relations to objects, in virtue of which we can not only perceive them but also focus our attention on them in a discriminating manner. When we are no longer in a position to perceive the object or to focus our attention on it, we can no longer think of it under the demonstrative mode of presentation which depends upon the existence of a suitable demonstrative relation.

What happens when the contextual relation to the object ceases to hold? As I have just pointed out, I can no longer think of a place as HERE if I no longer occupy that place. And I cannot think demonstratively of an object which I can no longer perceive. In both cases, however, *another* mode of presentation—another file, based on another relation to the object—becomes available as a substitute. For example, when a demonstrative mode of presentation comes out of existence because the demonstrative relation on which it is based no longer holds, another relation comes to hold, in virtue of which I *remember* the object. On that relation another mode of presentation is based, distinct from but closely related to the original demonstrative mode of presentation. Following Evans (1982), let us call the new mode of presentation a 'memory demonstrative'. Just as demonstrative modes of presentation are based on demonstrative relations in virtue of which one can perceive the object, memory demonstratives are based on certain relations in virtue of which one can *remember* the object. Through our memories of the object, we can focus our attention on it even after the perceptual encounter has ended. So we can say that the demonstrative THAT MAN [WHOM I SEE] is *converted into* a memory demonstrative THAT MAN [WHOM I SAW]. (Likewise, HERE can be converted into THERE, and NOW into THEN.) A first and rough answer to the question I raised ('What happens when the contextual relation to the object ceases to hold?') is therefore the following: When the contextual relation to the object is severed, the temporary file based on it disappears, but the information stored in the file does not disappear: it is transferred into the new file.[2]

I will return to the issue of 'cognitive dynamics' (conversion of files etc.) in Chapter 7. The issue we are at present concerned with is the existence and individuation conditions of mental file tokens. I said that the existence of a mental file token is contingent upon the existence of a suitable contextual relation to some entity which, in virtue of that relation, achieves the status of referent of the file. This suggests that a file cannot be tokened unless the relevant relation to the referent obtains, and this, in turn, entails that file tokens necessarily refer. This, it seems to me, is unduly strong and should be revised.

That the subject should stand in a suitable ER relation to some entity (the referent of the file) is a *normative requirement* corresponding to the function of the file. But there is no function without a possibility of malfunction. Since malfunctioning can always occur, there is no reason why a file could not be tokened even though the normative requirement is not met. For example, there may be no object to which one is R-related, or the information channel which the file token exploits may put us in relation to several objects instead of exactly one. In such cases the tokening will typically be infelicitous; but the file will be tokened nonetheless. So we should draw a sharp distinction between (i) the normative conditions on file tokening which follow from the function of files and (ii) the conditions under which a file token actually comes into existence. The normative requirement imposed by the file type on its tokens demands that, for the whole duration of the token's existence, there be a unique object y such that $\iota x\, R(\tau,x) = y$, where 'τ' is the token and 'R' is the relation to the token which exactly one object must bear in order to be the object the file is about. All the information in the file token will be

---

[2] 'Linking' also enables information to be saved through transfer into another file. On linking, see Chapter 4.

about that putative object, in such a way that exploitation and integration of that information can occur (e.g. if the file contains the predicates 'is happy' and 'is French', it will be possible to infer that someone is both happy and French). For a file token to come into existence, however, it is sufficient that there be a *presumption* that the normative conditions are (or will be) satisfied. The conditions in question need not be actually met: various cases in which they fail to be satisfied will be discussed in Part VI.[3]

3

I have described indexical modes of presentation as files which (ideally) exist only as long as the ER relations on which they are based (hence the possibility of gaining information about the object by exploiting the relations) exist. At this point, however, we need to introduce a distinction between two types of file based on ER relations.

'Proto-files', as I am going to call them, can *only* host information gained in virtue of the ER relation to the referent. For example, the proto-file SELF* can only host information gained 'from inside', in the first-person way; the demonstrative proto-file THAT MAN* can only host information gained by perceptually attending to the object. I call these files 'proto-files' (and mark them with an asterisk) rather than files *simpliciter* because I want files (properly speaking) to serve as individual *concepts*, i.e. thought constituents; and I take proto-files to lack a distinguishing characteristic of concepts.

---

[3] In some cases there is not even a presumption that the normative conditions are satisfied. For example, there may be no object at all serving as referent of the file, and the thinker may be aware that there is no object. As Segal puts it, 'empty files can arise either when someone falsely believes in the existence of a corresponding individual, or in cases of abstention, *or even in cases where the subject believes that there is no individual*' (Segal 2002: 81). He adds: 'you have a concept of Sherlock Holmes, don't you?' In such cases, I will argue, the file has a derived, metarepresentational function; it is an 'indexed file' (Chapters 14–15).

Concepts, in general, satisfy or ought to satisfy what Evans calls the Generality Constraint. Evans says that a subject in possession of a predicative concept *F* should be able to entertain thoughts in which that concept is applied to any object of which the subject has an individual concept; similarly,

> If a subject can be credited with the thought that *a* is *F*, then he must have the conceptual resources for entertaining the thought that *a* is *G*, for every property of being *G* of which he has a conception. This is the condition that I call 'The Generality Constraint'. (Evans 1982: 104)

In the mental file framework, predication is understood as follows: the file is what stands for the object of which something is predicated, and the predicate's location within the file means that it is taken to apply to the object in question. Translated into mental file talk, the Generality Constraint says that a file should be hospitable to any predicative concept in the subject's possession. Clearly, that is a constraint which proto-files do not satisfy. Take the proto-file SELF*: it can only host information gained from inside, through e.g. proprioception or introspection. Now, as I pointed out already,[4] there is much information about myself that I cannot gain in this way. My date of birth is something I learn through communication, in the same way in which I learn my parents' birthdates. In virtue of the Generality Constraint, it should be possible for that information to go into my SELF file, and that is the crucial difference between the SELF file and the (non-conceptual) proto-file SELF* from which it originates.

In contrast to proto-files, which are based on some ER relation and can only host information derived through that relation, a (conceptual) file based on a certain ER relation contains two sorts of information: information gained in the special way that goes with that relation (first-person information, in the case of the SELF file),

---

[4] See n. 8, p. 36.

and information not gained in this way but *concerning the same individual as information gained in that way*. Information about my birthdate is a case in point: I gain that information in a third-person way, through communication (as I might come to know anybody's birthdate), but I take that piece of information to concern the same person about whom I also have direct first-person information, i.e. myself; so that information, too, goes into the SELF file. I am therefore able to exercise my SELF concept in thinking 'I was born in 1952.'

It is because of that dual aspect of the SELF concept qua satisfier of the Generality Constraint that there are two types of 'I'-thoughts: those that are, and those that are not, immune to error through misidentification. When some information is gained from inside, that is, in virtue of the ER relation on which the SELF file is based, that information can only be about the subject: the way the information is gained determines which object it concerns (or, equivalently, in which file it goes). As a result, as Evans puts it, 'there just does not appear to be a gap between the subject's having information (or appearing to have information), in the appropriate way, that the property of being *F* is instantiated, and his having information (or appearing to have information) that *he* is *F* (Evans 1982: 221). But when some information about ourselves is gained from outside, it goes into the SELF file only in virtue of a judgement of identity.[5] The thought 'I was born in 1952' can thus be seen as the product of two thoughts: the thought that a certain person, namely the person I hear about in a given episode of communication, was born in 1952, and the thought that I am the person talked about. The thought that I was born in 1952 thus turns out to be 'identification-dependent', in Evans's terminology.

Despite the fact that they can host information not derived through the ER relation on which the file is based, the file is still based

---

[5] Or, in mental file talk: the information goes into the self file in virtue of a 'link' between that file and some other file.

on that relation. What this means is that, assuming the normative conditions associated with the file-type are met, *the file exists only as long as the relation exists,* and with it the special way of gaining information about the referent through the relation. Files should therefore be seen as an *expansion* of proto-files, including the proto-files themselves as their nucleus.[6] (The transition from proto-files to conceptual files is a difficult issue which I will touch upon in Chapter 8, §3 and in the appendix to that chapter.)

---

[6] Peacocke notes that when the subject falls prey to a perceptual illusion of which he is aware, the content of the illusion ought not to figure in the subject's conceptual file about himself, because, at the level of judgement, 'the subject rejects the content of his more primitive, pre-judgemental phenomenology' (Peacocke 2012: 84). This might be taken to argue against the inclusion of the primitive proto-file within the conceptual file. I acknowledge the difficulty, but cannot discuss the issue here.

6

Stable Files

Because files are based on (and their referent determined through) contextual relations, I advocated an indexical model, according to which files exist only as long as the relation they exploit contextually holds, or is presumed to hold. Indexical concepts such as those we express using indexical words or phrases like 'here' or 'that man' are thus construed as temporary files, which exist only as long as the context they are tokened in satisfies, or is taken to satisfy, the presupposition of the file.

In some cases, however, the file does not have a temporary character. Thus the SELF file is stable, in contrast to, say, demonstrative files. A demonstrative file exists only within a limited context: it exists only as long as the subject bears the demonstrative relation (whatever that relation is exactly) to some object x—a relation which makes it possible for the subject to focus his or her attention on x. If x disappears from view for sufficiently long, a change of context takes place and the file comes out of existence (or rather, it is converted into a memory demonstrative). In the SELF case, however, the relevant ER relation is the identity relation. The subject's self-identity is not a relation which holds in one context but not in another; it is a relation which, if it holds, holds forever and necessarily. So the idea that the SELF concept is indexical, or that the indexical model applies to the SELF file, has been subjected to criticism (see e.g. Millikan 1990).

I think we can discern two potential lines of criticism here. One first reason for denying indexicality in the case of the SELF file is the *permanence* of the file (in contrast to the temporary nature of indexical files such as the HERE file or demonstrative files). This reason I take to be rather superficial. What matters is less the duration of the file than its dependence on a contextual relation. If some contextual relation holds permanently, a file based on that relation will not be a temporary file, yet it will still possess the critical feature which makes it indexical. At this point, however, a deeper reason for denying indexicality to the SELF file emerges: in what sense, one might ask, is the subject's identity to himself or herself a contextual relation—a relation which may hold in one context but not in another? One paragraph back I conceded that the subject's self-identity is not a contextual relation in that sense. So the indexical model seems to break down, even if the temporary nature of the file is not taken to be essential.

In response, I wish to draw a distinction between two types of relation to objects of acquaintance. First there are the relations which the *subject* bears to the entities she or he is acquainted with. In the case of HERE, the subject bears a certain (contextual) relation to a place: she or he occupies it (and can think of it as HERE). In the demonstrative case the relation is what I called the demonstrative relation (the relation to objects which makes it possible for us to think of them demonstratively). Second, we have the relations between the mental files (tokens) and the same entities. These are the token-reflexive relations, properly speaking. They are typically characterized in terms of the former relations, that is, in terms of the subject's relations to the objects she or he is acquainted with. Thus if the subject bears relation R to some object x which, on the basis of that relation, he can gain information from in a certain way w, and if a file f in the subject's mind is used to store information gained in the way w, then, automatically, there will be a token-reflexive relation R^* between the file f and x. In the case of HERE that will be the relation which holds between a place and a mental file whenever the mental file is tokened in the mind of a person who occupies the place and serves to store information that person is in a position to gain in virtue of occupying that place. Likewise, the demonstrative relation between an individual and some object can be used to characterize the token-reflexive relation between a demonstrative file and that same object, namely the relation which holds between a file and an object whenever the file is tokened in the mind of someone who bears the demonstrative relation to that object and serves to store information that person is in a position to gain in virtue of standing in that relation to the object.

In the SELF case too, we can draw a distinction between the two types of relation. And this provides us with a response to the second line of criticism. Admittedly, the subject's relation to himself, namely identity, does not count as a 'contextual relation'. In this case as in the others, however, the subject's ER relation to the objects he gets information from (here, himself) gives rise to a derived relation between that object and the mental file in which that information is stored. In the SELF case the derived relation is that between the file and the individual in whose mind the file occurs. *That* is a contextual relation. The SELF file (type) is tokened in each of us, and in each case it refers to the individual to whom it bears the contextual relation $\lambda x \lambda y$ (x is tokened in y's mind and serves to store information y is in a position to gain about y in virtue of the fact that he is y). So the indexical model applies after all.[1]

---

[1] Earlier, I said that the ER relation on which it is based is what fixes the reference of the file, but that should be qualified in view of the distinction I have just drawn between two types of relations: the subject's relation to the object he is acquainted with and the token-reflexive relation between the mental file in the subject's mind and this object. It is, I submit, the token-reflexive relation which has the reference-fixing role, rather than the acquaintance relation in terms of which it is characterized. As Derek Ball pointed out to me, if it was the subject's acquaintance relations which directly fixed the reference,

2

There are other files that are relatively stable. Recognitional files are a case in point. Recognitional files are based on a relation to the object which I call 'familiarity'. An object is familiar to the subject just in case *multiple exposure to that object has created and maintained in the subject a disposition to recognize that object* (Recanati 2006a: 251).

Since recognitional files depend upon the continued existence of the subject's disposition to recognize the object, which disposition transcends particular encounters with the object, they are stable, in contrast to demonstrative files. Despite their stability, however, they still fit the indexical model. First, they depend for their very existence upon the existence of a contextual relation to the object, namely the relation of familiarity. Second, the reference of a recognitional file itself depends upon the context: it is that object (if any) multiple exposure to which has created and maintained in the subject the recognitional disposition which underlies the file. Which object that is depends upon the context. In a different environment, the very same recognitional device in place in the subject would have had the function of detecting another object than what it actually has the function of detecting in the actual environment.

we would have a problem in the demonstrative case. One can stand in the demonstrative relation to two distinct objects simultaneously. For example we can think, about two distinct objects: 'That is F but that is not F.' If it was the subject's acquaintance relation which fixed the reference, there would be a single referent for the two occurrences of the demonstrative in that thought, since both are based on the same acquaintance relation, namely the demonstrative relation. We do not have that problem if we say that what fixes the reference is the token-reflexive relation, namely the relation which holds between a file and an object whenever the file serves as repository for information gained by someone (the person in whose mind it is tokened) in virtue of that person's standing in the demonstrative relation to the object. Even if the subject simultaneously stands in the demonstrative relation to two objects, *a* and *b*, there will be two different files, A and B: A will refer to *a* in virtue of A's standing in the token-reflexive demonstrative relation to *a* while B will refer to *b* in virtue of B's standing in the token-reflexive demonstrative relation to *b*.

It is tempting—though not mandatory—to construe natural-kind concepts as recognitional files, distinguished from the above by the fact that their content is not an individual object.[2] We use the superficial or 'stereotypical' properties of water to detect water in the environment. What we detect is that substance (H_2O) multiple exposure to which has created and maintained in us the disposition to recognize it. In a different environment a different substance would possibly play the same role: it would have the same superficial characteristics and multiple exposure to *it* would have created and maintained in us the same disposition to recognize *it* via those characteristics. In such a context we would have a concept very similar to our WATER-concept and internally indistinguishable from it, but it would not be a concept of water. It would be a concept of twater or XYZ (however we call the substance which plays the role of water on Twin-Earth). On this familiar, Putnamian picture, the reference of our WATER-concept depends upon the context, even if the context at issue is much broader than the context relevant to determining the reference of HERE.

But as I said, construing natural kind concepts as indexical (more specifically, as a variety of recognitional concepts) it is not mandatory, far from it. After all, if I lost my capacity to recognize water, I would not necessarily lose my WATER file. I would still know all sorts of things about water. Similarly, I can recognize Obama, but my OBAMA concept does not reduce to a recognitional concept. I would not lose my concept if I lost my capacity to recognize Obama. The relevant concepts seem to be detachable from any specific informational relation to the referent. If that is

---

[2] Though not individual objects, natural kinds are *substances* in the sense of Millikan (1998, 2000). 'Paradigmatic substances....are individuals (Mama, the Empire State Building), stuffs (gold, milk), and natural kinds (mouse, geode)....The task of substance concepts is to enable us to reidentify substances through diverse media and under diverse conditions, and to enable us over time to accumulate practical skills and theoretical knowledge about these substances and to use what we have learned' (Millikan 2000: 1–2).

correct, does this not entail that the indexical model ultimately breaks down? I am going to argue that it doesn't.

3

So far, the files I have talked about are very closely tied to specific ER relations on which they are based. The file exists only as long as the relation (hence the possibility of gaining information about the object by exploiting the relation) exists, and for that reason the life expectancy of many files is rather short. As we have seen, there are exceptions—thus recognitional files, being based upon an enduring relation, are more stable and last longer than standard indexical files. All these files, however temporary and short-lived, are what we might call 'first-order' files, based on specific ER relations. But as we have just seen, we must allow room for more abstract files: files that are not based on specific contextual relations enabling us to gain information about the referent in particular ways. The question is whether the indexical model is thereby impugned.

In *Direct Reference*, I put forward the following picture. Some files (the *indexical* files) are based on specific contextual relations, such as one's relation of identity to oneself or the relation to what we hold in our hand, but others (the *encyclopedic* files) are based on a more general-purpose tracking relation. Thus my file about Mont Blanc contains all the information I can get about the mountain, *however it is gained.* It is not tied to a particular way of gaining information, nor to a specific ER relation. An encyclopedic file may exploit a number of ER relations to the reference of the file, in an opportunistic manner, instead of being based on a single one. Any relation will do, provided it preserves the link to the object. In this case, what determines the reference of the file is the overarching tracking relation: the relation between the file and the object it has been created to track (however it *is* tracked). Not being based on a specific ER relation, an encyclopedia entry is not short-lived, as the other type of file typically is. It survives when our contextual relation to the reference changes.

This might suggest that encyclopedic files are not based on ER relations, and that we should give up the indexical model in this case at least. Indeed, encyclopedia entries are more like *names* than they are like indexicals (Recanati 1993: 181–7). If, to deal with them, we introduce a second model in addition to the indexical model, this may lead us to re-analyse some of the files I have described as indexical. Thus Papineau, as we shall see in Chapter 7, holds that perceptual files in general are 'namelike': they are not indexical.

But I think we *can* fit encyclopedia entries into the indexical model. The only thing we need is to make room for a new sort of *relation* to the referent: a higher-order relation which holds whenever we stand in *some* ER relations to it. In other words, rather than say that some files are not based on relations to the referent, I draw a distinction between specific ER relations and the *higher-order ER relation* on which encyclopedia entries are based, namely

$$\lambda x \lambda y \, [(\exists R)(Rx,y)]$$

where 'R' ranges over ER relations. A subject (or a mental file in the subject's mind) x stands in that relation to an object y just in case there is/are some first-order ER relation(s) in which x stands to y. A file based on the higher-order relation hosts any information derived in virtue of that relation, that is, ultimately, any information derived in virtue of any of the first-order ER relations. Such files correspond to what Perry calls 'detached' files.[3]

---

[3] 'Think of the architecture of our beliefs as a three-story building. At the top level are detached files.... At the bottom level are perceptions and perceptual buffers. Buffers are new notions associated with the perceptions and used to temporarily store ideas we gain from the perceptions until we can identify the individual, or form a permanent detached notion for him, or forget about him. The middle level is full of informational wiring. Sockets dangle down from above, and plugs stick up from below' (Perry 2001a: 120–1; see also Perry 2012: 86–9).

Encyclopedia entries come at the top of a hierarchy of files. It is legitimate to speak of a *hierarchy*, for two reasons. First, files at each of the levels I have described presuppose files at the previous level. Proto-files are the most basic; conceptual files are generated from them (through what I called 'expansion'). Among conceptual files, first-order files are more basic, since higher-order files—encyclopedia entries—presuppose them. Second, files can be ordered in terms of how closely tied they are to specific ER relations. Proto-files are very closely tied to specific ER relations since they can only host information derived on the basis of these relations. This constraint in relaxed in conceptual files. Still, conceptual files remain closely tied to ER relations in the sense that their existence (like that of proto-files) is conditional upon the putative existence of specific ER relations to the referent. This second constraint is relaxed in encyclopedia entries, since they do not depend upon specific ER relations for their very existence, but only on there being some ER relation or other to the referent. Still, all types of file, including encyclopedia entries, are based upon ER relations to the object they are about, and their reference depends upon the ER relations on which they are based. That is the gist of the indexical model.

7

The Dynamics of Files

David Papineau has criticized the indexical model on the grounds that indexical words 'refer to different entities in different contexts of use', while a perceptual concept such as 'that bird', which Papineau himself is willing to construe as a mental file (see below), 'picks out the same bird whenever it is exercised'. Papineau therefore objects to the view that such concepts are 'demonstrative', and work like indexicals. They are, he maintains, more like proper names.

> You see a bird at the bottom of your garden. You look at it closely, and at the same time think *I haven't seen THAT in here before*. Later on you can recall the bird in visual imagination, perhaps thinking *I wonder if THAT was a migrant*. In addition, on further perceptual encounters with birds, you sometimes take some bird to be the same bird again, and can again form further thoughts about it, such as *THAT bird has a pleasant song...*
>
> In examples like this, I shall say that subjects are exercising *perceptual concepts*. Perceptual concepts allow subjects to think about perceptible entities. Such concepts are formed when subjects initially perceive the relevant entities, and they are re-activated by later perceptual encounters....
>
> It is quite wrong to classify perceptual concepts as demonstratives. If anything is definitive of demonstrative terms, it is surely that they display some species of *characterlikeness*. By this I mean that the referential

value of the term is context-dependent—the *sameself* term will refer to different items in different contexts. However, there seems nothing characterlike about the kind of perceptual concept illustrated in the above examples. Whenever it is exercised, your perceptual concept refers to the *same* bird. (Papineau 2006: 113)

What are perceptual concepts, then? According to Papineau, they are mental files associated with specific 'sensory templates':

> These templates will be set up on initial encounters with the relevant referents. They will then be reactivated on later perceptual encounters, via matches between incoming stimuli and stored template—perhaps the incoming stimuli can be thought of as 'resonating' with the stored pattern and thereby being amplified.... The function of the templates is to accumulate information about the relevant referents, and thereby guide the subject's future interactions with them... Note that this function of carrying information from one use to another highlights the distinction between perceptual concepts and demonstratives. Demonstrative terms do not so carry a body of information with them, for the obvious reason that they refer to different entities on different occasions of use. Information about an entity referred to by a demonstrative on one occasion will not in general apply to whatever entity happens to be the referent the next time the demonstrative is used. By contrast, perceptual concepts are suited to serve as repositories of information precisely because they refer to the same thing whenever they are exercised. (Papineau 2006: 114–15)

In the passages I have just quoted, Papineau offers two distinct objections to the indexical model. I do not think these objections succeed: the first one is easy to dispose of, while the second one can be met by appealing to the operation on files which I call 'conversion'. After rebutting these two objections (§2), I will turn to a third one which is potentially the most powerful (§3). That objection exploits the contrast, introduced in Chapter 4, between presumptions of identity and judgements of identity. To respond to the objection, I will introduce a new type of ER relation which plays a crucial role in the dynamics of files: *composite* ER relations (§4). As we shall see, composite ER relations, and the files based on them, rest on certain presumptions of identity.[1]

2

Papineau argues that the very idea of a mental file or 'repository' in which information can 'accumulate' is incompatible with the indexical model, for accumulation of information requires stability, while indexicals are unstable (their referent systematically shifts). That is the first objection. It can easily be disposed of, because demonstrative concepts do achieve stability within the context in which they exist.

It is simply not true that, on the indexical picture, demonstrative concepts shift their reference each time they are exercised. During an episode in which I look at a bird and entertain a demonstrative concept ('that bird'), I can form a number of demonstrative thoughts involving that selfsame concept which will then refer to the same bird, namely the bird to which I am demonstratively related for the whole duration of the perceptual episode. To be sure, when the demonstrative relation comes to an end, the demonstrative concepts disappears (or rather it is 'converted'), but during the temporal interval in which the demonstrative relation holds, it can be exercised as many times as we wish, and the demonstrative relation exploited to accumulate information about the bird.[2]

---

[1] Files based on composite ER relations correspond to the 'compound senses' Campbell talks about in 'Is Sense Transparent?' (Campbell 1987: 279–80).

[2] This shows that the type/token distinction is not sufficient and that we need a three-fold distinction between type, token, and occurrence (Recanati 2006b: 24–5). We need to distinguish the file token, which (in principle) comes into existence as soon as the subject stands in the relevant ER relation to the referent and goes out of existence when the relation no longer holds, and a particular occurrence (or 'exercise' or 'activation') of the file token in a given thought. The reference of the file (token) remains stable across occurrences, contrary to what Papineau suggests.

Nor is it an incidental feature of demonstrative concepts that they can persist through time in this manner, thereby making accumulation of information possible. It has often been pointed out that demonstrative thinking rests on an ability to keep track of objects, an ability that can only be exercised over time. Thus, according to Evans,

> We have to regard the static notion of 'having hold of an object at t' as essentially an abstraction from the dynamic notion of 'keeping track of an object from t to t'.' And the grasp, at t, of a thought of the kind suggested...requires a subject to possess at t an ability to keep track of a particular object over time. It is not precluded that one should have only a momentary grasp of [the] thought, for it is not precluded that, after an object has engaged with one's capacity to keep track of objects of that kind, one should lose track of it, and with it, the thought. Indeed it is an aspect of the capacity that the subject will, in general, know when this has happened. (Evans 1985: 311)

Campbell and Burge make related points. According to Campbell (1987: 287), being able to keep track of things over time is intrinsic to the capacity to use perceptual identifications of particular things in the context of observational judgements such as 'That table is round.'[3] Similarly, Burge claims that

> A certain sort of tracking is crucial in an individual's ability to perceive and have perceptual beliefs as of bodies. A sound basis for this requirement is that some such capacity is necessary for an individual to be representing bodies instead of events....Bodies are perceptually distinguishable partly and fundamentally through their continuity of

---

[3] 'One might be inclined to suppose that demonstratives should be thought of as instantaneous "snapshots" of objects, because one can after all make such a judgment as "that table is round" on the strength of a momentary glimpse of it. It may therefore be promising to suppose that someone could come to understand observational concepts without having the capacity to keep track of the things around him. The problem is that such a person would not be able to operate with the inferential structure that we use in marking the distinction between something's *seeming* to fall under an observational concept and its *really* doing so' (Campbell 1987: 287).

> boundary integrity over time. An ability to track by way of such continuity is a basic differentiating ability. Tracking the movement of bodies is one common realization of such an ability. Tracking a single unmoving object over some lapse of time is another. (Burge 2010: 198–9)

I conclude that demonstrative files exist over a period of time, corresponding to the period during which the demonstrative relation to the object holds. Within the relevant temporal interval, a demonstrative concept such as 'that bird' (Papineau's example) can be exercised repeatedly, and information about the referent can accumulate.

Papineau's second objection to the indexical model highlights the continuity between what I (mistakenly, according to him) describe as different files: demonstrative files, the memory demonstratives they convert into, and recognitional files. For Papineau there is just one file, which is initialized on the first encounter with the object, stored into memory (and possibility used in imagination), re-activated on further encounters as one recognizes the object as the same we experienced before, and consolidated as one becomes more and more familiar with the object. That this is always the same file, and not distinct files, is shown by the fact that information accumulates from one encounter to the next.[4]

What Papineau calls 'perceptual files' indeed correspond to three distinct types of file in my framework: demonstrative files, memory demonstratives, and recognitional files. Papineau denies that they are distinct files, and offers the 'accumulation of information' argument

---

[4] Papineau here tacitly appeals to a principle made explicit by Simon Prosser in the following passage: 'In the absence of identity beliefs, changes of opinion or lapses of memory a predicate will be retained and attached to a singular mode of presentation [a mental file] if and only if the same singular mode of presentation to which the predicate was originally attached is itself retained' (Prosser 2005: 373). This says, in effect, that the informational content of a file is retained only to the extent that the file itself is retained. That is precisely what I am about to deny. A piece of information may be retained despite a change of mental file (= an adjustment of mode of presentation), provided the new file inherits the content of the old file; so the fact that information is preserved cannot be used to argue that the mode of presentation (the file) has not changed.

in support of his claim that they are a single file. In response, I concede that, when an object is encountered and some information about it is gained, that information is typically preserved in memory and made available when the object is encountered again and recognized; new information can then enrich the initial body of information. This gives credibility to Papineau's claim that we are dealing with a single file. Yet the objection does not go through, because it is possible to account for the preservation of information across files within the indexical model.

It is a well-known property of indexical expressions that the content they express so depends upon the context that, if the context changes, the same content cannot be expressed again unless we adjust the indexicals to the new context. As Frege said,

> If someone wants to say today what he expressed yesterday using the word 'today', he will replace this word with 'yesterday'. Although the thought is the same its verbal expression must be different in order that the change of sense which would otherwise be effected by the differing times of utterance may be cancelled out. (G. Frege, 'Thought', in Beaney 1997: 132)

Similarly, an adjustment of indexical concepts, which is what I call *conversion*, must take place if the context changes. Conversion is at work when, for example, a demonstrative file gives way to a memory demonstrative. Conversion is the process through which information stored in a file is transferred into a successor file when the ER relation which sustains the initial file comes to an end.

By appealing to conversion, it is possible, within the indexical model, to do justice to Papineau's observations regarding the 'name-like' character of perceptual files. Information accumulates despite the distinctness of the files, because *one file inherits the content of another* (a feature which is definitive of conversion). This gives a sense in which demonstrative files, memory demonstratives, and recognitional files are 'the same file'. They are stages of the same evolving body of information. At *t* the subject sees the object, and can store information derived from the perceptual episode; the function of the perceptual buffer is to store that information. As the episode comes to an end, the subject stays, through memory, in contact with the object, but the relation to the object is different. Since the relation changes, I said that the perceptual file is replaced by a memory file, but the word 'replacement' hides the continuity between the memory file and the initial perceptual file: in a certain sense, it is the same file—the same body of information—that changes its status as the ER relation on which it is based changes. It is that continuity which the notion of conversion highlights. But this is compatible with the indexical model, according to which demonstrative files, memory files, and recognitional files are (in a different sense) distinct files. Files are supposed to fill the mode of presentation role, and there is no doubt that an object is *not* thought of under the same mode of presentation when one sees it for the first time, and when it is a familiar object one immediately recognizes.

I conclude that there are two distinct notions of file. First, there is the file qua evolving body of information putatively about a single object. Following Dean Pettit's suggestion, we may call it the 'pile' (for 'pile of information'). The file proper is more fine-grained. It involves a specific ER relation serving as information channel, in addition to a body of information gathered through that relation or through linking. The body of information, which may evolve within a given file, may also *survive* a change of file. In conversion, as we have just seen, one file succeeds another as the ER relation to the referent changes, but the body of information is preserved. Insofar as the pile is distinct from the file, and can survive a change of file, the persistence of the pile, and the fact that information about the referent accumulates, does not show that the file itself persists. So Papineau's argument does not go through.[5]

---

[5] Kaplan (1989a: 537–8) formulates the question of 'cognitive dynamics' as follows: What is it to retain an indexical belief, e.g. the belief that today is beautiful, over time? Here is a partial answer: Belief retention cannot involve retention of the file since the file

3

It is, I said, mental files in the fine-grained sense (files proper) which play the mode of presentation role. But this can be denied. Indeed, the criterion which, following Campbell, I used to distinguish the cases in which there is a single mode of presentation from the cases in which there are two seems to support Papineau's coarser-grained approach to file individuation.

As we saw in Chapter 4, mental files are a matter of information clustering. Clustering takes place when all the information derives from the same source, through the same ER relation, or is presumed to do so. The role of the file is precisely to treat all the information as if it concerned one and the same object, from which it derives. As Campbell emphasizes, this gives us a criterion for telling apart the cases in which there is a single file and the cases in which there are two. If the subject 'trades upon identity' and proceeds to integrate various pieces of information directly, without appealing to a further identity premise, that means that there is a single mode of presentation. That may well happen even if the relevant pieces of information are gained through distinct sense modalities. Campbell gives the example of someone looking at a glass and thinking: 'that glass is full', then touching the glass and judging: 'that glass is rigid'. In such circumstances the subject could make the following, cross-modal inference: 'that glass is full; that glass is rigid; so there is something that is both full and rigid'. Here the subject trades on the identity of the object seen and the object touched. No appeal is made to an identity premise 'that (seen) glass is that (touched) glass', but the identity is (fallibly) established through the subject's non-conceptual ability to 'track the object from modality to modality' (Campbell 1987: 283, 288). Such a tracking

has to change as the context changes (e.g. the thought that 'today is beautiful' gives way to the thought that 'yesterday was beautiful'); so what is retained can only be the pile. In order to play that role, the pile must be construed as a mental particular, just like the file. (I am indebted to Steven Hall for discussion of these issues.)

ability is as fundamental as the ability to track objects through time, Campbell argues: 'The unity and stability of the world is partly constituted by the fact that it is the *same* objects that are perceived at different times or through different sensory modalities' (Campbell 1987: 290). Again, the relevant cross-modal identities are not additional premises making the subject's reasoning enthymematic: they are presupposed by the subject's cross-modal clustering of information, which itself rests upon the subject's non-conceptual ability to track the object from modality to modality. Campbell concludes that 'ways of thinking of objects are intrinsically coarse-grained with respect to the underlying perceptual information' (ibid.).

Now Papineau could argue, along the same lines and on the basis of the same criterion, that the indexical model cuts modes of presentation too finely when it comes to cross-*temporal* inferences. Let us consider the phenomenon of recognition. According to the indexical model, it works as follows. The subject's initial perception of the object at *t* has left a memory file (resulting from conversion of the initial perceptual file), and that memory file gets 'linked' to the demonstrative file corresponding to the subject's current perception of the object at *t'*. Linking is the operation on files which enables information from one file to flow freely into the other; it corresponds to a judgement of identity (Chapter 4). In the case at hand, therefore, the subject implicitly judges: this object (which I see) = that object (which I saw). Or at least, that is what the indexical model predicts. Is that prediction correct? Arguably not. There are indeed cases in which the subject, at *t'*, entertains two distinct files, a demonstrative file corresponding to some object he sees at *t'*, and a memory demonstrative corresponding to some object he saw at *t*. Then, realizing that the 'two' objects are the same, the subject links the two files through a judgement of recognition.[6] But recognition need not take this form. It can be more

---

[6] See for example Perry (2002: 195–6): 'I see my friend Al limping toward me but cannot yet recognize him; I form a notion of this person. At that moment I have two unlinked notions of Al. Certain of my beliefs about Al I have twice over, such as that he

immediate: the file in memory can be *directly activated* by the current perceptual encounter. That, I think, is the sort of case Papineau has in mind when he talks of 're-activation' of the perceptual file. Indeed, Papineau insists that recognition involves a *single* file which is stored in memory between t and t' and re-activated at t'.

The Campbell criterion seems to support Papineau's coarse-grained individuation of files and to tell against the indexical model.[7] Suppose the memory file deriving from the initial encounter with the object contains the information 'was F'. And suppose that, on the new encounter with the object, one sees that it is G. In a case of immediate recognition, the subject will trade upon the identity of the seen object and the remembered object and will judge: 'That thing, which was F, is G' (or through existential generalization: 'something that was F is G'). This is exactly parallel to the cross-modal case and should lead us to conclude, with Papineau, that modes of presentation are intrinsically coarse-grained in the temporal dimension: since the information stored in memory and the perceptual information derived from the current encounter with an object one recognizes are immediately integrated, they should be construed as part of a single file, rather than distributed into two distinct files, as per the indexical model.[8]

4

To deal with the objection, we must concede that, in immediate recognition, the subject does *not* think of the object he perceives under a demonstrative mode of presentation distinct from the memory file

is a man. Others I have in one file but not in the other, such as that he has a limp. I accumulate information about him as he gets nearer; finally I recognize him as Al. At that point the notions become linked; the newly acquired perceptual information combines with the old information, and I say *Why are you limping, Al?'*

[7] Prosser (2005: 373 ff.) uses the Campbell criterion to argue for a coarse-grained ('dynamic') individuation of modes of presentation.

[8] Additional support for this claim can be derived from Evans's remarks on 'dynamic Fregean thoughts' (Evans 1982: 292–6, 1985: 309–11).

but, from the start, under a mode of presentation which somehow *incorporates* the memory file. That, however, does not mean that we have to give up the indexical model with its fine-grained individuation of files in terms of ER relations. What we should do, rather, is introduce *more* ER relations, and more types of file based on them. In particular, we should introduce *composite* ER relations.

In the case at hand, I suggest that the mode of presentation of the object one immediately recognizes is based on the following relation:

$\lambda x \lambda y$ (*x* has been acquainted with *y* in the past and is currently standing in the demonstrative relation to *y* once again)

I call that composite ER relation *the re-acquaintance relation*. It puts a well-functioning subject in a position to recognize the object and to cluster information derived from multiple sources: memory *and* perception. A file based on that relation is a third type of demonstrative file, in addition to standard demonstratives and memory demonstratives. I call it a *recognitional demonstrative*. A recognitional demonstrative is a variety of demonstrative file; it is not a recognitional file based on the familiarity relation. (It is less stable than a recognitional file because it requires a perceptual link to the referent, while a recognitional file only requires a recognitional disposition which transcends particular episodes.)

The re-acquaintance relation results from *compounding* the relations which underwrite memory files and demonstrative files. Memory files are based on the relation of having been acquainted with the referent in the past (or having stood in the demonstrative relation to it), while standard demonstrative files are based on the demonstrative relation. Positing yet another relation which results from compounding these two enables us to draw a distinction between the cases in which the subject has two distinct modes of presentation for the same object (one based on the demonstrative relation, and the other based on the past-acquaintance relation) and the cases of immediate recognition in which the subject thinks of the object he

86

(re-)encounters under a rich mode of presentation based on multiple relations to the object (Figure 3). Only in the first type of case does linking take place. In immediate recognition, there is no linking of files, as there is a single file (based on a composite relation). To be sure, it is *presupposed* that the object which the subject stands in the demonstrative relation to is the same object he has been acquainted with before and remembers; but the subject does not *judge* that the identity holds. Rather, the identity is established, at the sub-personal level, through the subject's non-conceptual capacity to recognize the object and track it over time.

To sum up, in a case of immediate recognition of an object one has perceived in the past, the memory file which results from the conversion of the initial demonstrative file (corresponding to the first perceptual encounter) is itself converted, through perceptual re-activation, into a file which rests on *multiple* information channels: the file hosts information gained in virtue of the subject's memory of the initial encounter *as well as* information gained in virtue of the current perceptual episode. The subject's relation to the object has changed: from a pure memory relation it has evolved into a composite memory-perception relation. This is an instance of *incremental conversion*: the successor relation consists of the predecessor relation R (here, the relation of having been acquainted with the object in the past) plus some extra relation (the current demonstrative relation). Through incremental conversion, the file grows an extra information link.

On this view, one maintains the fine-grained distinction between distinct types of file based on distinct types of ER relation (e.g. the demonstrative relation, the past-acquaintance relation, the

File A — (linking) — File B		File A — (conversion) ➝ File B	
R	R'	R	R+R'
			(Composite ER relation)

Figure 3. Linking vs incremental conversion

re-acquaintance relation, the familiarity relation). These files get united through the mechanism of conversion, which makes preservation of information possible. Thus the initial demonstrative file is converted into a memory demonstrative, and the memory demonstrative itself is converted into a recognitional demonstrative when the object is re-encountered. So the indexical model is upheld. Still, one accounts for the crucial feature of immediate recognition, namely the fact that the identity of the seen object and the remembered object is established through the subject's non-conceptual capacity to recognize the object. That capacity can operate because the subject stands in the re-acquaintance relation to the object. On that relation a special sort of mental file is based, which enables the subject to store information derived from multiple sources: memory, and current perception. That there is a single mode of presentation (based on the composite relation of re-acquaintance) rather than two is what distinguishes immediate from 'slow' recognition.[9] In slow recognition the subject judges that the seen object is the remembered object: there are two modes of presentation which are linked, while in immediate recognition cases there is a single mode of presentation based on a composite relation. Identity is presupposed in the latter sort of case, without being conceptually articulated in the form of an identity judgement.[10]

---

[9] On the distinction between the two types of recognition, see Wright (2012: §§7–8).

[10] The distinction arguably sheds light on alleged counter-examples to the claim that self-ascriptions of bodily properties directly based upon a first-person experience should be immune to error through misidentification (Recanati 2012a). In the so-called 'rubber hand illusion', one wrongly identifies the hand one sees as one's own, yet the self-ascription of ownership is directly based on a first-person experience. Here, I would say, the faulty 'identification' is built into the composite ER relation at stake, so it is not an error through misidentification in the usual sense, that is, one that involves a mistaken judgement of identity.

Part IV

Mental Files and Co-Reference

The mind can always intend, and know when it intends, to think
of the Same. This *sense of sameness* is the very keel and backbone
of our thinking.
(William James 1890: 459)

8

The Circularity Objection

1

When it comes to co-reference, several distinctions are in order. First, co-reference may be 'external' or 'internal'. Second, co-reference may hold between singular terms, or between pieces of information. These two distinctions cross-cut each other, so we end up with four distinct notions—even before the phenomenon of 'co-reference *de jure*', closely related to that of informational clustering (Chapter 4), has been introduced. The relation of co-reference *de jure* itself applies both to pieces of information and to singular terms, so at the end of the day we shall have six different notions to deal with, as shown in Table 1 below (p. 95).

Let us start with external co-reference (or co-reference *tout court*). This is an easy matter: Two singular terms are co-referential just in case they refer to the same object, and two pieces of information are co-referential just in case they are about, and concern, the same object (which standardly means that the information causally derives from that object). *Internal* co-reference can now be characterized in terms of (external) co-reference: two pieces of information, or to singular terms, are internally co-referential just in case they are *taken to be*, or *represented as*, co-referential in the simpler, external sense.

Now there are two kinds of internal co-reference. This roughly corresponds to the distinction between cases in which identity is presupposed and cases in which it is asserted, or—as I put it in Chapter 4—between 'presumptions of identity' and 'judgements of identity'. In Kit Fine's terminology, something may be 'represented as the same', or it may be 'represented as *being* the same' (Fine 2007). Fine proposes the following test to tell the two cases apart:

> A good test of when an object is represented as the same is in terms of whether one might sensibly raise the question of whether it is the same. An object is represented as the same in a piece of discourse only if no one who understands the discourse can sensibly raise the question of whether it is the same. Suppose that you say 'Cicero is an orator' and later say 'Cicero was honest,' intending to make the very same use of the name 'Cicero.' Then anyone who raises the question of whether the reference was the same would thereby betray his lack of understanding of what you meant. (Fine 2007: 40)

There is, as I will say from now on, *de jure* co-reference between two singular terms (tokens) in a piece of discourse just in case *anyone who understands the discourse knows that the two terms co-refer if they refer at all*.[1] Anaphora is a good example. An anaphoric pronoun or description is *de jure* co-referential with its antecedent. Consider (1), an example from Pinillos we will discuss in Chapter 9:

(1) The Prime Minister invited Smith₁ but he₁/the bastard₁ did not show up

It is, of course, possible to wonder whether the pronoun 'he' (or the description 'the bastard') refers back to the Prime Minister, or to Smith, or refers to some other person (e.g. some man made salient by the speaker's pointing finger or the direction of her gaze). But *anyone who raises these issues is someone who has not (yet) understood the utterance.* One does not understand (1) unless one knows that the pronoun/ description is anaphoric on 'Smith', and one does not know that

---

[1] See Pinillos 2011. A similar characterization in terms of conditional co-reference can be found in Chastain 1975: 210 and Donnellan 1978: 53.

unless one knows that the two terms (the name 'Smith', and the pronoun/description) co-refer if they refer at all. Contrast this with an identity statement such as 'Cicero is Tully'. Here, the two names are presented as co-referring, so there is 'internal co-reference', but it is perfectly possible for someone who fully understands the utterance to wonder whether the two names are really co-referential, or even to doubt that they are. (Understanding the identity statement does not require believing it to be true.)

The distinction between external, internal, and *de jure* co-reference is reminiscent of that drawn by Evans, in his article 'Pronouns', between 'three notions associated with the term *coreference*' (Evans 1985: 246), but it is not exactly the same. The first of Evans's three notions is external (or, as Evans puts it, 'extensional') co-reference. His second notion, 'intended coreference', corresponds to *de jure* co-reference. It is a notion which 'can apply both to a pair of expressions one of which is a proper name and the other of which is a pronoun which has that name as antecedent, and also to two occurrences of the same proper name' (Evans 1985: 240), but *not* to a pair of distinct names such as 'Cicero' and 'Tully'. (On the same page Evans mentions, but explicitly puts aside, a broader interpretation of the notion of intended co-reference such that 'one who sincerely utters an identity statement does intend that the two terms be coreferential'. The broader notion *would* correspond to what I call 'internal co-reference'.) Evans's third notion is the notion of 'referential dependence', which is a special case of co-reference *de jure*. If a term A is referentially dependent upon another term B, as the pronoun is upon the name in (1), A and B are *de jure* co-referential, but this is only a special case—there can also be *de jure* co-reference without referential dependence (as when the same proper name is used twice). As Evans points out, referential dependence is an asymmetrical relation, while co-reference *de jure* is symmetrical (Evans 1985: 243–4). Figure 4 summarizes the types of co-reference between singular terms.

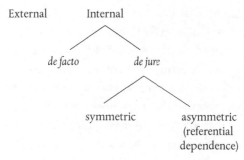

Figure 4. Types of co-reference between singular terms

As the figure shows, any instance of internal co-reference that does not qualify as *de jure* co-reference in virtue of passing Fine's test is categorized as *de facto* co-reference.

The distinction Fine draws between two types of internal co-reference between singular terms—*de jure* and *de facto*—also applies to (internal) co-reference between two pieces of information; but to see that we need the mental file picture. According to the mental file picture, two singular terms (tokens) are *de jure* co-referential—their referent is 'represented as the same'—if they are associated with the same mental file. If two singular terms are taken to be co-referential without passing Fine's test—that is, if it makes sense to wonder whether they really are co-referential—that means that they are associated with two distinct files that are linked. Now, when two distinct files are linked, information is allowed to flow freely between them; so information from one file can flow freely into the other, and be integrated with the information there. Two pieces of information can therefore end up in the same file, and be taken to concern the same object, even if the object they concern is 'represented as being the same' rather than 'represented as the same'. They are represented as being the same, rather than represented as the same, because co-reference is established through linking. The stronger form of internal co-reference obtains between two pieces of information when they end up in the same file *without the benefit of a prior linking operation*. Only in such a case can we say that two pieces of

Table 1. Varieties of co-reference

	Between pieces of information i and j	Between singular terms a and b
External co-reference	i and j concern the same object	a and b refer to the same object
Internal co-reference	i and j are taken to concern the same object (in virtue of presuppositions *or* judgements of identity)	a and b are taken to refer to the same object
De jure *co-reference*	i and j occur in the same file without the benefit of a prior judgement of identity or linking operation	a and b are associated with the same file, not with two files that are linked

information are *de jure* co-referential. That two pieces of information occur in the same file makes them internally co-referential but not necessarily *de jure* co-referential.

Table 1 recapitulates the distinctions we have made between the six types of co-reference.

2

A common objection which any theory of mental files has to address is the circularity objection.[2] There are two versions of the objection: one—the simplest version—targets the mental file account of internal co-reference between pieces of information, while the other targets the mental file account of identity judgements. I start with the simplest version and will introduce the other one later in the section.

---

[2] An early statement of the objection can be found in Lawlor's dissertation: 'In the context of building from the ground up an account of what constitutes coreferential thinking…[the theorist] owe[s] an account of what makes information belong to a single file. And [she] cannot provide this account in terms of a thinker's capacity for coreferential thinking. That would be viciously circular' (Lawlor 2001: 80).

The mental file account says that two pieces of information are taken to concern the same entity (internal co-reference) just in case they occur in the same mental file. But what is it for two pieces of information to occur in the same mental file? If the theory answers by saying that the two pieces of information are taken to concern the same entity, then it is circular and does not advance our understanding. So the simplest version of the circularity objection goes.

In a first draft of this chapter, I tentatively responded to the objection by saying that, according to the Campbellian account I have put forward, two pieces of information occur in the same file just in case *the subject uses them* (or is disposed to use them) in a certain way, namely, in an 'integrated' manner.[3] That is what it means for two items of information to occur in the same file. However, that response is not sufficient to defuse the circularity objection. Integrative behaviour on the part of the subject is a *symptom* of informational clustering, but it is not what constitutes, or accounts for, informational clustering. So the question: 'What is it for two pieces of information to occur in the same file?' cannot be answered simply by appealing to the subject's integrative behaviour. On the mental file account, the subject's integrative behaviour is *explained* by the hypothesized clustering of information. The further question, 'what explains the clustering?', still awaits an answer, and this is where circularity looms (Goodsell 2011: 7–8). For it is hard to answer that question without appealing to the fact that the subject takes the relevant information (that which goes into the file) to concern one and the same object. This immediately raises the circularity objection, as one of my graduate students, Gregory Bochner, pointed out:

> Many advocates of mental files...acknowledge—as if this were compatible with what they claim—that a mental file is created when an

---

[3] For example, the subject who has the predicates 'is well-read' and 'is bald' in his Cicero-file is thereby disposed to infer that some bald man is well-read.

object is *taken to be* one by the subject.[4]...But...if you already need to think of the object *in order to* determine that it is a single object deserving a single location in your syntax, then this means that you must be able to think of the object *prior* to the attribution of a vehicle or mental file. And, presumably, if some identity mistake is made in this early process of syntactic assignment—if, for instance, two different vehicles are created for a unique object taken to be two distinct objects—it will be *that* early mistake that will explain cognitive significance, not the fact that there are two vehicles....All of this is incompatible with the idea... that it is differences in syntax that determine differences in cognitive significance, and, instead, squarely supports the opposite view that it is differences in cognitive significance that determine differences in syntax. (Bochner 2010)

As I mentioned earlier, a related version of the objection targets the analysis of identity judgements in terms of a linking operation on files. If, as Bochner claims, belonging to a single file is a matter of 'being taken to be about the same object', then the account of judgements of identity in terms of an operation on files leads us into a regress, since the files themselves presuppose identity judgements: what goes into the file is whatever information we gain concerning *the same object as* information already in the file. To break the circle, Bochner claims, we must account for identity judgements in terms of modes of presentation that are more basic than files—more basic in the sense of not presupposing prior identity judgements. Bochner takes this to argue in favour of Descriptivism and old-fashioned Fregean senses.

---

[4] At this point Bochner quotes Forbes, who writes: 'When we receive <u>what we take to be</u> *de re* information which we have an interest in retaining, our operating system may create a locus, or dossier, where such information is held; and any further information <u>which we take to be</u> about the same object can be filed along with the information about it we already possess....The role of a name is to identify a file for a particular object—as I shall put it, we use names to "label" dossiers. In sum, then, on coming across a new name, one <u>which is taken to stand for</u> some particular individual, the system creates a dossier labeled with that name and puts those classified conditions into it which are associated with the name' (Forbes 1990: 538; Bochner's emphasis).

But the idea that various pieces of information cluster into a single file when they are 'taken to concern the same object' can be understood in a way that does *not* presuppose a prior identity judgement. It may be entirely a matter of subpersonal binding of information. Thus in the case of proto-files at least it is the cognitive system, not the subject, that takes the pieces of information to concern the same object and cluster them within a file. The subject does not judge that the pieces of information concern the same object. Identity is presupposed, it is built into the way the information is (subpersonally) packaged. Bochner's twofold objection can therefore be met by appealing to the subpersonal mechanisms underlying informational clustering: the cognitive system tracks the source of information by distributing information into files based on distinct ER relations, and *that* is what accounts for informational clustering.

This response, however, works only for proto-files. As another of my graduate students, Michael Murez, has made clear, the real difficulty comes from the introduction of *conceptual* files (the sort of files which are thought constituents and which are exercised when we make judgements). We saw in §4.3 that a piece of information goes into a (conceptual) file based on a certain acquaintance relation R if that piece of information has been obtained through R or *if it is taken to concern the same individual as* information obtained through R. The circularity objection therefore holds against what Murez calls the 'sophisticated theory' of mental files, that is, the theory that goes beyond proto-files and makes room for conceptual files (Murez 2009: 62). The related objection to the analysis of identity judgements also holds: Judgements of identity are accounted for in terms of a certain operation on files (linking), but the files in question, because they are conceptual, constitutively depend upon certain identity judgements: what goes into the file is information derived through the ER relation on which the file is based, *plus whatever information we gain concerning (what we take to be) the same object as* information already in the file.

To sum up, the two related versions of the circularity objection are as follows:

- *Objection 1 [pertaining to internal co-reference]:* What is it for information to cluster into a single (conceptual) file? The answer appeals (*inter alia*) to the fact that information in the file is taken to concern the same object, and that is circular.

- *Objection 2 [pertaining to identity judgements]:* If conceptual files themselves depend upon identity judgements (in order to be fed the 'alien information' they need to achieve the status of conceptual files, i.e. information *not* derived through the acquaintance relation on which the file is based), then we cannot analyse identity judgements in general in terms of a linking operation on files, as I have done, without launching a regress.

3

To answer the second objection, we must take advantage of the hierarchy of files and the distinction of levels it is based on. The regress can be avoided if we introduce a clear distinction between, on the one hand, whatever operation on the proto-files makes it possible for them to host alien information (information not derived through the relevant ER relation) and achieve the status of conceptual files, and, on the other hand, linking as it operates on the conceptual files which result from the prior linking operation. The prior operation we can refer to as 'proto-linking'. It is similar to linking because linking makes it possible for information to flow between files and, therefore, makes it possible for information not derived through the ER relation on which a certain file is based to end up in that file nevertheless. So linking and proto-linking alike allow 'alien' information to flow into a file (or a proto-file). Still, I submit, they are distinct operations, and to the extent that they are, the regress can be avoided. Let us see how.

Identity judgements are accounted for in terms of an operation on (conceptual) files, namely linking. The very notion of a conceptual file itself presupposes some operation similar to linking (since it enables information to flow into the file from without); but there is no circularity because the operation which the notion of a conceptual file presupposes—proto-linking—is *not* the linking operation which accounts for identity judgements. In Chapter 4 I described conceptual files as having a dual structure: the *nucleus* of the file consists of information derived through the relevant ER relation, while the *periphery* consists of information not derived through the relevant ER relation but through linking. Proto-linking operates on proto-files, allowing alien information into them and expanding them accordingly, while linking operates on already constituted conceptual files with a dual structure (nucleus + periphery) which it exploits but does not affect or modify. Because the files on which proto-linking operates are proto-files, whose proper functioning does *not* rest on identity judgements, no circularity is involved in analysing identity judgements as establishing a link between two conceptual files, which themselves are analysed as resulting from a proto-linking operation on proto-files.

Now what *is* proto-linking? Since contextual files *result from* proto-linking, proto-linking itself cannot be conceptual: it must be a form of identification which takes place at a preconceptual level. We have considered such cases already: in Campbell's cross-modal example, what the subject sees is identified with what she touches, but the identification takes place at the subpersonal level. No judgement of identity intervenes. In Chapter 7 I accounted for (some varieties of) subpersonal identification in terms of *incremental conversion*. Through incremental conversion, a file based on a certain relation R grows an extra information link: it is converted into a file based on a composite relation $R + R'$. Exercise of the new file presupposes the identity of the object to which the subject bears R and the object to which the subject bears R', yet no identity judgement is made. Incremental conversion makes it possible to feed alien information (namely information derived through R') into the file, and it does so by converting the file into a successor file with respect to which the information in question is *not* 'alien'. So the mechanism of incremental conversion accounts, or should account, for what I dubbed the 'expansion' of proto-files. Expansion, I submit, is nothing but a variety of incremental conversion.[5]

What about Objection 1—the 'simplest objection', as I called it? I think it is essentially right and should *not* be resisted; but I also think it is a mistake to view the objection as undermining the mental file framework. One cannot, without circularity, account for internal co-reference (the fact that two pieces of information are taken to concern the same object) in terms of the occurrence of that information within a single file. If anything, it is the other way round: Two pieces of information go into the same file if they are taken to concern the same object. Now when are two pieces of information taken to concern the same object? Well, there are two possibilities. Either the cognitive system binds these pieces of information together directly because they are gained through the same ER relation; or a judgement of identity occurs which enables information originally in one file to end up in another and join information originally there. In both cases, two pieces of information are taken to concern the same object and end up in the same file. The mental file framework sheds light on both cases, even though no attempt is made—or should be made—to 'reduce' the relation of internal co-reference between pieces of information to their occurring within the same file.[6]

---

[5] Of course, this is not the whole story—we haven't accounted for the crucial property of conceptual files—their satisfying the Generality Constraint. See the appendix for speculative remarks on this issue.

[6] I am indebted to an anonymous reviewer, and also to Thea Goodsell, for comments which led me to rewrite this chapter.

Appendix: Incremental Conversion and the Origin of Concepts

I said one should account for 'expansion'—the transition from proto-files to conceptual files—in terms of incremental conversion.[7] This makes conceptual files very similar to proto-files. For, on that account, what goes into the 'expanded' file resulting from proto-linking is nothing but what is delivered through the relevant (composite) relation on which that new file is based. Expanded files are not different from the original proto-files, in this regard. The only difference is the composite nature of the relations underpinning the expanded files. In both cases, however, the file can only host information derived through the relevant (and possibly composite) ER relation.

But conceptual files are not just any old expanded files based on composite relations. They satisfy the Generality Constraint and can accommodate *any* information about the referent, however it is gained. This crucial feature has to be accounted for. How can we do so? The issue here is that of the origin of concepts. It goes well beyond the limits of the present enquiry. What follow are highly speculative suggestions which the reader should feel at liberty to skip.

One obvious option would be to say that the new information link which grows out of incremental conversion is the *higher-order information link* which characterizes encyclopedia entries. On this view a conceptual file based on relation R is nothing but a file based on the composite relation $R + R^*$, where 'R^*' is the higher-order relation. But this account puts the cart before the horse. Encyclopedia entries are a variety of conceptual files; it hardly makes sense to appeal to them (and to the characteristic relation on which they are based) to account for the emergence of conceptual files in general.

A better option appeals to the relation of mediated acquaintance which language provides. The name of an object is itself an object of perceptual acquaintance. Just as for other objects, I can stand in all sorts of relation to the name, for example the demonstrative relation (when I attend to a particular token of the name) or the familiarity relation (when I have acquired a disposition to recognize the name). Now, by perceiving the name of an

---

[7] On expansion, see Chapter 5, §3; on incremental conversion, see Chapter 7, §3.

object, I can gain information not only about it (the name), but also about what it names (the object). I can gain information about the object by listening to what users of the name say when using it. Acquisition of a name therefore provides a new information link to the object—or rather, a variety of information links, corresponding to the variety of relations to the name itself.[8] Thus the demonstrative relation to the name generates a discourse-demonstrative relation to the object, through which I can think of it ('that object I'm hearing about'). Similarly, the familiarity relation to the name generates a discourse-familiarity relation to the object, through which I can think of it ('that object I know as NN'). This a stable relation which enables us to accumulate information about the object across linguistic encounters.

Typically, names are acquired by ostension: I see the object while hearing its name. Just as, when I am in a position both to see and touch an object, I think of it through a file based on a composite relation, so when I see an object while hearing its name I think of it under a mode of presentation involving a multiple information link. This is an instance of composite relation, but what is special here is the fact that the linguistic relation to the object permits the acquisition of any information about it (provided that information can be transmitted through language). Or at least, this is the case for the linguistic relation to the object that goes together with mastery of (hence familiarity with) its name. I submit that the Generality Constraint will be satisfied by any file involving that relation in its composite relational base.

Proto-linking can also operate so as to compound the familiarity relation in virtue of which you are disposed to recognize the object (and to access information stored on previous encounters with it) and the discourse-familiarity relation in virtue of which you are disposed to recognize its name (and to access information about the object stored on previous encounters with the name). Compounding these relations yields what we may call a proto-encyclopedia entry: a stable file which enables you to accumulate information about the object gained through either experience or testimony.

---

[8] See Millikan 2000: 88–91.

9

Co-reference *De Jure:*
The Transitivity Objection

1

In a recent paper, Angel Pinillos argues that 'third object' accounts of *de jure* co-reference (of which the mental file account is an instance) are bound to fail.[1] According to such accounts, Pinillos says, two terms are co-referential *de jure* if and only if they are associated with a single entity (e.g. a single mental file) which constitutes or determines their shared cognitive significance. (That entity is the 'third object'.) Pinillos's alleged knock-down objection to such accounts is that being co-referential *de jure* is not a transitive relation (Pinillos 2011: 314–16). It is possible for A and B, and for B and C, to be co-referential *de jure*, even though A and C are not. But if the relation of *de jure* co-reference rested on the identity of the mental files respectively associated with each of the terms, it should be transitive, since identity is a transitive relation.

Pinillos gives two groups of example to show that *de jure* co-reference is not a transitive relation:

Type 1 examples
(1) We were debating whether to investigate both Hesperus$_1$ and Phosphorus$_2$; but when we got evidence of their true identity, we immediately sent probes there$_{1,2}$.

---

[1] The first argument to that effect is due to Kit Fine (2007: 119).

(2) As a matter of fact, my neighbour John$_1$ is Professor Smith$_2$, you will get to meet (the real) John Smith$_{1,2}$ tonight.

(3) Hesperus$_1$ is Phosphorus$_2$ after all, so Hesperus-slash-Phosphorus$_{1,2}$ must be a very rich planet.

Type 2 examples

(4) Smith$_{1,2}$ is wearing a costume, and (as a result) Sally thinks he$_2$ is someone other than Smith$_1$.

(5) He$_{1,2}$ was in drag, and (as a result) Sally thought that Smith$_1$ wasn't Smith$_2$.

Pinillos argues that in each example, there are three terms A, B, and C such that A and B are co-referential *de jure*, B and C also are co-referential *de jure*, yet A and C are only co-referential *de facto*. In (1) and (3), 'Hesperus' and 'Phosphorus' are co-referential *de facto* (as they feature in the informative identity judgement 'Hesperus is Phosphorus'), yet both 'Hesperus' and 'Phosphorus' are *de jure* co-referential with 'Hesperus/Phosphorus' in (3) or with the anaphoric 'there' in (1). Example (2) works like (3): 'John' and 'Smith' are co-referential *de facto* (as shown by the informative identity 'my neighbour John is Professor Smith'), yet both are *de jure* co-referential with 'John Smith' in the second clause. Type 2 examples are a bit more complex, since they involve an attitude ascription ('Sally thinks that ...', 'Sally thought that ...'), but according to Pinillos they also feature three terms A, B, and C such that A and B, and B and C, are co-referential *de jure*, while A and C are co-referential *de facto*.

I do not find Pinillos's argument convincing, and I reject his conclusion (to the effect that third-object accounts fail to account for the data). But I think the two types of example call for different reactions. In the next two sections, I will argue as follows. In type 2 examples, all of the three terms A, B, and C *are* co-referential *de jure*, despite Pinillos's assertion to the contrary; so I simply deny that there *is* a failure of transitivity in these examples. But I accept Pinillos's claim that type 1 examples exhibit non-transitivity: the co-reference relation that holds between A and B and between B and C does not hold between A and C. It follows that *de jure* co-reference is not just the 'identity-of-associated-mental-file' relation—to that extent, Pinillos is right. But, I will argue, this does not object to the mental file account, nor to third-object accounts in general; for Pinillos's initial characterization of such accounts is incorrect. Properly stated, third-object accounts say that two terms are co-referential *de jure* if they are associated with a single entity (e.g. a single mental file). They do not say that to be *de jure* co-referential *is* to be associated with such an entity. Dropping the biconditional in favour of a simple conditional is enough to meet Pinillos's objection, I will argue.

2

The paradigmatic type 2 example is (4), of which Pinillos offers a detailed analysis (Pinillos 2011: 315–16):

(4) Smith$_{1,2}$ is wearing a costume, and (as a result) Sally thinks he$_2$ is someone other than Smith$_1$.

The first occurrence of the name 'Smith', as the subscripts indicate, is *de jure* co-referential both with the pronoun 'he' (which is anaphoric on it) and with the second occurrence of the name 'Smith' at the end of the sentence. The basic criterion for *de jure* co-reference is, roughly, that *anyone who wonders whether the two terms are co-referential (instead of taking for granted that they are) is someone who does not fully understand the utterance.*[2] In other words, *de jure* co-reference entails knowledge of co-reference on the part of the competent language users. But, Pinillos argues, the pronoun and the second occurrence of the name 'Smith' *cannot* be *de jure* co-referential: they can only be *de facto* co-referential. It follows that *de jure* co-reference is not a transitive relation (since it holds between A and B, and between B and C, but not between A and C).

---

[2] See the quotation from Fine 2007 in Chapter 8 above (p. 92).

Why does Pinillos believe that in (4) the pronoun 'he' and the second occurrence of the name 'Smith' cannot be *de jure* co-referential? He thinks that follows from another criterion for *de jure* co-reference, which we can formulate as follows:

A Prioricity
If two terms *a* and *b* are *de jure* co-referential in a sentence 'blah...*a*...*b*...blah', then whoever grasps the sentence knows that it follows from it that there is an *x* such that blah...*x*...*x*...blah

Pinillos gives the following example to show A Prioricity at work:

(6) The Prime Minister invited Smith$_1$ but he$_1$/the bastard$_1$ did not show up

Both variants of the sentence (with 'he' or 'the bastard') entail 'there is an *x* such that the Prime Minister invited *x* and *x* did not show up'. The entailment is known a priori, i.e. it is known to hold by anyone who understands the utterance.

Let us go back to (4). If 'he' and the second occurrence of 'Smith' in (4) were *de jure* co-referential, Pinillos claims, then in virtue of A Prioricity it would follow that the sentence entails '∃*x* Sally thinks *x* is someone other than *x*' in an a priori manner. But there is no such entailment (he says): (4) may be true without Sally's irrationally believing of anyone that he is not himself or herself. Conclusion: 'he' and the second occurrence of 'Smith' are not *de jure* co-referential.

This is too swift. I see no reason to deny that the a priori entailment at issue holds. In this situation I can say: 'Sally thought that someone was someone else'.[3] This entails that for some *x*, she thought that *x* was distinct from *x*. In saying this, however, I do not necessarily ascribe an irrational belief to Sally. I can also say, in the same sort of case: 'Sally thought that someone was his own father' ('∃*x* Sally

---

[3] 'Thinking one thing is another' is the title of the first chapter of Joseph Camp's book *Confusion* (Camp 2002). (Insofar as I can tell, it is in John MacFarlane's 2007 review of that book that the phrase 'coreference *de jure*' first appears.)

thought x was x's father'), again without taking Sally to hold irrational beliefs. This is like Russell's example: 'I thought your ship was longer than it is' (Russell 1905: 169–70). There are two readings: one reading on which the ascribed thought is irrational, and a *de re* reading in which it is not. In the case of (4), the conclusion that for some x, Sally believes that x (or better: believes of x) that he is not x indeed follows a priori, on the *de re* reading. So there is no reason to deny that the two occurrences of the name 'Smith' are *de jure* co-referential in (4). It follows that this type of example does not establish that *de jure* co-reference is not a transitive relation.

In addition to A Prioricity, Pinillos appeals to another principle, Attitude Closure, which we can formulate as follows.

Attitude Closure
If two terms a and b are *de jure* co-referential in a sentence 'NN believes that ... a ... b ...', then whoever grasps the sentence knows that it follows from it that NN believes that there is an x such that ... x ... x ...

From Attitude Closure it follows that, if there is *de jure* co-reference between 'he' and the second occurrence of 'Smith' in (4), the sentence should entail not only '$\exists x$ Sally thinks x is someone other than x' (as predicted by A Prioricity), but also 'Sally thinks $\exists x\, x$ is someone other than x.' Now *that* ascribes an irrational belief to Sally. Since (4) does not actually entail that Sally believes any absurdity, Pinillos concludes that the pronoun and the second occurrence of 'Smith' are not *de jure* co-referential in (4).

What reasons do we have to believe in Attitude Closure? Pinillos gives examples in which the characteristic entailment (from 'NN believes that ... a ... b ...' to 'NN believes there is an x such that ... x ... x ...') holds; but I take (4) and (5) to be counter-examples. What does the failure of Attitude Closure in such cases show? According to Pinillos, it shows that the singular terms in the scope of the attitude verb are not *de jure* co-referential. According to me, however, it only shows that the attitude report is given the transparent or *de re* interpretation. For Attitude Closure to work, the report must not be given a transparent or *de re* interpretation. When the report is given the transparent interpretation, the two singular terms are *de jure* co-referential *for the speaker and his addressee* (and whoever correctly understands the utterance), but this is not meant to track *de jure* co-reference *within* the reported thought.[4]

3

In example (1), Pinillos says, transitivity fails:

> (1) We were debating whether to investigate both Hesperus$_1$ and Phosphorus$_2$; but when we got evidence of their true identity, we immediately sent probes there$_{1,2}$.

Transitivity fails because 'Hesperus' and 'Phosphorus' are only *de facto* co-referential, while 'there' is *de jure* co-referential with both of them. As Pinillos puts it,

> Anyone who fully understands [the utterance] will know of 'there' and 'Hesperus' that they refer to the same thing if they refer at all. The same goes for 'there' and 'Phosphorus'. However, people who fully understand (1) do not have to know that 'Hesperus' and 'Phosphorus' refer to the same thing if they refer at all. Imagine a person being presented with some evidence that 'Hesperus' and 'Phosphorus' refer to distinct planets so that she thereby does not count as knowing that the expressions are coreferential. This person is still able to understand someone else's use of (1), although she does not know of the 'Hesperus' and 'Phosphorus' occurrences that they refer to the same thing (if they refer at all). Hence, those occurrences are not *de jure* coreferential. (Pinillos 2011: 315)

---

[4] See Chapter 14 for the subtle interplay between the point of view (and the files) of the speaker and the point of view (and the files) of the ascribee in the interpretation of attitude reports.

Here, I agree with Pinillos: type 1 examples like (1) do show that *de jure* co-reference is not a transitive relation. Pinillos concludes that third objects account fail. According to such accounts, he says,

> Occurrences A and B in a discourse are *de jure* coreferential because they stand in a certain relation R to a single object X (e.g. a single mental file).

This cannot be right, Pinillos points out, for if it were—if *de jure* co-reference was a matter of identity (identity of mental file, say)—it would be a transitive relation; but example (1) establishes that it is not.

Again, I agree with Pinillos that example (1) shows that *de jure* co-reference is not a transitive relation; but I deny that this argues against the mental file account (or third object accounts in general). It does argue against a strong version of such accounts, namely:

> Occurrences A and B in a discourse are *de jure* co-referential (i.e. pass Fine's test) *just in case* they stand in a certain relation R to a single object X (e.g. a single mental file).

But it does not argue against a weaker version of the theory, according to which being associated with a single mental file (or any relevant third object) is sufficient, though not necessary, for *de jure* co-reference:

> Occurrences A and B in a discourse are *de jure* co-referential if they stand in a certain relation R to a single object X (e.g. a single mental file).

This weaker version leaves open the possibility that two occurrences A and B might be *de jure* co-referential, and pass Fine's intuitive test, for some other reason than their being associated with the same mental file.

Like Pinillos, I characterize *de jure* co-reference in terms of a priori knowledge of (conditional) co-reference: two terms are *de jure* co-referential just in case anyone who understands the utterance in which they occur knows that they co-refer it they refer at all. Now, if two terms have the same sense, understanding the terms (knowing their sense) entails knowing that they co-refer if they refer at all; that follows from the constraint that sense determines reference. So identity of sense entails *de jure* co-reference. But why should the entailment be bidirectional? There may be other sources of a priori knowledge of (conditional) co-reference than sense-sharing. Indeed, I will argue, that is exactly what is going on in examples of type 1: a priori knowledge of conditional co-reference is secured, but the source of such knowledge is not the identity of the associated mental files (or the identity of sense, more generally).

In each example in the first group, we find that two terms (say, 'Hesperus' and 'Phosphorus') are associated with distinct files—so they are only *de facto* co-referential—but there is also a third file (say the 'Venus' file or, better, the 'Hesperus/Phosphorus' file) which is created when one learns that the two terms actually co-refer. That third file is what the 'merge' model posits: it says that, upon understanding and accepting an identity, one feeds all the information from the two initial files into a third file, and suppresses the initial files.[5] On the weaker 'link' model I advocate, one does not (automatically) suppress the initial files, but that does not prevent one from opening a file for the unique object which is the referent of the two initial files. When an inclusive file is created and the initial files retained, I say there is 'partial merging'. It is, I take it, the function of slash-terms such as 'Hesperus/Phosophorus' to be associated with inclusive files in situations of partial merging. Be that as it may, given the way the inclusive file is introduced and its role, it is a priori that it co-refers with each of the initial files if it refers at all. So it is a priori that 'Hesperus' and 'Hesperus/Phosphorus' co-refer (if they refer at all). Likewise it is a priori that 'Phosphorus' and 'Hesperus/Phosphorus'

---

[5] 'On receipt of an identity-statement invoking two ... clusters, the two appropriate cards are withdrawn and a new card is prepared, bearing both the names of which one heads one of the original cards and one the other, and incorporating the sum of the information contained in the original cards; the single new card is returned to stock and the original cards are thrown away' (Strawson 1974: 56).

co-refer (if they refer at all). It follows that both 'Hesperus' and 'Phosphorus' are *de jure* co-referential with 'Hesperus/Phosphorus'. Yet these terms are *not* associated with the same file: 'Hesperus' and 'Phosphorus' are associated respectively with what I called the 'initial files', while 'Hesperus/Phosphorus' is associated with what I called the 'inclusive file'.[6] In this case, therefore, we have an instance of *de jure* co-reference that is not accounted for in terms of a shared file, but in terms of a relation other than identity between two distinct files: the relation—whatever it is exactly—that holds between the initial files and the inclusive file. Such cases can be accounted for within the mental file account, so they do not argue against it; they only argue against an implausibly strong version resting on the (unargued) premise that *only* the identity of associated files can be responsible for a priori knowledge of conditional co-reference.

[6] Considering such cases, Fine says: 'it is not that the merged file represents the individual as the same as the earlier files, since that would require that the earlier files represent the individual as the same. Rather, the new file, *if* I choose to create it, will represent the individual as *being* the same as the earlier files' (Fine 2007: 69). In this passage in which he talks about the mental file account, Fine seems to suggest that 'Hesperus' and 'Hesperus/Phosphorus' are not co-referential *de jure*, even though they pass his own intuitive test. But I think one should stick to the test and acknowledge that they *are* co-referential *de jure*, while distinguishing co-reference *de jure* from an even stronger notion ('co-reference-de-jure-in-virtue-of-identity-of-associated-file'). Note that Fine's argument for resisting the idea that the merged file is *de jure* co-referential with the earlier files is not convincing: if the merged file represents the individual as the same as the earlier files, that does *not* require that the earlier files represent the individual as the same.

Part V

Epistemic Transparency

10

Slow Switching

1

I said that co-reference *de jure* is a kind of *internal* co-reference. There is internal co-reference whenever two terms are represented as co-referring or taken to co-refer. Now there may be internal co-reference without external co-reference. For example, if I mistakenly say 'A is B', I present 'A' and 'B' as co-referring, but I am wrong: they do not actually co-refer. So there can be internal co-reference without external co-reference, just as there can be external co-reference without internal co-reference.

If that is so, and if co-reference *de jure* is a kind of internal co-reference, then should it not be possible also for two terms to be co-referential *de jure* without being externally co-referential? Of course this cannot happen in a case of anaphora, since the anaphor's reference is constitutively parasitic on its antecedent's reference.[1] But consider the following example, due to Herman Cappelen (p.c.). There are two guys, A and B, who bear the same name (say 'Cicero'). John thinks there is a single guy: so he freely mixes information he gets from A with information he gets from B and feeds everything into a single file. Having heard of A (referred to as *Cicero*) that he is bald and of

---

[1] Anaphors are 'referentially dependent' upon their antecedent (Evans 1985: 243–4). Referential dependence entails, but is not entailed by, co-reference *de jure*. See Chapter 8, p. 93.

B (also referred to as *Cicero*) that he is well-read, he concludes that some bald guy is well-read. John takes the occurrences of 'Cicero' targeted at A and the occurrences of 'Cicero' targeted at B to co-refer, not because he has two files that are linked, but because he has a single file. This is very much like co-reference *de jure*. Yet it is not true that John 'knows' that the two terms co-refer if they refer at all. In this situation, Cappelen points out, the two terms do *not* co-refer: one occurrence of 'Cicero' refers to A, the other to B.

This case can be described as an inverse Paderewski case. Paderewski cases are cases in which a subject associates two distinct files with a single name. Inverse Paderewski cases are cases in which there are two names but the subject associates them with a single file. The question posed by Cappelen is: should we not treat inverse Paderewski cases as cases of co-reference *de jure*, despite the lack of actual co-reference? If the answer is positive, that means that we should characterize co-reference *de jure* in *non-factive* terms: Instead of saying that anyone who understands the discourse 'knows' that the two terms co-refer if they refer at all, we should rather say that he or she 'takes them' to co-refer.

The factivity issue is closely related to another issue which has been the focus of much attention in the literature on self-knowledge. That is the *epistemic transparency* issue.[2] Reference, as we all know, is not epistemically transparent. The subject may not realize that two terms refer to the same object, or that they refer to distinct objects. In both cases the subject may be deluded. What about sense? It seems that, in contrast to reference, sense (mode of presentation) *must be* transparent. If modes of presentation themselves are not transparent, there is no reason to move from pure referential talk to mode of presentation

---

[2] The term is introduced by Michael Dummett in the following passage: 'It is an undeniable feature of the notion of meaning…that meaning is *transparent* in the sense that, if someone attaches a meaning to each of two words, he must know whether these meanings are the same' (Dummett 1978: 131). Boghossian (1994: 36) breaks up the transparency thesis in two parts: the transparency of sameness and the transparency of difference.

talk in the explanation of rational behaviour. The appeal to senses (as opposed to sheer reference) in psychological explanation *presupposes* the transparency of sense as opposed to the non-transparency of reference. As Boghossian puts it,

> we...ascribe thoughts to a person...for two related purposes; on the one hand, to enable assessments of his rationality and, on the other, to explain his behavior. As these matters are currently conceived, a thought must be epistemically transparent if it is to play these roles. Without transparency, our conceptions of rationality and rational explanation yield absurd results. We manifest recognition of this fact by barring *de re* thoughts—thoughts which intuitively lack epistemic transparency—from figuring in assessments of rationality and psychological explanation. However, if we abandon transparency even for *de dicto* thoughts, and hence in effect altogether, then we must either jettison the notion of rationality and with it the practice of psychological explanation that it underwrites, or we must show these notions can be refashioned so as not to yield absurd results. The problem is that the first suggestion is wild and there appears to be no satisfactory way of implementing the second. (Boghossian 1994: 39–40)

Summarizing the debate on this topic, Laura Schroeter writes that 'most philosophers of mind accept the...thesis that you have *transparent* access to the contents of your own thoughts: provided that you're minimally rational, you simply cannot mistake one conceptual content for another' (Schroeter 2007: 597).[3] Indeed a rational subject must be capable of reflecting critically upon his or her own thoughts; that sort of reflexive control over one's thoughts is possible only if they are transparently accessible. Transparency follows from rationality.

Schroeter cashes out transparency as follows: If it seems to you that two tokens 'obviously and uncontrovertibly' mean the same,

---

[3] A notable exception to the consensus is Ruth Millikan: see her *White Queen Psychology* (Millikan 1993) and *On Clear and Confused Ideas* (Millikan 2000).

then they do mean the same and co-refer (if they refer at all). She gives the following examples which all involve co-reference *de jure*:

> i. *Pleonastic identity claims:* You think to yourself, 'George Bush is George Bush'. If you understand this claim in the standard way, it won't strike you as an open question whether the two names co-refer: your thought simply presents itself to you as about a particular man being identical with himself.
>
> ii. *Pleonastic self-interpretations:* After entertaining the claim 'Bush smirks', you go on to think: 'That thought was about Bush'. Here too, it won't strike you as an open question whether you're thinking of a single man twice over.
>
> iii. *Pleonastic transitions in reasoning:* You think 'Bush smirks' and 'Bush swaggers'. You then draw the conclusion, 'Someone both smirks and swaggers'. Once again, the sameness of the man in question won't strike you as up for dispute: your thoughts simply present themselves to you as co-referential.

> These three kinds of case have received separate attention in the literature on self-knowledge. But for each of them, philosophers have endorsed a transparency thesis: rational subjects, it is thought, cannot be wrong in taking their uses of 'Bush' to co-refer in these examples. (Schroeter 2007: 598)

At this point, however, it is hard not to invoke the duality of sense. Sense is both what accounts for rational behaviour, and what determines reference. Because of its role in psychological explanation, sense must be transparent, as we've just seen. Insofar as it determines reference, however, it cannot be (fully) transparent. Reference is known to depend upon external factors, of which the suject may be unaware. Such factors are constitutive of the reference-determining sense of the expression, and to that extent, sense is bound to share the non-transparency of reference. So, in Cappelen's example, the two occurrences of 'Cicero' carry distinct senses (they have to, since sense determines reference and the two occurrences refer to distinct objects), but the subject for whom they are co-referential *de jure* is simply not aware of that. For the subject in question, the two occurrences have the same sense: she associates them with the same mental file, thereby making them co-referential *de jure*. That is clearly a mistake on the subject's part. This type of case shows that we should distinguish between 'sense' (mode of presentation) in the narrow sense, and 'sense' (mode of presentation) in a broad sense. Sense, broadly understood, is world-involving, so it is not transparent. But sense, in the narrow sense, must be transparent.[4]

Now if we draw a distinction between sense (mode of presentation) in the broad and the narrow sense, corresponding to the roles of sense qua cognitive significance and qua reference-fixer, then we open the way to a similar distinction between two kinds of co-reference *de jure*, an 'internal' kind (co-reference *de jure* in the narrow sense) and an 'external' one (co-reference *de jure* in the broad sense). This sets limits to transparency. Transparency, as characterized by Schroeter (see above), entails the following principle: 'If it seems to you that two tokens "obviously and uncontrovertibly" mean the same, then they do mean the same and co-refer (if they refer at all).' But if co-reference *de jure* can be given a 'narrow' interpretation, then it will be possible for a subject to treat two occurrences as *de jure* co-referential (to associate the same mental file with them), *even though these occurrences are not even co-referential*. That is the situation described by Cappelen, and if the description is correct, co-reference *de jure* is an internal affair and it does not entail actual co-reference.

In this chapter, however, I will defend the factive characterization of co-reference *de jure* which, following Fine and Pinillos, I put forward in the previous chapters. I will do so by taking a stance in the debate

---

[4] As Schroeter says, 'the Fregean notion of sense is supposed to fulfil at least three different roles: (i) reflecting the subjective appearance of *de jure* co-reference, (ii) reflecting the subject's substantive understanding of what it takes to be the reference, and (iii) fully determining the actual reference. It's the first role that is crucial to the transparency debate. If reference externalism is true, then no single theoretical entity can perfectly satisfy all three roles' (Schroeter 2007: 600 n.).

about the compatibility of externalism and self-knowledge.[5] I will side with the 'compatibilists' and defend the transparency of sense—properly understood—against the alleged counter-examples. One important class of such counter-examples features the phenomenon of 'slow switching', to which I now turn. (Inverse Paderewski cases will be dealt with in the next chapter.)

2

We are concerned with cases in which a subject deploys a single file several times in a train of thought, thereby securing co-reference *de jure* between what we may describe as distinct 'occurrences' of the file. Externalism says that the reference of a file depends upon external relations between the file and some entity in the context. An immediate consequence of externalism is this: if we vary the context across occurrences, so as to change the entity which bears the relevant relation to the file, we change the referent of the file. Now, occurrences of the file which refer to distinct objects must carry distinct reference-determining senses. (To say that sense determines reference is to say that the same sense cannot determine distinct referents—any distinction at the level of reference entails a corresponding distinction at the level of sense.) It follows that, if the contextual change which induces a change of reference takes place without the subject being aware of it, epistemic transparency is threatened: the subject will unwittingly entertain distinct senses through deployment of what is internally the same file.

If one is a 'compatibilist', that is, if one seeks to reconcile externalism with epistemic transparency, one will question the nature of the contextual change which induces a change in reference (hence, allegedly, a change in sense). An important yet arguably irrelevant class of cases

---

[5] On that debate, see the papers collected in Ludlow and Martin (1998) and in Nuccetelli (2003); see also Brown (2004). 'Self-knowledge' in the debate means something like 'transparency for mental content'.

involves *counterfactual* changes. One's WATER file refers to water in virtue of being embedded in a water-environment on Earth. In externalist thought-experiments, we reason that, if the stuff that fills lakes and rivers and descends from the sky as rain was XYZ instead of H_2O, our WATER file would refer to XYZ instead of referring to water. But, the compatibilist will insist, this does not threaten epistemic transparency. The subject in the actual situation refers to water and entertains the water-determining sense of 'water' *whenever* she deploys her WATER file. The counterfactual subject in the counterfactual situation refers to XYZ and entertains the XYZ-determining sense of 'water' *whenever* she deploys her twin file. A problem arises for transparency only if, for the same subject but unbeknown to her, distinct occurrences (deployments) of the same file refer to distinct entities. For that to be the case, the relevant change should not take us from an actual situation to a counterfactual situation: the world must be fixed, and the reference-inducing change must take place within that world. So we have to think of 'Twin-Earth' as a distant planet in *our* world; and the subject must be allowed to travel from Earth to Twin-Earth.

Travel to Twin-Earth does not automatically induce a change of reference, however. In Putnam's story (Putnam 1975), when the scientists land on Twin-Earth and start experimenting, they find out that the watery stuff there *is not water*. That means that their WATER file keeps on referring to water, even on Twin-Earth (where the watery stuff is not water, but twater). It does not change its reference, which is fixed by the context of acquisition (the Earth) rather than the context of deployment (Twin-Earth). We can, however, get a reference change by letting the traveller *stay* on Twin-Earth long enough. This is what Burge (1988) described as a 'slow-switching' case:

> The thoughts would not switch as one is switched from one actual situation to another twin actual situation. The thoughts would switch only if one remained long enough in the other situation to establish

environmental relations necessary for new thoughts. So quick switching would not be a case in which thoughts switched but the introspection remained the same. But slow switching would be such a case. (Burge 1988: 652)

Following Burge, let us imagine a subject who, unbeknownst to him, is switched to Twin-Earth at an early stage in his life and stays there forever. When he arrives, his water thoughts refer to water and when, pointing to lakes and rivers on Twin-Earth, he says (or thinks), 'This is water', he is wrong: the propositions he entertains are false (since the stuff is actually twater, not water). But after many years on Twin-Earth the subject's water thoughts, or some of them at least, will no longer be water thoughts: they will be regular twater thoughts. If, after twenty years of life on Twin-Earth, the subject looks at the glass in front of him and thinks 'This is water', his thought will be *true* if the glass in front of him is filled with twater. That's the Burgean intuition about slow switching cases, and like other writers on the topic, I find it hard to resist. Whether the new concept the subject now expresses with the word 'water' (or through deployment of his mental file) refers only to twater or indifferently to water-or-twater is an issue I need not go into:[6] what matters is that the file, which once referred to water (to the exclusion of twater), has changed its reference through prolonged interaction with twater on Twin-Earth.

Slow switching cases defeat the principle of epistemic transparency understood as the principle that

> rational introspection...provide[s] subjects with all they need to determine sameness and difference in belief. Nothing more than introspection is needed to determine whether or not the belief they entertain, express or reject today is the same as or different from the belief they entertained, expressed or rejected yesterday. (Owens 1990: 158)

[6] See Burge 1998: 352–4 for the distinction between 'Disjoint Types Cases' and 'Amalgam Cases'.

What the slow switching examples show is that reference, hence belief content, may change over time even though no internally detectable change occurs: the same mental file which refers to some entity at t_1 comes to refer to a distinct entity at t_2.

But does this really threaten epistemic transparency? One may argue that it does not, because epistemic transparency should not be understood as diachronic, contrary to what the above quotation from Owens implies. As Owens himself notes, 'the *only* reason for retaining [epistemic transparency] is the role it plays in the Cartesian model of the *rational* subject as the one who would never subscribe to contradictory beliefs. This conception of rationality... presupposes that the fully rational subject can introspectively determine sameness and difference in belief' (Owens 1990: 170).[7] Indeed, as Boghossian says in the passage I quoted earlier, 'Without transparency, our conceptions of rationality and rational explanation yield absurd results' (Boghossian 1994: 39). But the relevant notion of transparency—the notion that matters as far as rationality is concerned—is *synchronic* transparency. Schroeter spells it out as follows:

> *Synchronic Transparency*: In a normally functioning thinker, at any given time two deployments of the very same mental file must be assigned the very same object (kind, property) as reference. This revised constraint allows for shifts in the reference of a mental file over time, but rules out divergent assignments to co-temporal deployments of a file. (Schroeter 2007: 604)[8]

[7] 'Agents can be censured for maintaining inconsistent mental states, but such censure would be out of place if it were not within their power to determine that they were doing so. An inconsistency that is hidden from introspection should not impugn rationality; hence content, at least in the sense assumed in rational norms, must be perspicuous' (Cumming 2011: 2–3).

[8] Note that this way of characterizing transparency (in terms of mental files and their reference) makes the epistemic transparency thesis immune to the objections Wikforss raises to 'metalinguistic' or 'metaconceptual' characterizations. Transparency boils down to the 'requirement on the theory of content that content should capture the subject's cognitive perspective' (Wikforss forthcoming); it is not something over and above that requirement (as Wikforss assumes in her critique). See also Stalnaker (2008) for a critique of transparency analogous to Wikforss.

The reason why only synchronic transparency matters is that a fully rational subject must be able to detect contradictions between thoughts held *at the same time*—within the same train of thought. This synchronic condition is explicitly built into the standard Fregean characterization of modes of presentation as relevant to rational explanation.[9]

Does this mean that slow switching cases do not threaten epistemic transparency? No, because, arguably, slow switching also brings about failures of *synchronic* transparency. This point has been much emphasized by Boghossian, who points out that not all deployments of the file switch in slow switching cases:

> It seems right to say that some tokens of 'water' will shift from meaning **water** to meaning **twater**. But it seems to me equally compelling to say that certain *other* tokens of 'water' *won't* shift. Specifically, it seems to me that those tokens of 'water' occurring in *memories*, and in *beliefs about the past* based upon them, will retain their Earthly interpretations, despite being tokened on Twin-Earth. Such thoughts, unlike, for instance, beliefs with undated general contents, or thoughts about one's present surroundings, are caused and sustained by *previous* perceptions long gone. In the normal case, they owe little, if anything, to current perceptions and cognitive transactions with one's environment. From a purely intuitive standpoint, they would be expected to

---

[9] I have in mind the Fregean criterion, according to which two singular terms '*a*' and '*b*' differ in sense if it is possible for a rational subject to assent to '*a* is F' while *at the same time* witholding assent to (or rejecting) '*b* is F'. Dickie and Rattan (2010) challenge the synchronic condition on the grounds that 'there can be rational engagement between attitudes held at different times and by different subjects, so a notion of sense which can explain rational engagement wherever it arises…must be individuated more widely than [Frege's synchronic criterion] allows' (Dickie and Rattan 2010: 146). Though I am sympathetic to their project, I am not convinced by Dickie's and Rattan's argument because it rests on the Pinillos biconditional which I rejected in Chapter 9: they take two terms to be *de jure* co-referential (i.e. such that full understanding of these terms entails knowledge that they co-refer) if and only if they have the same sense. Thus on p. 147 they say: 'full understanding of υ and μ involves knowledge of co-reference iff υ and μ share a sense'. I think this is wrong. In the diachronic example they discuss, two distinct mental files are involved but they are united through the mechanism of incremental conversion (Chapter 7, §4), so this may well be a case in which there is co-reference *de jure* despite a distinctness in sense (in which case Dickie's and Rattan's argument collapses).

retain their Earthly interpretations, despite the admitted shift in their syntactic cousins. (Boghossian 1994: 38)

If this is right, then we can imagine a synchronous train of thought involving both shifted and unshifted deployments of the same file simultaneously. Boghossian gives an example in which Peter, the slow switching subject, has both memories of a striking encounter he had with Pavarotti (whom he saw floating on Lake Taupo shortly before the switch to Twin-Earth) and 'undated general thoughts' about Pavarotti which refer to twin Pavarotti (the singer he regularly reads about in Twin-Earthian magazines). He concludes:

> In the situation described, Peter's externally individuated thought tokens are not epistemically transparent to him. In particular, Peter's language of thought contains tokens expressions that possess different semantic values, despite being of the same syntactic type....Tokens of 'Pavarotti', 'water', and 'Lake Taupo', in sentences expressing memories and beliefs about that memorable occasion, will refer to Pavarotti, water and Lake Taupo, respectively; whereas other tokens of that type, in sentences expressing beliefs about his current environment, or current desires, will intuitively mean twater and twin Pavarotti. From the inside, however, there will be no indication of this : as far as Peter is concerned, they will appear to express precisely the same contents. (Boghossian 1994: 39)

In this situation, there can be co-reference *de jure* without actual co-reference, or so it seems. Boghossian imagines that Peter entertains the following instance of what he (wrongly) takes to be *modus ponens*:

1. Whoever floats on water, gets wet
2. Pavarotti once floated on water
3. Pavarotti once got wet

In this inference there is co-reference *de jure* between the occurrences of 'water' in the first and second premise respectively, yet these occurrences are not actually co-referential, so the reasoning is invalid:

[The first premise] by virtue of expressing a general quantified proposition, is to be regarded as having Twearthly content, i.e. as being about twin-floating and twin-water....The second premise, by virtue of expressing a belief that is rooted in an Earthly experience, will be about Earthly floating and Earthly water. (Boghossian 1994: 45)[10]

The question is: How can the compatibilist account for such prima facie counter-examples to epistemic transparency?[11]

3

Boghossian treats both premises in the above reasoning as true, but the reasoning itself as fallacious through equivocation. There is equivocation because the reasoner 'trades on the identity' of two distinct things. Epistemic transparency fails because there is a mismatch between how things are internally (a single file/term) and how they actually are (two distinct entities). Burge, however, has attempted to

---

[10] Surprisingly, Boghossian adds that in this case, 'True premises, aided by a failure of univocity that Peter is in principle not in a position to introspect, will combine to produce a false conclusion.' But the conclusion is not false—Pavarotti actually got wet during the encounter on Lake Taupo. Still, the reasoning is invalid. (Maybe Boghossian takes 'wet' in the conclusion to express the concept *twin-wet* which it inherits from the occurrence of the same term in the first premise, while 'Pavarotti' in the conclusion inherits from the second premise the reference to Earthly Pavarotti. If that is so, then the conclusion says that Earthly Pavarotti once got twin-wet, and that is false indeed—assuming it makes sense to talk of twin-wetness.)

[11] One straightfoward option for the compatibilist is simply to *deny* the existence of Boghossian-type cases where synchronic transparency fails. Such a position is described in Sainsbury and Tye (2012: 92–5): 'With the switch to twin-earth, after sufficient time has gone by, Paul's concepts change, and he comes to believe of the liquid in his memory images that it is twater and of certain water-involving historical events [which he remembers] that they are twater-involving' (Sainsbury and Tye 2012: 93; see also Ludlow 1995: 158–9 and Tye 1998). On this view, the memory images are retained, but they are re-interpreted by means of the post-shift concepts currently in the subject's repertoire. No violation of synchronic transparency ever occurs because, after the semantic shift, the file refers to twater *whenever* it is tokened. In what follows, however, I will grant that Boghossian-type cases are possible, thereby assuming the worst-case scenario for epistemic transparency. (According to Ludlow 1995, Boghossian cases are not merely possible, they are common. See Gerken 2009 for discussion.)

show that epistemic transparency does *not* fail in such examples. He argues that, by enrolling the two occurrences of 'water' in a chain of reasoning in which they are co-referential *de jure*, one *makes* the second occurrence refer to the same entity as the one referred to by the first occurrence. The natural tendency of water thoughts based on Earthly memories to refer to water rather than twater is thus overridden. As Burge writes,

> Anti-individualism does not say that every thought's content is fixed by the type of object that occasions the thought. Although free-standing memories normally evoke the concepts utilized in or appropriate to the remembered contexts, the exigencies of reasoning will often take precedence. One commonly utilizes concepts used earlier in an argument to identify objects in memories invoked in later steps. (Burge 1998: 367)

In Boghossian's example we start with a general premise with Twearthly content: this, according to Burge, constrains the second premise to *inherit* the Twearthly content of the first, even though the grounds for asserting the second premise are provided by memories of Earthly events. So, for Burge, the second premise is *false*: it asserts that Pavarotti once floated on twater, something that never happened.

Actually Burge does not discuss Boghossian's specific example, but another example of the same type. In Burge's own example, the first premise is the one that is based on Earthly memories, so it is the one that starts the anaphoric chain and determines the reference of all occurrences in the chain. Burge first describes the example the way Boghossian would:

> Alice might remember an event of picking up, and feeling the light weight of, some aluminum on earth, before she was switched; and in remembering the event, she might think correctly that she picked up some aluminum at that time. Then remembering a sample of twalumium on twin earth that she saw yesterday, she might think that yesterday there was

some twaluminum beside her....She might reason from these premises, fallaciously, to the conclusion that she once picked up the same sort of thing that was beside her yesterday. The word form 'aluminum' undetectably expresses for Alice two different concepts. The concepts used in the reasoning are supposed to be different because whereas the earth concept is evoked by the memory of the long past event of picking up aluminum, the twin earth concept is supposed to be evoked by the memory of what is in fact twaluminum on twin earth. The inference appears to Alice to be valid; but because of the switch in concepts, it is invalid. (Burge 1998: 366)

This description of the example is incorrect, according to Burge:

In determining what Alice is thinking in the second premise, one must remember that both the substantive memory of yesterday's experience, and the preservative memory of the use of the concept in the first premise, are operating in Alice's thinking. What it is to carry out valid arguments in thought is to connect premises, holding them together in a way that supports the conclusion....Insofar as we think that Alice is not making a mistake in reasoning, it is natural...to take her to be holding constant, through preservative memory throughout the argument, the concept used in the first premise in her thinking the second premise. The role of the concept aluminum in the reasoning is primary in her thinking, and preservative memory takes the occurrence of the concept in the first premise as a basis for its reuse in the second premise....

Given this usage by Alice, the second premise is false: She is mistaken in applying her concept aluminum, preserved from the first premise and originally evoked by her experience on earth, to her experience yesterday on twin earth. She is using the concept obtained from the first premise to *identify* the metal she remembers seeing, as expressed in the second premise. The mistake is a mistake of memory identification, not one of reasoning. Variations on this point apply to all of Boghossian's examples. (Burge 1998: 367)

To sum up the debate: Boghossian says that in slow switching inferences the premises are both true but the reasoning is fallacious because the two occurrences fail to be co-referential even though they are associated with the same mental file. That they are not actually co-referential despite being *de jure* co-referential shows that epistemic transparency fails. Burge defends epistemic transparency: the two occurrences *are* co-referential. But he takes the second premise to be false, because it inherits the reference of the first premise. (If the second premise was free-standing instead of being enrolled in the reasoning it would not be forced to inherit the reference of the first premise and would, presumably, be true.)

4

Is Burge right, or is Boghossian? Before presenting my own view, I would like to mention Schroeter's critical discussion of Burge (Schroeter 2007: 609–13). Schroeter constructs a Boghossian-type example in which the beliefs expressed by the two premises 'were formed independently and only subsequently put together in conscious thought' (Schroeter 2007: 609), and argues that in such cases Burge's anaphoric analysis is arbitrary and implausible. In Schroeter's example, the first premise is based on earthly memories from before the switch, while the second premise is based on her current perception on Twin-Earth. The subject, Peter, remembers how his sister Jo used to love playing in the water when she was a kid (on Earth, before the switch), and at the same time he notices the fastidious (twin) Jo who is unwilling to venture into (twin) water despite general coaxing. 'Peter is suddenly struck with the juxtaposition of these two thoughts—his memory and his perceptual belief—and he begins to wonder how Jo could have changed so much' (Schroeter 2007: 606). In drawing the conclusion that his sister has changed, Peter trades on the identity of Jo (the person his memory is about) and twin-Jo (the person his current perception is about). In this context, Schroeter argues, Burge's interpretative strategy is implausible:

> Burge suggests that whichever belief occurs second in Peter's conscious train of thought will change its normal reference (and

concepts) so as to match that of the belief that precedes it in conscious thought. If Peter's memory occurs first in his reasoning, then both the occurrent memory and the occurrent perceptual belief involve Peter's Earthly concepts Jo_1 and $water_1$; but if Peter's perceptual belief occurs first, then the whole train of reasoning involves Peter's distinct Twin Earthly concepts, Jo_2 and $water_2$. On this account, the reference and conceptual structure of Peter's child-hood memory shifts, depending on what else Peter happens to be thinking about when the memory surfaces in consciousness. This is a highly counterintuitive result. Normally, we don't think that a particular standing attitude can change its reference and concepts, depending on which *other* thoughts the subject is consciously enter-taining at the moment. It's much more natural to suppose that the standing attitudes retain their truth conditions and conceptual structure whenever they surface in Peter's consciousness. (Schroeter 2007: 610; see also Brown 2004: 178)

Like Schroeter, I think we should reject Burge's claim that, in *all* the relevant cases, one of the two premises is false because its content quasi-anaphorically depends upon the content of the other premise; for this gives too much weight to the order of the premises. As Pollock pointed out,

> In philosophy it is customary to think of arguments as linear sequences of propositions, with each member of the sequence being either a premise or the conclusion of an inference (in accordance with some reason scheme) from earlier propositions in the sequence. However, this representation of arguments is an artifact of the way we write them. In many cases the ordering of the elements of the sequence is irrelevant to the structure of the argument. (Pollock 2008: 452–3)[12]

This suggests that, in *some* cases at least, the premises are on the same footing—neither depends upon the other for its content. Since that is

---

[12] I am indebted to Michael Murez for bringing that passage to my attention.

so, I agree with Schroeter: it must be possible to construct Boghossian-type cases for which Burge's anaphoric strategy does not work.[13]

Let us assume that the Schroeter example is one such case, and that, as she claims, neither of the premises in the reasoning is anaphorically dependent upon the other. She concludes that epistemic transparency fails in such cases, but that conclusion is not forced upon us. I think we can maintain a principle of transparency, even with respect to such cases.

Consider Peter's train of thought in Schroeter's example:

1. JO once loved playing in **WATER**.
2. JO does not like playing in **WATER** now.
3. JO has changed.

Boghossian and Schroeter both think that the premises are true but the reasoning invalid through equivocation. I reject that analysis. On the analysis I favour, the reasoning is valid, as it is for Burge, yet the premises are on the same footing, as on the Boghossian–Schroeter analysis. Boghossian and Schroeter take premises 1 and 2 to be both true, under distinct interpretations for 'Jo' and 'water' (the Twearthly interpretation for premise 2, the Earthly interpretation for premise 1). Burge takes the Earthly interpretation fixed by the first premise to dominate the whole train of thought so that premise 2 comes out false. In contrast, I take both premises (and also the conclusion) to be *neither true nor false* in this train of thought. On my view, the mental file JO (or WATER) which the subject deploys several times in the reasoning is one that is not appropriately related to a single entity, as it should, but to two: one on Earth, one on Twin-Earth. It therefore fails to refer much like a definite description such as 'the author of *Principia Mathematica*' fails to refer.

[13] According to Mikkel Gerken, 'it may be argued that no single account is plausible for every specification of the slow-switch scenario'. Burge's anaphoric account marks a psychological possibility, but 'it is plausible that Boghossian's account according to which Peter's reasoning exhibits the fallacy of equivocation also marks a psychological possibility' (Gerken 2011: 389).

On this construal of the alleged counter-examples to epistemic transparency, they are not really counter-examples: That the two occurrences fail to co-refer even though they are *de jure* co-referential does not show that the subject is mistaken and that transparency fails. Indeed the factive characterization of co-reference *de jure* can be maintained in the face of such examples: the subject *knows* that the two occurrences co-refer if they refer at all. In the cases at hand, precisely, the two occurrences do *not* refer. In Schroeter's example, the subject Peter is confused: he mixes up two persons, namely Jo and twin-Jo, and his mental file fails to refer for that reason. This sort of case is compatible with epistemic transparency, and we can maintain that:

> If it seems to you that two tokens 'obviously and uncontrovertibly' mean the same, then they do mean the same and co-refer (*if they refer at all*)

Unicity of reference is a built-in presupposition of the file. Cases in which there are two objects are cases of presupposition failure and in such cases, arguably, there is no reference. On my view, therefore, as on Burge's, transparency holds: the subject knows that the two occurrences co-refer if they refer at all—on this he cannot be mistaken. What the subject does not know is *whether or not* the occurrences refer; for that depends upon external factors, and the subject can be mistaken in assuming that his file is contextually related to a single object. If there is no object, or more than one, the file does not refer.

11

Transparency and its Limits

The slow switching cases we discussed in Chapter 10 all involve a train of thought in which a singular term arguably shifts its reference across premises. In Schroeter's example, repeated below, the name 'Jo' refers to Jo in the first premise and to twin-Jo in the second premise; yet the subject, unaware of the switch to Twin-Earth, is unaware of the shift in reference. This defeats transparency. Internally there is *de jure* co-reference between the two occurrences of 'Jo' in the premises, yet, externally, these occurrences are not even co-referential.

(1) **JO** once loved playing in **WATER**.
(2) **JO** does not like playing in **WATER** now.
(3) **JO** has changed.

Following Burge, I argued that, appearances notwithstanding, no reference shift occurs across premises in this type of example. But instead of aligning the reference of the term in one premise on its reference in the other, as Burge does, I claimed that there is *reference failure* in both cases. Because of his state of confusion, Peter, the slow switching subject, does not manage to properly refer.

There is a prima facie objection to this account, however. When Peter sees (twin) Jo unwilling to venture into (twin) water and thinks 'Jo does not like playing in water', there is no doubt that, by 'Jo', he refers to the person he is watching, namely twin-Jo. The belief he entertains is a *perceptual belief*, and the object a singular perceptual belief is about is the object the underlying perception is about. Intuitively, therefore, Peter *succeeds* in referring, even though, unaware of the switch to Twin-Earth, he mistakes the person he is seeing for his biological sister Jo. This is similar to Kripke's example: 'Jones is raking the leaves'—where the individual the subject sees raking the leaves is Smith, not Jones (Kripke 1977: 263–4). Kripke contrasts semantic reference and speaker's reference in such cases: Smith, the man the speaker is seeing, is only the speaker's referent. But Kripke was concerned with the semantic reference of words, and the name 'Jones' does *not* semantically refer to Smith. If, instead, we are concerned with mental acts, the dialectical situation changes dramatically: there is no doubt that, in the circumstance Kripke describes, the speaker mentally refers to the man he is seeing, namely Smith, whom he mistakes for Jones (hence his use of the name 'Jones', which semantically refers to Jones, to express the thought). If what we are concerned with is the speaker's thought, speaker's reference is all that matters. Likewise, in Schroeter's example, Peter mentally refers to the person he is watching, namely twin-Jo, whom he mistakes for his biological sister Jo (hence his use of the name 'Jo' to express the thought). All this suggests that the subject succeeds in referring to the person he is watching, and to predicate something of her, so there is no compelling reason why his thought should be deemed 'neither true nor false', as I have claimed it is.

A similar objection can be voiced in connection with the first premise in the reasoning. When Peter remembers his biological sister Jo playing in the water on Earth, there is no doubt that the person his memory is about is Jo, his biological sister. Peter's thought inherits the reference of the memory on which it is based: Peter therefore succeeds in mentally referring to Jo. Why, then, should his thought be deemed neither true nor false? Why talk of reference failure in such cases?

My response is the same in both cases. Even though the subject's memory is of Jo, and his perception is of twin-Jo, still the *way* the thinker attempts to refer in thought to the object of his perception or memory is not a purely demonstrative way.[1] (If the thought was purely demonstrative, that would enable it to simply inherit the object of the experience on which it is based.) The subject *recognizes* the person he is watching as his biological sister Jo; likewise, he thinks of the person his memory is about as the same person he has been interacting with for many years after the switch and is currently watching. The mental file through which the subject attempts to refer is not a purely demonstrative file but what I called a *recognitional file*, which embodies a certain presupposition of identity. The presupposition fails, and therefore the subject fails to refer through that file. The subject's thought, thefore, is neither true nor false, even if there are thoughts 'in the vicinity' that are true and to which the subject would naturally retreat if he realized his mistake: those are the purely demonstrative thoughts directly based on the perception or the memory.

In short: Schroeter's story would be correct if the thoughts reported in premises 1 and 2 were simple demonstrative thoughts; but they are not. If they were, the subject would be deploying two distinct files in premise 1 and premise 2: a demonstrative file in premise 2, a memory demonstrative in premise 1. Thus construed the reasoning would be fallacious, as Schroeter argues. But in premises 1 and 2 the same mental file is deployed. That file is anchored to two distinct individuals and it fails to refer because of the confusion on which it is based.

---

[1] What I mean by a 'purely demonstrative' mode of presentation is a non-composite mode involving either perception or memory but not both.

2

Schroeter might respond to me in the way she responded to Burge: by pointing out that the premises might be 'formed independently and only subsequently put together in conscious thought' (Schroeter 2007: 609). Let us assume that this is indeed the case, and that the thoughts serving as premises in the reasoning do involve a demonstrative and a memory file whose referents ought to diverge given the respective sources of these files. Still, when the subject, Peter, enrols the thoughts into the above piece of reasoning, thereby 'trading upon the identity' of two distinct informational sources, he relies on a false presupposition of identity (Stalnaker 2008: 126–7). Here, however, we have *stipulated* that the files invoked in the premises were a demonstrative and a memory file *rather than* a composite file presupposing the identity of the seen individual and the remembered individual. If there are such cases (which I doubt), this shows that a presupposition of identity can be operative in the reasoning even if it is not built into the modes of presentation (mental files) under which the referents are thought of in the premises.

One problem with this idea is that, if the presupposition is not built into the files but added as an extra premise, the reasoning has to be described as enthymematic. But in Chapter 4 I laid much emphasis on Campbell's idea that when one trades upon identity, there is no missing premise that the two things the confused subject treats as one are identical. I contrasted the cases in which identity is presupposed (and no extra premise is involved) with the cases in which identity is asserted. Now we are considering a mixed possibility: identity is presupposed, but there is an extra premise, namely the presupposition itself. The presupposition is not built into the modes of presentation, yet it is at work nonetheless.

In discussing a related case, Stalnaker has attempted to make sense of the idea that a 'tacit presupposition' may serve as hidden premise in a piece of reasoning.[2] If this is correct, 'trading upon identity' comes in two varieties: one variety on which, as Campbell says, there is a single sense (a single file), and the identity presupposition is built into the mode of presentation; and another variety in which the presupposition is operative without being built into the modes of presentation. Only in the former case are the premises devoid of truth-value because of reference failure. In the stipulated Schroeter case, analysed à la Stalnaker, the explicit premises ('Jo$_2$ does not like to play in the water', and 'Jo$_1$ used to like playing in the water') are both true, the hidden premise (the presupposition Jo$_1$ = Jo$_2$) is false, and the conclusion ('Jo has changed') is devoid of truth-value because, in contrast to the explicit premises, it involves a composite file resting on the false presupposition.

We have retained the idea of reference failure for the conclusion though not the premises. On this interpretation of the example, three distinct modes of presentation are involved: a memory demonstrative in the first premise, a perceptual demonstrative in the second premise, and a composite, identity-presupposing mode of presentation in the conclusion. But we can easily imagine a variant of the case in which (as in Burge's 'aluminum' example) the conclusion is purely general and involves no singular mode of presentation: 'there is an x that is both F and G' (where 'F' and 'G' are the predicates featuring in each of the premises). In this case the conclusion is true or false (as the case may be) but it does not follow from the explicit premises, since the presupposition of identity is false. What should we say about this case? Is the reasoning fallacious, as Schroeter and Boghossian would say? If we build the (false) identity presupposition into

---

[2] Stalnaker imagines a variant of Perry's *Enterprise* example in which there are two different ships seen in the Oakland harbour but they are taken to be the same ship. The subject reasons as follows:

This ship (pointing to the bow) is an aircraft carrier;
That ship (pointing to the stern of the second ship) is British;
Therefore there is a British aircraft carrier.

[continued overleaf]

the reasoning, we have to consider it as fallacious through equivocation. But if, like Stalnaker, we spell out the identity presupposition as
a suppressed premise, even though it is neither articulated in the subject's reasoning nor 'subpersonally encoded', then perhaps we can
maintain that the reasoning is valid. Indeed, the conclusion *would*
follow if the suppressed premise *were* true. Either way, transparency as
I understand it is not threatened. Two different files are invoked in the
premises, as per the initial stipulation. To be sure, their co-reference is
presupposed; but for transparency to fail, there has to be a single file,
referring to two distinct objects (on two distinct deployments).

This takes us back to the 'normal' interpretation of the Schroeter
example. Normally, in a train of thought like Peter's, the identity presupposition which pervades the reasoning does affect the modes of
presentation involved in the premises. That is why, in section 1, I said
that the files invoked by the premises are not distinct demonstrative
files based on perception or memory, but a single recognitional file.
When there is a single file, I maintain that there is reference failure,
due to the falsity of the presupposition built into the file. So there is
no shift of reference, and transparency is preserved.

3

It can be objected that, even if there is a single file, there can be
reference shift rather than reference failure. When the file at issue is
based on a composite relation, as in our example (on the 'normal'
interpretation), and a fortiori when it is an encyclopedia entry, there

Stalnaker suggests we should represent the reasoning as involving 'a false tacit
presupposition, a suppressed premise'. He writes: 'This way of representing the reasoning does not assume that John has entertained the possibility that the two [things] are
different...or that the presupposition [that they are the same] is in any way encoded at
some perhaps subpersonal level in John's internal cognitive apparatus. Most of what we
presuppose is presupposed simply by not recognizing the possibilities in which the presuppositions are false. The explicit statement of the tacit premise is part of the theorist's
representation of the situation' (Stalnaker 2008: 127).

will typically be distinguishable *regions* in the informational content of the file, corresponding to the diversity of information links on which the file is based. And these regions may be more or less strongly activated in a given case. As we shall see, this gives rise to a form of context-sensitivity which threatens transparency.

In our example, the file rests upon a memory link and a perception link. Some of the beliefs stored in the file derive from memory, others from current perception. Let us assume that the memory-based region of the composite file is more strongly activated in the context in which premise 1 is entertained. (Following Schroeter, we suppose that the thoughts serving as premises are formed independently of each other.) In this sort of case, arguably, the subject *may* succeed in referring to the source of the memory, despite the fact that (i) the memory beliefs are stored in the composite file, and (ii) the composite file embodies a false presupposition of identity. The fact that the 'other' region of the file is not (strongly) activated may be sufficient to render the presupposition failure harmless and to prevent it from making the file-invoking premise truth-valueless. Likewise, if the perception-based region of the file is more strongly activated (as is arguably the case when premise 2 is entertained), the subject *may* succeed in referring to the object he is perceiving, despite the fact that (i) the perceptual beliefs are stored in the composite file, and (ii) the composite file embodies a false presupposition of identity. Conclusion: even if a single file is deployed twice in the premises, it is theoretically possible for that file to succeed, on each deployment, to refer to a distinct object than what it refers to on the other deployment.

I think such situations, in which only some aspect of a given file is strongly activated, raise interesting issues and should be taken on board. I also think that in such situations, the failure of the presupposition built into the file may be harmless, indeed. This means that reference shifts will be possible in such cases even though a single file is deployed twice (in contexts that lead to the activation of different regions of the file). But *such situations will arise only if the presupposition of identity has no relevance to the current train of thought*. In the Schroeter example the fact that we exploit the identity in reasoning makes the presupposition relevant and forces us to activate not just the memory (or the perception) region of the file, but the whole recognitional file.

This relates to an important issue I have so far neglected regarding the reference of rich files such as encyclopedia entries.[3] I said that, in general, the reference of a file is determined relationally: the reference of a file is the object to which the subject (or the file in the subject's mind) stands in the relevant ER relation. But in the case of encyclopedia entries there is an arbitrary number of distinct (first-order) ER relations. The file keeps growing new information links in an opportunistic manner. How is the reference of such a file determined? Is the reference the object which *initially* justified opening the file? That seems unlikely—the more information we store in the file, the more ER relations we exploit in so doing, the less it matters what the initial source of the file was. The reference seems to be, as Evans (1973, 1982) suggested, the *dominant source* of information in the file.[4]

But what is dominant may depend upon the purposes at hand. In particular it may depend on which region of the file is more strongly activated. There will typically be distinguishable information clusters *within* the file, corresponding to distinct information links. Depending on which cluster (or region) is more strongly activated, the 'dominant source of information' will possibly vary. So the fact that one region might be more strongly activated than another one depending on the context introduces a measure of context-sensitivity in the semantics of files: the reference of a file *may* shift through modulation of the activated regions. That is admittedly a failure of

---

[3] I am grateful to Michael Murez for raising that issue, and making interesting suggestions, in discussing this chapter.

[4] Murez suggests that the presupposition of unicity underlying the file is the presupposition of unicity of the dominant source of information in the file. This prevents cases of minor confusion from making the file contentless through presupposition failure.

transparency, since transparency does not allow a single file to refer to distinct things. But, again, that situation will arise only if the presupposition of identity has no relevance to the current train of thought. The failure of transparency is therefore very limited: it will hardly ever entail a failure of rationality. That is so because, whenever the subject 'trades upon the identity' of two distinct informational sources, she or he will exploit the presupposition of identity on which the composite file rests, and that, arguably, entails failure of reference for all occurrences of the file in the train of thought.

4

A last objection to the account I have put forward takes us back to inverse Paderewski cases. Remember Cappelen's example (§10.1):

> There are two guys, A and B, who bear the same name (say 'Cicero'). John thinks there is a single guy: so he freely mixes information he gets from A with information he gets from B and feeds everything into a single file.

The objection runs as follows. Suppose John sees B raking the leaves, and says 'Cicero is raking the leaves.' Here, arguably, John refers to B. 'Cicero' is a name for B (as well as a name for A) and in this context the subject's perceptual relation to B disambiguates the name so that the subject, by using that name in that context, unambiguously refers to B. Likewise, there will be contexts in which the subject's use of the name 'Cicero' will unambiguously refer to A. These uses of 'Cicero', which refer to distinct objects, are associated with a single mental file in John's mind, so this is a case where there is co-reference *de jure* between tokens of 'Cicero' without actual co-reference. Yet it cannot be said that the name 'Cicero' fails to refer in such cases. The correct description, rather, is that the name is ambiguous and refers to both A and B. Admittedly, the subject is confused—he does not know that the name is ambiguous—but that does not prevent contextual disambiguation from taking place in at least some cases, and in these cases at least the name refers. This shows that there can be co-reference *de jure* between two non-co-referential occurrences even though the occurrences in question do refer. This is an objection to my account of the confusion in terms of reference failure.

I respond that mentally, the subject *is* confused: he uses a single mental file to refer to two distinct objects. This can only generate reference failure: the file the subject deploys in thought does not refer. What arguably succeeds in referring in the examples is the *public name* 'Cicero': in the example there are two homonymous names each of which has its own semantic referent. If the subject, while watching B, says 'Cicero is raking the leaves', what he says is true, for the context makes it clear that the name he uses is the name for B. But what we are concerned with, again, is the speaker's *thought*, not his utterance. And what he deploys in his thought is the file he associates with the ambiguous name 'Cicero'. That file is irreducibly equivocal, and fails to refer.

One may counter that the subject *uses the name in thought*. The thought, because it uses the public name, inherits the reference of the latter. In Part VI, indeed, I will discuss (and endorse a version of) 'Instrumentalism', the view that we *can* use public words in thought. But with respect to the Cappelen example, this will not help. One uses a public word in thought whenever one bases a mental file on the word through some kind of 'deferential' mechanism. However, a necessary condition of deferential inheritance is that the name on which the file is based possess a unique referent. If the word one bases one's mental file on is ambiguous (as the name 'Cicero' is in the example) the file is equivocal and does not refer. In other words: For the thought to inherit the reference of the name, the name itself has to be disambiguated; it must be a 'common currency name' in the terminology of Kaplan (1990). This is what happens in ordinary deference. In real life, there is a single Cicero. Upon hearing of Cicero in class, the subject may create a mental file CICERO which deferentially inherits the reference of the name. In the Cappelen example, however, the mental file is *not* based on the common currency name 'Cicero' as a name for some particular person—it is based on the ambiguous name-type 'Cicero' which (qua name-type) does not refer. There can be no deferential inheritance in that sort of situation. So I maintain that the subject fails to refer in that example through deployment of the equivocal CICERO file.[5]

---

[5] Kaplan is even more radical than I am: 'when two different common currency words are wired together in this way… nothing whatsoever is being said' (Kaplan 1990: 109). I maintain that the subject's *thought* is neither true nor false in such situations, but I am prepared to concede that, in certain cases at least, the subject's utterance may still express a definite content. (See Evans 1982: 67 ff. for the difference between saying something and thinking it.)

Part VI

Beyond Acquaintance

12

Descriptive Names

1

I have argued that singular thought about an object involves a non-descriptive mode of presentation of that object, that is, a mental file based on some acquaintance relation to the object. If that is right, then singular thinking requires acquaintance. That consequence may seem hard to swallow, however. As several philosophers, and most prominently Robin Jeshion, have emphasized, 'we are capable of having *de re* thought about objects with which we lack acquaintance' (Jeshion 2004: 594; by '*de re* thought' she means what I mean by 'singular thought'). How can this be if the story I have told is correct?

That acquaintance is not necessary for singular thinking is supposed to be established by a type of case, discussed by Grice, Kripke, Donnellan, Evans, Kaplan, and others, in which the subject only knows some object 'by description' yet seems to be able to express a singular thought about that object. The cases in question involve the use of a singular term (e.g. a proper name or a demonstrative) to refer to whatever satisfies a certain description. Thus the name 'Jack the Ripper' was introduced to refer to whoever committed certain murders, and 'Neptune' was introduced to refer to whatever planet causes certain perturbations in the orbit of Uranus. (Both examples are due to Saul Kripke.) On the same pattern, Evans coined the descriptive name 'Julius' which refers, by stipulation, to whoever invented the zip, and Kaplan coined 'Newman 1' which refers, by stipulation, to the first baby to be born in the next century. If, by using such names, it is possible to express singular thoughts about those objects, this provides prima facie counter-evidence to the claim that singular thinking requires acquaintance.

But there is no general agreement about descriptive names and whether or not sentences involving them really express singular thoughts. Evans holds that they do not. Qua proper name, the name 'Julius' is rigid: the associated description ('whoever invented the zip') only serves to fix its reference. Still, the thought expressed is descriptive:

> The thought expressed by 'Julius is F' may equivalently be expressed by 'The inventor of the zip is F'...Someone who understands and accepts the one sentence as true gets himself into exactly the same belief state as someone who accepts the other. Belief states are distinguished by the evidence which gives rise to them, and the expectations, behaviour, and further beliefs which may be derived from them (in conjunction with other beliefs); in all these respects, the belief states associated with the two sentences are indistinguishable. We do not produce new thoughts (new beliefs) simply by 'a stroke of the pen' (in Grice's phrase)—simply by introducing a new name in the language. (Evans 1982: 50)

Donnellan comes to the same conclusion: 'the fact that a name is introduced as a rigid designator does not by itself put a person in a position to have *de re* propositional attitudes toward the entity rigidly designated' (Donnellan 1977: 23).[1] If it did, then Leverrier—the astronomer who introduced the descriptive name 'Neptune' after inferring that a hitherto unknown planet was responsible for certain perturbations—would have been able to gain a piece of astronomical knowledge (to the effect that, if some planet causes the relevant perturbations, it is Neptune which does) simply by performing an act of

---

[1] Kim 1977: 616 argues for the same conclusion.

linguistic stipulation. The unacceptability of that conclusion establishes that the introduction of a descriptive name is not sufficient for singular thought (though it gives us rigidity). As Donnellan puts it, the acquaintance constraint 'account[s] for why the sort of stipulations we have been discussing do not put us in a position... to know anything about the entity for which we have introduced a rigid designator' (Donnellan 1977: 25).

But the principle Evans appeals to (that we cannot produce new thoughts 'by a stroke of the pen') runs counter to a no less plausible principle which Kaplan calls the 'Instrumental Thesis' and which, he says, follows from the causal/historical chain picture of the reference of names:[2]

> The notion that the referent can be carried by a name from early past to present suggests that the language itself carries meanings, and thus that we can *acquire* meanings through the instrument of language. This...provides the opportunity for an *instrumental* use of language to broaden the realm of what can be expressed and to broaden the horizons of thought itself.
>
> On my view, our connection with a linguistic community in which names and other meaning-bearing elements are passed down to us enables us to entertain thoughts *through the language* that would not otherwise be accessible to us. Call this the *Instrumental Thesis*. (Kaplan 1989b: 603)[3]

One of the applications of the Instrumental Thesis, Kaplan points out, is to the case of descriptive names:

> The introduction of a new proper name by means of a dubbing in terms of description and the active contemplation of characters involving *dthat*-terms—two mechanisms for providing direct reference to the denotation

---

[2] This picture, Kaplan says in a footnote (1989b: 602–3), first appears in print in Donnellan 1970 (thus antedating Kripke). Kaplan forgets Geach, who explicitly put forward the picture in 'The Perils of Pauline', published in 1969. See the quotation from Geach pp. 31–2.

[3] For a similar view, see Millikan 2000: chapter 6.

of an arbitrary definite description—constitute a form of cognitive restructuring; they broaden our range of thought. (Kaplan 1989a: 560 n. 76)

We can introduce a name by describing the referent...Such names are still directly referential and, in my view, still have the capacity to enlarge what we can express and apprehend. If we were to discover that Aristotle had been predicted and dubbed one year before his birth...the name...would still be a *name*, with all its attendant powers. (Kaplan 1989b: 605)

So we cannot simply *assume* that no new thought is introduced via a mere linguistic stipulation. This, rather, is part of what is in question. Kaplan himself holds that, simply by manipulating the linguistic apparatus of direct reference, it is possible to entertain a singular thought about an object known to us only by description.

2

How can we settle the issue? Our intuitions in this area vary from case to case, Jeshion points out (Jeshion 2010: 113–18). Moreover, they are not very sharp. To adapt an example from Stephen Schiffer (1981: 49, 1995: 92), suppose I see big footprints in the sand and say 'He must be a giant.' Do I, or do I not, express/entertain a singular thought about whoever made these footprints? If we say I don't, as singularists are prone to do, what about the case in which someone has been buried into the sand and just one toe is emerging? Here, if I say, 'He must be a giant', it is hard to resist the intuition that a singular thought is expressed. With the help of such examples, it is not too difficult to imagine a continuum of cases between straightforward instances of knowledge by acquaintance and straightforward instances of knowledge by description, most instances in between being intermediate cases with a more or less tenuous informational link to the referent.[4] With respect to such intermediate cases, our intuitions tend to be shaky (Azzouni 2011). Perhaps Kripke's examples of real-life

---

[4] See Kaplan 1989a: 560–1 for the related idea that there is a continuum of cases between pure referential uses and pure attributive uses of both names and descriptions.

descriptive names—'Neptune', 'Jack the Ripper'—fall into that category, for singularists seem to oscillate between two positions, betraying the lack of firm intuitions about these cases.[5] The first position consists in insisting that, for example, Leverrier expressed no singular thought by his stipulative use of 'Neptune' (see Donnellan's argument above), or that the introducers of the descriptive name 'Jack the Ripper' only had descriptive thoughts about the referent when they introduced the name. Alternatively, however, philosophers sometimes feel the temptation to accept that there *is* singular thought in e.g. the Jack the Ripper case, and to account for this by appealing to some kind of informational connection to the referent: the bodies of the victims, and the various pieces of evidence left by the murderer on the crime scenes, link the introducers of the name (the Scotland Yard people, presumably) to the referent and make it possible for them to entertain singular thoughts about him.[6] Similarly, though Homer is known to us only as the author of the *Iliad* and the *Odyssey*, still the works themselves may be thought to constitute a link between Homer and us, which enables us to entertain singular thoughts about him.[7] Now, Hawthorne and Manley (forthcoming: §2.10) point out, 'If one can have singular thoughts about Homer in the presence of his works and Jack the Ripper in the presence of his deed, why not Neptune in the presence of its perturbations?' Indeed they cite a contemporary astronomer—Herschel—who insisted that we can 'see' Neptune through the perturbations it causes.

The general murkiness of the situation leads Hawthorne and Manley to conclude that the best way to secure 'our grip on the presence or absence of singular thought is via certain kinds of propositional attitude reports: True reports that "quantify in" (where a variable within the report is bound by a quantifier outside it) as well as true reports with a referential term in the that-clause, require the presence of a singular

---

[5] As Kim points out, 'Kripke's own position on this issue seems ambivalent' (Kim 1977: 616).

[6] See the quotation from David Lewis on pp. 34–5 (n. 5).

[7] I assume that a single male person wrote the *Iliad* and the *Odyssey*.

thought' (Hawthorne and Manley forthcoming: §1.5). Accordingly they put forward the following principle they call 'Harmony' (Hawthorne and Manley forthcoming: §2.1):

> HARMONY Any belief report whose complement clause contains either a singular term or a variable bound from outside by an existential quantifier requires for its truth that the subject have a singular thought.

But given the link thus established between singular thought and the appearance of singular terms or externally bound variables in true belief ascriptions, 'reflection of our practices of belief-reporting provides a strong prima face case for liberalism', they say. 'Liberalism', for Hawthorne and Manley, is the denial of *any* acquaintance constraint on singular thought.

I believe Hawthorne and Manley are right, up to a point: *If* one accepts Harmony, one has to give up acquaintance as a constraint on singular thought. Consider the following, rather extreme case (an instance of what Kaplan calls the 'pseudo-*de re*').[8] Ann is a 6-year-old girl, whom John has never met and whose existence he is unaware of. But John believes that every 6-year-old can learn to play tennis in ten lessons. So, meeting Ann, I tell her: 'John believes that you can learn to play tennis in ten lessons.' There is a sense in which this is true. (Admittedly, there is also a sense in which this is false.) Harmony therefore entails that John has a singular thought about Ann, even though he is not acquainted with her.[9] So there can be singular thought without acquaintance.

---

[8] See Kaplan 1989a: 155 n. 71. Note that the example I give is rather special, and significantly different from the examples of pseudo *de re* reports discussed by Kaplan. That example was discussed in Gilles Fauconnier's graduate seminar in the early 1980s.

[9] I raised the issue in a seminar in St Andrews in November 2008, and Hawthorne and Manley, in response, seemed to accept this extraordinary conclusion (that John has a singular thought about Ann, in the described scenario).

For a singularist, this result is clearly unacceptable. The thought that every 6-year-old can learn to play tennis in ten lessons is the paradigm of a *general* thought—a higher-level thought about properties. So if the criterion for singular thought is given by attitude reports, as per Harmony, we lose the very distinction we were trying to account for. A descriptivist is likely to welcome this result, but a singularist cannot accept it. This means that a singularist must reject Harmony. One may do so in two ways. One can maintain the link between singular thought and *de re* reports, but draw a distinction between 'genuine' *de re* reports and 'pseudo' *de re* reports—the example of Ann and John belonging to the latter category.[10] Or one may reject the whole methodology of relying on *de re* reports to characterize singular thought. Personally, I think it's a bad idea to start from attitude reports, given the complexity of their semantics and their high level of context-sensitivity. (Similarly, I hold it's a bad idea to start from locutionary reports in theorizing about 'what is said'.[11]) We should rather start from the theory of thought (and, in particular, the distinction between singular and general thoughts) and use elements from that theory, along with a number of other ingredients, in trying to understand the multi-faceted phenomenon of *de re* attitude reports (see *Direct Reference*, chapter 20).[12] To be sure, as Hawthorne and Manley point out, 'those who accept [the acquaintance constraint] but reject [HARMONY] face the challenge of explicating the relevant notion of singular thought while allowing it to float free from the semantics of belief reports' (Hawthorne and Manley

[10] For Kaplan, pseudo-*de re* reports are 'distorted' and involve unjustified 'falsification'. He concludes: 'I do not see that the existence of the *pseudo de re* form of report poses any issues of sufficient theoretical interest to make it worth pursuing' (Kaplan 1989*a*: 555–6 n.).

[11] See Recanati 2004: 14–16. Reliance on 'said-that' tests led Cappelen and Lepore (2005) to absurd consequences, thus providing what I take to be a *reductio* of the methodology. (Cappelen and Hawthorne 2009 acknowledge the failure of 'said-that' tests but stick to the methodology and try to come up with a better variant.)

[12] As Kamp puts it, 'only when a sufficiently detailed theory of the attitudes is in place, can we tackle the theory of attitude reports with any chance of success' (Kamp 1990: 87).

forthcoming: §2.7). But that is precisely what the notion of mental file is supposed to do for us: to provide a cognitive explanation, independent of our reporting practice.

I admit, of course, that there is some vagueness in the division between cases in which the acquaintance constraint is met and cases in which it isn't, and a corresponding lack of firm intuitions with respect to intermediate cases. But this should not be considered a problem for the acquaintance theorist. In cases in which it is unclear whether or not there is acquaintance, it will likewise be unclear whether or not a singular thought is expressed. This is to be expected, from the acquaintance theorist's point of view.

Far from being a problem, the lack of firm intuitions regarding ordinary examples of descriptive names such as 'Neptune' or 'Jack the Ripper' actually *protects* the acquaintance theorist from the standard argument in favour of 'acquaintanceless singular thought'. That argument is based on two premises:

1. In cases like Jack the Ripper (or Jeshion's favourite example: Unabomber), the introducers of the descriptive name are not acquainted with the reference.

2. Such cases nevertheless elicit intuitions of singularity.

Anti-acquaintance theorists argue that the best overall theoretical response to these facts is to drop the acquaintance requirement on singular thought. What singularity intuitions track, Jeshion (2010) says, is not the presence of acquaintance but the presence of some other feature which is independent of acquaintance, and which the theorist has to discover. The presence or absence of *that* feature will explain why some instances of descriptive names elicit intuitions of singularity while others (e.g. Schiffer's footprint example) do not. The premises of the argument can be questioned, however, or at least qualified. Acquaintance is arguably a matter of degree, and the Scotland Yard people have got some (admittedly tenuous) information link to the murderer. The existence of such a link goes against premise 1 to a certain extent, and—to the very same extent—against premise 2, insofar as the link in question should be sufficient to blur our intuitions to some degree. To make a convincing case for acquaint-anceless *de re* thought, therefore, the right sort of example to use is one like Kaplan's Newman 1 (the first child to be born in the next century), for which the first premise is uncontroversial. But such examples do *not* elicit singularity intuitions.

Be that as it may, it is not my intention to contest the premises of the anti-acquaintance argument. I admit that, by and large, the subject's access to the referent is mainly descriptive, in the relevant examples; and I find Kaplan's Instrumental Thesis sufficiently attrac-tive to seriously consider the possibility that the subject, by using a name or a demonstrative, puts herself in a position to entertain a sin-gular thought about the referent. What I want to claim is that such a view is fully compatible with my framework. This may come as a surprise, since the phenomenon of acquaintanceless singular thought seems incompatible with my claim that singular thoughts involve mental files based on some acquaintance relation to what the thought is about. But, as I am now going to argue, it isn't.

3

The mental file framework rests on two principles:

1. The subject cannot entertain a singular thought about an object *a* without possessing, and exercising, a mental file whose referent is *a*.

2. To possess and exercise a mental file whose referent is *a* the subject must stand in some acquaintance relation to *a*.

These two principles together seem to entail that no singular thought can be entertained unless the subject is acquainted with what her thought is about. Principle 1 says that singular thinking requires possession of a mental file, and Principle 2 says that possession of a mental file requires acquaintance with the referent of the file. The conclusion that there is no singular thought without acquaintance seems to follow. But it does not really follow.

Principle 2 says that a mental file requires a suitable relation to the referent. As I pointed out earlier (§5.2), that is a *normative* claim, distinct from the *factual* claim that there is no mental file tokening without some acquaintance relation to the referent. In other words, we should distinguish between *de facto* and *de jure* conditions on singular thought. In *Direct Reference* (Recanati 1993: 178–9), I introduced a similar distinction in connection with Russell's view that the use of a genuine proper name demands that the user be acquainted with the referent of the name. According to the non-standard interpretation of Russell's claim I put forward in that book, a genuine proper name may well be tokened (*de facto*) even though its *de jure* requirements are not met: a proper name imposes certain epistemic demands on its users, but the demands may or may not be satisfied. Similarly, one may argue, a mental file can come into active use (*de facto*) even though the epistemic requirement stated in Principle 2 is not satisfied. If this is right, then an acquaintance theorist may (and, I think, should) countenance the phenomenon of acquaintanceless singular thought.

In *Direct Reference* I presented Russell's view of names (on the non-standard interpretation) as follows:

> Along with the well-known view that ordinary proper names such as 'Bismarck' are not genuine proper names, because genuine proper names require direct acquaintance with their referents (a type of acquaintance possible only with oneself and one's sense data), Russell seems to have held a slightly different view, namely : that 'Bismarck' is a genuine proper name, but that we are unable to entertain the thoughts which our utterances including this name are meant to express. The thought we think when we hear or say 'Bismarck was an astute diplomatist' is not the thought this utterance purports to express, Russell claimed, because this thought is unavailable to us; it is available only to Bismarck himself. It is

because ordinary proper names such as 'Bismarck' *are* genuine proper names, on this view, that they require their users to be acquainted with their referents (a condition that is not fulfilled when someone other than Bismarck uses the name 'Bismarck'); this is also why an utterance including a name such as 'Bismarck' is meant to express a singular thought—a thought which an ordinary user of the name is unable to entertain.

In [this] framework…a proper name is a word which *must* be used in a certain way, even though it may happen to be used in other ways. A genuine proper name is defined (normatively) by what it demands; Russell thus speaks of 'the direct use which (a proper name) *always wishes to have*' (my emphasis). In the case of 'Julius', as in the case of 'Bismarck' (in Russell's framework), there is no reason to deny that the name itself is a genuine proper name, which requires that its reference be thought of nondescriptively. This is perfectly consistent with the fact that the reference of the name *happens* to be thought of descriptively. (Recanati 1993: 178–9)

In this passage I endorse Evans's view that, in the case of 'Julius', a user of the name can only think about its referent descriptively (as 'the inventor of the zip'). I will get back to that issue shortly.[13] What matters for present purposes is that, in that case as in the case of 'Bismarck' according to Russell, the normative requirement associated with the use of names is not satisfied: the subject is unable to think of the referent non-descriptively, as he should given that he is using a name. But that does not prevent him from actually using the name.

Exactly the same sort of position can be upheld with respect to mental files, by giving a normative interpretation of Principle 2 above. I sketched such a position in *Direct Reference*, when I said that descriptive names such as 'Neptune' or 'Jack the Ripper' are 'created only in the expectation that more information about the bearer will accumulate, thus eventuating in the possibility of thinking of the

---

[13] As will become apparent in Chapter 13, I no longer wholeheartedly accept Evans's view that one cannot produce new thoughts simply 'by a stroke of the pen' (i.e. by introducing a name for some object known by description). I am now open to the view that, in *certain* cases (namely cases in which one is justified in one's expectation of a forthcoming acquaintance relation), one can think a singular thought by mentally tokening a descriptive name.

latter nondescriptively. This possibility is simply *anticipated* by the use of a descriptive name' (Recanati 1993: 180). One way of interpreting this suggestion is that the user who knows the referent only by description nevertheless *opens a file for it* because he anticipates that he will soon be acquainted with it and needs a place to store information about it. On that interpretation, a file may be opened *before* the epistemic requirement is met. The epistemic requirement still holds, however. The only *reason* to open a file in such cases is that the user expects to stand in the appropriate relation to the referent. So *a mental file still requires, for its justification, that the subject stand in a suitable, information-bearing relation to the referent*. This, I take it, is the defining feature of acquaintance-based views such as the one I have been defending in this book.

Several options are available, within that general framework. According to one option, there is singular thought only if there actually is acquaintance with the object of the thought. This rules out acquaintanceless singular thought. But nothing prevents an acquaintance theorist from choosing a more 'liberal' option and holding that *there is singular thought as soon as there is a mental file*, whether or not the associated *de jure* requirement is actually satisfied. On this view, *as soon as* one opens a file for an object (even if one knows that object only by description, as in the Leverrier–Neptune case), one puts oneself in a position to entertain singular thoughts about that object. This view accommodates acquaintanceless singular thought, yet it is compatible with the idea that mental files are governed by an acquaintance constraint, normatively understood.

To sum up, the view I have presented, based on Principles 1 and 2, is compatible with the phenomenon of acquaintanceless singular thought, provided Principle 2 is interpreted as being about the normative (*de jure*) requirements of singular thought. Cases in which, *de facto*, the requirements are not satisfied do not object to a principle that says what the requirements *are*.[14]

---

[14] As Vendler puts it, 'the fact that a tool can be misused does not alter the function of the tool' (Vendler 1967: 51–2).

13

Singular Thought without Acquaintance

1

In Chapter 12 (§3) I described two possible options for the acquaintance theorist faced with the phenomenon of 'acquaintanceless singular thought'. In this section, I will consider the arguments that can be adduced in favour of each and the objections they raise. This will lead me to make room for an intermediate position.

The first position I have described may be called the *Strong Acquaintance View*. It is the view which anti-acquaintance people target, as if acquaintance theorists had no other options available. According to that view, singular thought requires actual (*de facto*) acquaintance with the referent. So, descriptive names do not allow their users to grasp/ entertain singular thoughts. It is that view which I ascribed to Evans.

A possible objection to that view is that it tends to underestimate the potential impact of language on thought. Coining a name, or using a demonstrative, for what one is thinking about descriptively arguably goes some way toward changing our perspective on the object, thus paving the way for singular thought about it. This is the gist of Kaplan's Instrumental Thesis.[1]

---

[1] Kaplan actually holds something stronger: that mentally tokening a name or a demonstrative is sufficient for singular thought (not merely that it 'paves the way' for it). But the Instrumental Thesis, as Kaplan formulates it (i.e. vaguely), is compatible with a

Anti-instrumentalism, i.e. the view that there is *no* such incidence of language on thought, does not seem very plausible.

But the Strong Acquaintance View need not be committed to Anti-instrumentalism. Thus someone like Evans might argue as follows. Coining a name for the inventor of the zip does provide us with a new vehicle for thought: we now have a name, 'Julius', that we can use in thought. So much is conceded to Instrumentalism. But the name in question (or, rather, its mental counterpart) is only a constituent of the thought-*vehicle*. By tokening a thought-vehicle involving such a name, we *try* to think a singular thought (not in the sense of thought-vehicle, but in the Fregean sense of thought-*content*), and we may or may not succeed.[2] As Evans used to put it, we 'essay' a singular thought. But there are many circumstances in which we similarly essay a singular thought and actually fail to think one. When Leverrier tried to think a singular thought by tokening another descriptive name, 'Vulcan', he failed because the name was empty. An empty name (just as an empty demonstrative of the sort one can token in hallucination) is an improper vehicle for singular thinking since, in the absence of a reference for the name or the demonstrative, no semantically evaluable thought is expressed by using them.[3] This does not mean that the user of the singular term is not thinking anything: there are other thoughts in the vicinity, which the subject is arguably entertaining. Evans discussed that issue in connection

weaker position according to which coining and using a name 'broadens the horizons of thought' even if further conditions have to be satisfied for such use to give rise to full-blooded singular thinking. Be that as it may, I draw a distinction between 'Instrumentalism', the view that linguistic resources (and in particular the apparatus of direct reference) can be exploited to broaden the horizons of thought, and Kaplan's own version, which I call 'Radical Instrumentalism' (see below). On Instrumentalism, see also Harman 1973: 84–8, 1977: 174–5, Millikan 2000: 88–91.

[2] On the neo-Fregean distinction between thought-vehicle and thought-content, see Recanati 1993: 98–103.

[3] There are well-known exceptions to this generalization: negative existentials or belief reports involving empty singular terms are truth-evaluable. See Chapters 14–15 for discussion of these cases.

with hallucination, but in the 'Vulcan' case it is clear that the 'thoughts in the vicinity' will include general thoughts involving the definite description which is supposed (but fails) to fix the reference of the name: 'the planet that causes the perturbations in the orbit of Mercury'.

What about the 'Neptune' case, or the 'Julius' case? Here, in contrast to the 'Vulcan' case, the reference-fixing description has a denotation. Still, in conformity to the Strong Acquaintance View, one may argue that no singular thought (in the sense of: thought-*content*) is thinkable when one uses such a descriptive name, for the following reason: the thought-vehicle involves a mental name or mental file without the appropriate informational relation to the referent, and what fixes the reference of the name/file is the relation, as we have seen. In the absence of the grounding relation, no referent can be determined, and no singular thought entertained. Again, a singular thought-vehicle is tokened, but it fails to determine an evaluable thought-content. What are entertained are only the thought contents in the vicinity, including the general thought involving the reference-fixing description.

I do not find this argument absolutely compelling. It is true that what fixes the reference of the file is the grounding relation, not the content of the file (the information it contains). But in the case of de scriptive names the situation is very special: what is given before the relevant relation R actually comes to obtain is not only the vehicle (the name/file) through which the subject tries to think singularly but *also* the referent. The descriptive name is introduced, by stipulation, as a name for a given object *a*. It will become an ordinary name when, and only when, a certain relation R (making information flow possible) holds between the file and *a*. Maybe that will never happen, but if that ever happens (i.e. if the subject gets acquainted with *a*) the referent of the file cannot be anything other than *a*. In other words, the referent is *determined in advance*, by stipulation. Its determination, therefore, does not have to wait until relation R actually comes about:

the file and the referent are both given ahead of relation R. The only thing that can be argued is that the referent in question really becomes 'the referent' only when the relation R actually obtains. If the relation R never comes about, no connection is established between the singular vehicle and a, such that a can be deemed the referent of the file. But assuming the subject is right in his anticipation that R is going to come about, then what reason is there to deny that, through the singular vehicle and its (delayed) connection to a, the subject is able to think a singular thought about a?

One reason that might be adduced is that 'the future is a realm of possibilities and, therefore, contains no identifiable individuals' (Gale and Thalberg 1965: 195). On this view, held by Prior (1959) and discussed by Gale and Thalberg, anticipation or prediction cannot ground singular thought.[4] Prior (1959/1968: 72) and Gale (1968: 167) both cite Peirce who said that 'the possible is necessarily general... It is only actuality, the force of existence, which bursts the fluidity of the general and produces a discrete unit' (Peirce 1967b: 147; quoted in Prior 1959/1968: 72 and Gale 1968: 167). A possible individual, like the first child to be born in the next century, cannot be referred to, on this view; it can only be described. As Gale emphasizes, the informational relations which make singular reference possible are temporally oriented: the past leaves traces that we can exploit, but the future does not.

Whatever we think of this argument, it is not directly relevant, for Jack the Ripper was *not* a 'future individual' for the people who coined the name; nor was Neptune for Leverrier. What was future was *the informational connection to*, not the existence of, the referent (and its traces). That is precisely the issue we are dealing with: can a *future informational connection to the referent* make a present thought singular?

---

[4] See also Ryle (1954: 27): 'Statements in the future tense cannot convey singular, but only general propositions, where statements in the present and past tense can convey both.' This and other references can be found in Gale (1968) in the chapter on 'Future Individuals'.

Those who give a negative answer presumably do so because they take it as obvious that what one is thinking now—the nature and content of one's thought—cannot depend upon what will happen in the future. But the ultimate source of that reaction may well be the intuitive pull of Cartesian internalism. Given that suspicion, one should be cautious and keep an open mind on this issue—until an explicit argument establishes the bearing of what Gale (1968) calls the 'logical asymmetries between the past and the future' on this specific debate. The argument ought to establish that these asymmetries set limits to the influence of external factors upon thought content.

Pending the articulation of such an argument, I am inclined to take a step further in the direction of Instrumentalism, and to accept that, through a descriptive name (or the acquaintanceless mental file that corresponds to it in thought), one may be able to think a singular thought. Still, that *need not* be the case: certain conditions have to be satisfied for the tokening of a singular vehicle in thought (involving a mental file) to be successful and constitute thinking a singular thought. So the semi-liberal view for which I am trying to make room is very different from the second of the two options I mentioned in Chapter 12—an option we may call 'Radical Instrumentalism'.

Radical Instrumentalism says that, *simply* by coining a mental name, opening a file, or using a mental demonstrative, one can think a singular thought.[5] As I have already said, even that extreme position seems to me to be compatible with my framework. To be sure, on that position, singular thought is no longer constrained by acquaintance, whether present or future. But singular thought involves tokening a singular vehicle in thought (a mental file, or a mental name); and a singular vehicle, qua type, is individuated in terms of its function, which is: the storing of information gained

---

[5] See Kaplan 1989a, Borg 2004, and the Crane–Azzouni symposium on 'Singular Thought' in *Proceedings of the Aristotelian Society*, supp. vol. 85 (2011).

through acquaintance. So *singular thought is still defined in terms of acquaintance*, even if there can be singular thought in the absence of (present or even future) acquaintance.

Be that as it may, I reject Radical Instrumentalism, for the reason I gave above. Like Evans, I take it that certain conditions have to be satisfied for the tokening of a singular vehicle in thought (involving a mental file) to be *successful* and constitute thinking a singular thought. In particular, reference must be achieved. If reference is not achieved, no singular truth-condition is determined and the thought cannot be evaluated as true or false. That is what happens in the 'Vulcan' case.[6] In the 'Vulcan' case, the reference-fixing description fails to denote anything, but even when the description has a denotation, that in itself is not sufficient for the descriptive name to achieve reference. The referent of a descriptive name is 'determined' by the reference-fixing description (and it is so determined as soon as the name is introduced), but the object whose *identity* is thus determined is confirmed as *referent* only through some acquaintance relation R. The acquaintance relation may arguably be anticipated without undermining the reference relation which is based on it, but if the acquaintance relation never comes about, the reference relation does not either.

On the view I arrive at, actual acquaintance is not necessary to open a mental file; expected acquaintance is sufficient; yet opening a mental file itself is *not* sufficient to entertain a singular thought (in the sense of thought-content). Mental file tokening is sufficient to entertain a singular thought only in the sense of thought-*vehicle*. Entertaining a singular thought-vehicle by mentally tokening a descriptive name (or, equivalently, by opening a file in anticipation) will—at best—enable us to entertain a singular thought-

---

[6] In Chapter 14 I will deal with exceptions to this generalization: thoughts like 'Leverrier believed that the discovery of Vulcan would make him famous', which are clearly truth-evaluable despite the occurrence in it of an empty vehicle.

content only if we are right in our anticipation of some forthcoming informational relation R to the stipulated referent.[7]

2

Let us take stock. We think singular thoughts about individuals by tokening singular vehicles in thought (mental files). I have argued that such files, qua types, are best characterized by their function: to store information gained in virtue of acquaintance relations to the reference of the file. If this is right, acquaintance is involved in the very concept of a singular thought. But this does not mean that one can think a singular thought only if one is acquainted with the referent. So the standard anti-acquaintance argument (based on acquaintanceless singular thought) misses its target. That singular thinking involves mental files, whose role is to store information gained through acquaintance relations to the reference, is compatible with the view that one can think a singular thought in the absence of acquaintance.

What, then, are the necessary conditions for thinking a singular thought? To answer that question, I have argued, we need to draw a crucial distinction (familiar in the neo-Fregean literature) between thought-vehicle and thought-content, and a corresponding distinction between the conditions necessary for tokening a singular thought-vehicle and the conditions necessary for

---

[7] What does it take to be right in one's anticipation? This is a difficult question. Suppose an astronomer opens a mental file for the (as yet unknown) perturber of the orbit of Uranus, and tries to discover it just as Leverrier did, but dies shortly before the planet is actually discovered. (This example is adapted from one given by Cian Dorr during the Barcelona conference on Singular Thought where these ideas were presented.) Suppose, in addition, the astronomer did not communicate with other people regarding the planet she was looking for. My account entails that the astronomer did not think a singular thought when using the descriptive name, since the proper acquaintance relation never came about. Whether or not that conclusion is acceptable, I do not know. If one finds it unacceptable, one may perhaps argue that the astronomer *was* right in her anticipation of a forthcoming informational relation. For, had she not died accidentally, she would have got acquainted with the perturber, as expected.

successfully thinking a singular thought-content. In this section, I recapitulate the conditions in question.

To think a singular thought in the sense of vehicle, one must activate a mental file. The role of a mental file is to store information gained through acquaintance with the referent, but can one open such files in the absence of acquaintance? I have argued that one can, provided one has a good reason to do so.

That there are necessary conditions for tokening a singular vehicle is something that is widely accepted. Even Kaplan, who holds that one can freely generate singular thought-vehicles by exploiting the resources of the language, says that one does so only if one has a good reason. He writes:

> Normally one would not introduce a proper name or a *dthat*-term to correspond to each definite description one uses....What purpose...is served by direct reference to whosoever may be the next president of Brazil? The introduction of a new proper name by means of a dubbing in terms of description and the active contemplation of characters involving *dthat*-terms—two mechanisms for providing direct reference to the denotation of an arbitrary definite description—constitute a form of cognitive restructuring; they broaden our range of thought. To take such a step is an action normally not performed at all, and rarely if ever done capriciously. The fact that we have the means—without special experience, knowledge or whatever—to refer directly to the myriad individuals we can describe does not imply that we will do so. (Kaplan 1989*a*: 560 n. 76)

Jeshion says something similar. She rejects 'the view that there are no substantive conditions of any sort on having singular thought [so that] we can freely generate singular thoughts at will by manipulating the apparatus of direct reference' (Jeshion 2010: 106). She says that singular thinking (which, for her as for me, proceeds through the manipulation of mental files) is not free but obeys certain constraints or conditions. Which constraints or conditions? 'A mental name', she says, 'can be initiated only if the individual-to-be-named is in the relevant way significant to the thinker' (Jeshion 2010: 126).

In the cases which elicit singularity intuitions, 'subjects have interests, goals, knowledge and affective states tied to the subject of thought' (ibid.). So 'a mental file is initiated on an individual only if that individual is significant to the agent with respect to her plans, projects, affective states, motivations' (Jeshion 2010: 136).

Even though Jeshion criticizes Kaplan for holding that 'we have a means of generating "singular thought on the cheap"' (Jeshion 2010: 106) her view seems to me broadly comparable to that sketched by Kaplan in the passage I have just quoted (which she cites). For both Jeshion and Kaplan, we think singular thoughts about individuals by tokening singular vehicles in thought. By using the resources of natural language, we can generate such vehicles even in the absence of acquaintance. But the generation is constrained: we token a singular vehicle only if certain conditions are satisfied.[8]

I, too, think we don't open a mental file unless we have a good reason to do so. The most typical reason (in the absence of actual acquaintance) is that we expect that acquaintance with the referent will enable us to gain information from it, information which will go into the file.[9] When an object is 'significant to the agent with respect

---

[8] Emma Borg, who explicitly embraces Radical Instrumentalism, says that 'singular concepts, on this approach, are cheap: we can, whenever we wish, create a singular concept for a given object, simply by introducing a demonstrative (or other referential) expression for descriptive information we already possess' (Borg 2004: 187); yet even she admits that 'introducing such a concept will be worthwhile (cognitively useful) *only if* certain conditions are satisfied (Borg 2004: 193). Crimmins (1992) defends a similar view.

[9] In 'Descriptive Descriptive Names', Jeshion criticizes what she calls the 'Anticipation Response': Descriptive names are not introduced because one anticipates a future time in which one will be speaking and thinking about the named object in a psychologically neutral fashion. It is rather to begin (*now*—with the introduction of the name) speaking and thinking of the object directly, with no privileged mode of presentation' (Jeshion 2004: 606). But there is nothing here with which I have to disagree. In optimal circumstances, a descriptive name enables us to think about the object directly, i.e. to entertain a singular thought, as soon as it is introduced. But the name enables us to do that only because it corresponds to a mental file whose *raison d'être* is the storage of *information* about the referent. The (expected) existence of an information link is what *justifies* opening a file. This is compatible with Jeshion's point that such a file, once it exists, gives us a way of thinking of the object in a psychologically neutral fashion.

to her plans, projects, affective states, motivations', the agent typically expects to come into various sorts of relation with it, hence Jeshion's significance requirement can hardly be met without the potential acquaintance requirement also being satisfied.[10] Yet, like Jeshion, I do not think that, in the absence of actual acquaintance, expected acquaintance is *necessary* to open a mental file. Jeshion mentions cases like the following:

> Imagine a well-adjusted adoptee of loving adoptive parents, who, because of his closed-adoption, lacks all access to knowledge of his biological parents. Yet he yearns to know them, especially his biological mother. He wonders what she is like, fantasizes about meeting her, writes letters to her in the hopes that he may someday get to know her. He says 'I'll do anything to finally meet her.' (Jeshion 2010: 117)

Such cases, I think, rest on *imagined* acquaintance. Imagined acquaintance, just like expected acquaintance, justifies opening a file and tokening a singular term in thought.[11] Moreover, as I mentioned above and will emphasize later, one may open a mental file to do other things than what it is the normal function of mental files to do—things that have nothing to do with acquaintance. (See §3 below, on 'derived' functions for mental files.) For example, thinking about the average mid-twentieth-century American, I may give him a name and predicate things of him.[12] When one uses a name in such a way, there is no doubt that the name has a function, distinct from, though parasitic on, the normal function of names. So I think one should be definitely 'liberal' with regard to the generation of mental files. The natural and primary function of mental files is to store information, so the typical reason for opening a mental file is that one expects to

---

[10] As Crimmins (1992: 87) puts it, 'a file will not be opened in just any case in which there is reason to believe that there is [an object] of interest': unless there is some (forthcoming) information link to that object, 'the file would be useless'.

[11] Jeshion gives an even better example: a child's imaginary friend (Jeshion 2010: 136).

[12] This is related to the phenomenon of 'arbitrary reference' discussed in Breckenridge and Magidor (2012).

get information, but even if one has no such expectation, one may have other reasons for thinking through a singular vehicle.

Besides the conditions on the *generation* of mental files, however, we must follow Evans in also making room also for conditions on their *success*. Opening a mental file is sufficient to entertain a singular thought only in the sense of thought-*vehicle*. It is not sufficient to entertain a singular thought in the sense of thought-*content*.[13]

What are the conditions on successfully thinking singular thought-*contents*? I have argued that singular thoughts are fundamentally non-descriptive: their object is determined relationally, not satisfactionally. That entails that one can express a singular thought only in virtue of some relation to the referent. But, I have tentatively argued, the relation need not necessarily hold at the time of tokening the singular thought: it can (perhaps) be anticipated, as in most cases of descriptive name use (e.g. 'Jack the Ripper'). In such a case, one can think a singular thought (content) by opening a mental file even if, for the time being, one has only the description to rely on, provided one is right in anticipating that one will come into relation to the denotation of the description and be in a position to gain information from it. (Unless one is correct in one's anticipation, one can only think of the object descriptively.)

Admittedly, this position is very tentative. If, because of the (yet to be articulated) argument from temporal asymmetries, one rejects the idea of singular thinking by anticipation, one should revert to the Strong Acquaintance View. Whichever option one takes, however, the conditions on singular thought-content are more stringent than

---

[13] Failure to draw the vehicle/content distinction (or to draw the right consequences from it) is the main weakness of Radical Instrumentalism. Let us grant that mentally tokening a name or demonstrative is sufficient to entertain a singular thought-vehicle. The important question (which the radical instrumentalist ought to address) is: Is this sufficient to think a singular thought-content? Since the name or demonstrative in question may well be empty, it is pretty clear that the answer must be negative. (Emma Borg attempts to reconcile Radical Instrumentalism with the vehicle/content distinction but she manages to do so only by equivocating on the notion of 'content'. See next footnote.)

those on singular thought-vehicles. One may think a singular thought-vehicle even if one does not expect to be acquainted, but to think a singular thought-content one must *at least* expect acquaintance and be right in one's expectation. That is so, again, because of the fundamentally relational character of singular thought.

To be sure, there is nothing to prevent a theorist from using 'singular thought' in the sense of 'singular thought-vehicle'. I have no quarrel with the claim that Leverrier entertained a 'singular thought', thus understood, when he said to himself 'The discovery of Vulcan will make me famous.' In that harmless sense, I concede to the anti-acquaintance theorist that there can be singular thought in the absence of acquaintance, whether actual or potential. But this is perfectly compatible with the view that singular thought is based on acquaintance relations to the referent.[14] My defence of acquaintance rests on two claims: (i) singular thought-vehicles are *typed* by their (primary) function, which involves acquaintance; (ii) singular thought-*contents* can only be grasped in virtue of (possibly anticipated) acquaintance relations to their objects. This is compatible with the fact that singular thought-vehicles can be tokened even if their primary acquaintance-involving function is not fulfilled.

---

[14] Emma Borg says that she 'reject[s] wholesale the idea that there are epistemic (or indeed any other substantial) kinds of constraint on singular content' (Borg 2004: 169), while, at the same time, acknowledging that the 'singular concepts' she says one can freely create by manipulating the apparatus of direct reference are nothing but . . . vehicles, i.e. syntactic objects in the language of thought, objects which 'themselves possess both content and character' (Borg 2004: 195). She admits that a singular concept in this sense actually possesses content only if certain conditions are satisfied (so that no content is carried if the name/demonstrative is empty), but maintains that a singular content is expressed even in such cases! The inconsistency is avoided through her distinction between the content of an utterance (which content is a thought-*vehicle*) and the content of the thought-vehicle in question. So, when she says that there are no substantial constraints on singular content, she simply means that, by manipulating the apparatus of direct reference, one can generate mental vehicles which, themselves, may or may not carry content. This, of course, is compatible with the acquaintance view.

3

So far I have distinguished the following types of case:

Case 1: (Normal referential communication) A singular thought vehicle
is tokened and it is successful, since the vehicle's referential function is
fulfilled. It is fulfilled because, as soon as it comes to exist, the file plays
the role it is designed for. As a result, a singular thought-content is
grasped.

Case 2: (Neptune) A singular thought vehicle is tokened and it is arguably successful, since the vehicle's referential function comes to be fulfilled (though not immediately). As a result, a singular thought-content
is grasped, or so I am tempted to argue. (I acknowledge that, because of
the delay it takes for the vehicle's function to be fulfilled in this case, it is
controversial whether, through that vehicle, a singular thought-content
can be grasped *from the start*.)

Case 3: (Vulcan) A singular mental vehicle is tokened but it is unsuccess-
ful. The vehicle's referential function is not fulfilled. As a result, no singular thought-content is grasped.

I now want to introduce a fourth type of case which takes us further
away from the cases of normal referential communication. Not only
can singular mental vehicles be tokened even though their referential
function (which depends upon acquaintance) is not fulfilled, as in
the Vulcan case. I believe that singular mental vehicles may also
acquire and serve *derived functions* whose fulfilment does not require
acquaintance.

Among the derived functions of singular vehicles, there is what
we may call the *actualizing function*. It is not clear that there are genuine 'actuality operators' in natural language, but descriptive names
such as 'Julius' serve that function well. Coining and using a name for
an object we know only by description means that we open a file for
it. The primary function of mental files, if what I said is correct, is to
store information derived through acquaintance, but by, as it were,
pretending to be acquainted with some object and referring directly

to it—even though as a matter of fact we know it only by description—we manage to bracket the descriptive condition through which we think of the object and focus on *it* in imagination, keeping it fixed as we consider counterfactual circumstances (circumstances in which, possibly, it does not satisfy the description). In this way, through actualization, we achieve rigidity and succeed in entertaining a thought which is both descriptive and truth-conditionally singular. This I take to be is a good example of 'an *instrumental* use of language to broaden the realm of what can be expressed and to broaden the horizons of thought itself' (Kaplan 1989b: 603).

Another derived function for singular vehicles, also involving the imagination, is what we may call their *discourse-referential function*. The notion of 'discourse referent' was introduced in connection with the familiarity theory of definiteness, according to which a definite (e.g. 'the cat', 'it') is used to refer to something that is already familiar, while an indefinite ('a cat') is used to introduce a new referent.[15] The problem with the theory is that it treats definites and indefinites as referring expressions, despite the fact that in many linguistic environments (e.g. quantificational contexts or negative contexts), such expressions have *no referential function whatsoever* (Heim 1983: 225–6). Heim gives the following examples:

(1) Every cat ate *its* food.
(2) John didn't see *a cat*.

Example (1), she points out, 'has a reading where "its", a personal pronoun, i.e. a type of definite NP, functions as a so-called "bound variable pronoun" and doesn't refer to any particular cat'. Similarly, she says, 'Under the preferred reading of (2), with negation taking widest scope, the indefinite "a cat" fails to refer.' So it will not do to say that a definite (e.g. 'the cat', 'it') is used to refer to something that

---

[15] On the familiarity theory of definiteness, see Hawkins 1978.

is already familiar, while an indefinite ('a cat') is used to introduce a new referent. In (1) and (2) there is no reference at all, whether familiar or not. So the theory must be reformulated, and that, Heim tells us, is what Karttunen did:

> In order to avoid untenable claims about reference, Karttunen reformulates the familiarity theory by using a new notion, that of 'discourse reference', in place of 'reference'. So...a definite NP has to pick out an already familiar *discourse* referent, whereas an indefinite NP always introduces a new *discourse* referent. Since discourse reference is distinct from reference, and since, in particular, an NP may have a discourse referent even when it has no referent, this reformulation makes the familiarity theory immune to the objections encountered by its traditional version....
>
> But what are discourse referents?...[They can] be identified with what I will call 'file cards', i.e. elements of a so-called 'file'... A listener's task of understanding what is being said in the course of a conversation bears relevant similarities to a file clerk's task. Speaking metaphorically, let me say that to understand an utterance is to keep a file which, at every time in the course of the utterance, contains the information that has so far been conveyed by the utterance. (Heim 1983: 225–6)[16]

Now what relation is there between ordinary referents and discourse referents? The notion of discourse referent may be treated as a primitive of semantic theory, a 'theoretical construct' (Heim 1983: 225), and referential uses (i.e. cases in which there is a referent in the ordinary sense) as a particular case: the case in which, as Hans Kamp puts it, the discourse referent is *anchored to* some real individual (Kamp 1990: 49–64; see also Kamp and Bende-Farkas 2006 and Genabith, Kamp, and Reyle 2011).[17] From a psychological point of view, however, it

---

[16] Heim (1988: 404) says of the file metaphor, which 'must have been used many times before', that it was brought to her attention by Angelika Kratzer.

[17] Kamp and his colleagues distinguish *internal* (or *formal*) from *external* anchors. It is external anchors that anchor a discourse referent to a real individual. In contrast, a discourse referent is *internally* anchored just in case *the subject takes himself to be* suitably

makes more sense to proceed in the other direction and to treat as basic *the mental files individuated by their referential function*—the sort of thing we need in theorizing about referential uses—while accounting for discourse referents and non-referential uses in terms of that basic notion. That is how Karttunen proceeded in his original paper.

Karttunen's original suggestion was that, when we process discourse, we treat even non-referential pronouns *as if* they referred to objects, and store the information conveyed about the objects in question (the 'discourse referents') in files, just as, in processing referential discourse, we store information conveyed about ordinary referents in files.[18] Consider one of his examples:

(3) I don't believe that Mary had a baby and named her 'Sue'

To interpret the indefinite 'a baby' in the embedded clause, Karttunen says, one must 'tentatively set up a referent', that is, open a file in which we can store the information we get about the tentative referent in question (to the effect that it is a baby and that Mary had her). In virtue of the familiarity rule, the definite pronoun 'her' in the second conjunct of the clause refers to the *same* discourse referent so that the new information it is associated with (to the effect

related to some external object, that is, just in case there is a presupposition of external anchoring. (In my framework, the presumption that the subject is suitably related to something external is a built-in feature of mental files. What corresponds to a mental file in the DRT framework is therefore the *internally anchored discourse referent*.)

[18] Among later theorists, some take the same perspective as Karttunen. Thus Landman introduces the notion of 'pegs' characterized as 'objects we postulate in conversation as stand-ins for real objects. They are means of keeping track of what we talk about in information exchange...We talk about them as if they have independent existence, existence outside of us, like real objects' (Landman 1990: 277). Note that, in his seminal DRT paper, Kamp presents indefinite descriptions like 'a baby' as 'referential terms, not existential quantifiers' (Kamp 1981: 192). Contrast this with textbook presentations of DRT, where it is commonly said that 'definite and indefinite NPs are neither quantificational nor referential' (Kadmon 2001: 27). The tension between these two ways of talking is relieved by taking seriously the idea that discourse referents are pseudo referents or quasi–referents, i.e. are *treated as* referents for tracking purposes.

that Mary named her Sue) goes into the same file. However, as soon as, moving up the syntactic tree, we reach the embedding prefix 'I don't believe that', the pretence that the baby exists comes to an end (and co-reference by means of definites is no longer possible). As Karttunen says, 'After considering the whole sentence beginning with "I don't believe that...", [the interpreter] may decide that there is no such baby, after all. In short, a text interpreter must keep track of the status of referents it has established and delete them when necessary' (Karttunen 1976: §1.3).[19] So in analysing discourse we should distinguish several levels (corresponding to levels in syntactic structure). At the top level is 'the world as seen by the speaker'. This world is populated with permanent referents which exist for good. The levels below the top level correspond to situations we describe *in the course of* characterizing situations at the top level.[20] These ancillary situations have their own population of *short-term referents* corresponding to a portion of text and 'existing' only in a limited 'realm'. In our example, the situation at the top level is a situation in which the speaker does not hold a certain belief; immediately below is the situation which is said *not* to obtain, namely a situation in which the speaker does hold the belief; still below is the situation that corresponds to the *content* of the belief (a situation which would obtain if the belief was true). In *that* situation the baby exists (and it is named 'Sue'). Since that situation is not believed by the speaker to obtain, the baby which exists in that situation does not exist in the global situation at the top level; so it cannot be referred to—that is why the occurrence of the pronoun 'her' in (3) is non-referential, just like the occurrence of the pronoun 'its' in (1). Still, in describing the innermost situation, we use the same

---

[19] See also Chastain: 'Embedded in a wider context, [a referential expression] may still purport to refer or it may cease to do so. In the latter case I will say that its purported reference has been *canceled*—in other words, it cannot be referentially connected with anything beyond the boundaries of the context' (Chastain 1975: 203).

[20] This is my terminology, not Karttunen's. Karttunen does not talk about 'situations'.

devices—indefinite antecedents, definite pronouns anaphoric on them—as we do when we talk about actual situations at the top level.

In Karttunen's framework, the apparatus of discourse referents is clearly an extension of the ordinary referential apparatus. To me at least this suggests the following picture. The singular vehicles, or mental files, we use to cope with simple referential communication (and which have counterparts in the realm of perception), have evolved new, derived functions which enable them to be used also in thinking complex thoughts such as those expressed in (1), (2), and (3), that is thoughts which, because they involve negation, quantification, conditionals, attitude ascriptions, or modals, simultaneously describe situations at several levels. We need a distinction between the cases like 'Vulcan' in which the referential function of the file is not fulfilled (even in a delayed fashion) and the cases discussed by Karttunen because, in contrast to the 'Vulcan' case, no one would be tempted to say that the speaker expresses *a singular thought about a cat* by means of (1), or *a singular thought about a baby* by means of (3), even though in both cases a definite is used. I conclude that the 'singular vehicles' which are used to keep track of discourse referents in e.g. quantificational discourse are no longer bona fide singular vehicles with a referential function (which may be fulfilled or unfulfilled): these devices have acquired a new, derived function. Still, we need some evolutionary story to explain how and why these devices have come to acquire the new function, and any such story will have to take account of the original function of the devices, which made them fit to play the new role. (Note that we also need some evolutionary story to connect the use of mental files in ordinary referential communication to their arguably more basic use in perception.)

Once in place, the idea of derived function can be appealed to to account for some problematic cases that are similar to the 'Vulcan' case but only up to a point. Suppose I say to myself: 'My son believes that Santa Claus will come tonight.' In thinking this thought, I token the mental name (file) 'Santa Claus' in non-referential fashion. Should we say that, by tokening the singular thought-vehicle, I fail to entertain a singular thought-content (like Leverrier in the 'Vulcan' case)? 'Failure' seems to be the wrong term to use here. I prefer to say that, in this case, I successfully use the mental name with a derived function, in order to ascribe to my son what I called a 'pseudo-singular belief' (Recanati 1998: 557, 2000: 226).[21] The derived function of files on such uses is their *metarepresentational function*, to which I now turn.

[21] To entertain a pseudo-singular belief is to have a singular mental sentence tokened in one's belief box, but one that fails to express any proposition. If I say or think 'Leverrier believed that the discovery of Vulcan would make him famous', it seems that I successfully use the empty name 'Vulcan' to ascribe to Leverrier a pseudo-singular belief.

Part VII

———

Vicarious Files

14

Mental Files in Attitude Ascription

1

Normally, the mental files that provide the sense of occurrences of linguistic expressions reflect the speaker's own way of viewing the world; but that is not always the case. Recall the example from Pinillos I discussed in Chapter 9:

> (1) We were debating whether to investigate both Hesperus and Phosphorus; but when we got evidence of their true identity, we immediately sent probes there.

The speaker of (1), at the time he utters (1), knows that Hesperus is Phosphorus; he is aware that there is a single planet, Venus. So he should associate the same mental file (namely the 'inclusive file' which gives the sense of 'there' at the end of the sentence) with both 'Hesperus' and 'Phosphorus'.[1] Yet, following Pinillos, I analysed the example by saying that 'Hesperus' and 'Phosphorus' in that sentence are *not* co-referential *de jure*, as they would be if they were associated with the same mental file.[2] 'Hesperus' and 'Phosphorus' in (1) are

---

[1] I am indebted to Peter Pagin for emphasizing that point.

[2] The reason for that is that one can understand the first conjunct (containing the names 'Hesperus' and 'Phosphorus') even if one doubts that, or wonders whether, Hesperus really is Phosphorus.

associated with separate files whose distinctness reflects the *earlier* doxastic state of the speaker and his group (before they learnt the identity of Hesperus and Phosphorus). The point of the sentence is precisely to report the earlier doxastic state of the speaker and his group, and the transition from it to their current doxastic state.

It is a characteristic of attitude reports that often, the words in the embedded clause are associated with the ascribee's mental files rather than, or in addition to, the speaker's own files. This corresponds to the opaque reading of such reports. In (1), the first sentence is an attitude ascription: the embedded interrogative complement features two referring expressions, 'Hesperus' and 'Phosphorus', which are read opaquely. One cannot substitute 'Hesperus' for 'Phosphorus' in the complement clause, even though (for the speaker, as for us) Hesperus is Phosphorus:

*We were debating whether to investigate both Hesperus and Hesperus; but when we got evidence of their true identity, we immediately sent probes there.

This suggests that the modes of presentation associated with 'Hesperus' and 'Phosphorus' in the ascription are the ways *the ascribee* thinks of the reference of these terms. These ways of thinking correspond to the two separate mental files which characterize the doxastic state of the subject before learning the identity. (In contrast, the mode of presentation associated with 'there' at the end of the sentence is the inclusive file which characterizes the doxastic state of the subject *after* learning the identity.) So, in belief ascriptions, the files associated with linguistic occurrences do not necessarily reflect the speaker's current point of view, but may reflect the ascribee's point of view. In other words, attitude ascriptions allow files to be used *vicariously*.

This introduces us to the metarepresentational function of mental files. Mental files are primarily singular terms in the language of thought: they serve to think about objects in the world. But they have a derived, metarepresentational function: they serve to represent how other subjects think about objects in the world. A special case is the case, illustrated by (1), in which the ascribee is the subject at an earlier stage of his doxastic development. The files which (before learning the identity) the subject used to deploy in thinking about Venus, namely the HESPERUS file and the PHOSPHORUS file, are still available after learning the identity but their status has changed: their role is now to enable the subject to represent how he thought of Venus previously.

To account for the vicarious use of files, we need the notion of an *indexed file*. An indexed file is a file that stands, in the subject's mind, for another subject's file about an object. An indexed file consists of a file and an index, where the index refers to the other subject whose own file the indexed file stands for or simulates. Thus an indexed file $<f, S_2>$ in S_1's mind stands for the file f which S_2 putatively uses in thinking about some entity. So there are two types of file in S_1's mind: regular files which S_1 uses to think about objects in his or her environment, and indexed files which she or he uses vicariously to represent how other subjects (e.g. S_2) think about objects in their environment.

Two remarks about indexed files:

1. Since, in order to think about S_2 and his thoughts, the subject must have a mental file about S_2, we may think of indexed files as sub-files (files within files): the indexed file $<f, S_2>$ will be a file embedded within S_1's file about S_2 and specifically representing S_2's way of thinking about some entity.

2. Indexed files are recursive: the file component of an indexed file may itself be an indexed file. Thus S_1 may think about S_2's way of thinking of S_3's way of thinking of some entity, and to that effect may entertain the indexed file $<f, S_3>, S_2>$.[3]

Given the existence of two types of files in the subject's mind (regular files and indexed files), and the general mechanism of linking that

---

[3] See the discussion of Schiffer's Floyd example in Chapter 15 (§2).

operates between files, there are two possibilities for a given indexed file. Either the indexed file, which represents some other subject's way of thinking about some entity, is linked to some regular file in the subject's mind referring to the same entity (and corresponding to the subject's own way of thinking of that entity); or it isn't. If it isn't, the subject's only access to the entity in question is via the filing system of other subjects. For example, S_1 may not believe in witches, but may still ascribe to S_2 thoughts about *a certain witch* which S_2 thinks has blighted his mare (Geach 1967; Edelberg 1992). In this case S_1 does not refer to the witch in the full-blown sense of the term; he does not express a genuine singular thought about the witch, but only a vicarious singular thought—a singular thought by proxy, as it were. This is the free-wheeling, or unloaded, use of indexed files, illustrated by the Santa Claus example I mentioned earlier.

The other possibility for an indexed file is to be linked to a regular file in the subject's mind.[4] In such a case the subject has two ways of thinking of the object: a way of thinking of his own (a regular file) and a vicarious way of thinking (the indexed file). If the subject uses the indexed file to think about the object, that use is 'loaded' and has existential import, in contrast to the free-wheeling use.[5] Even though the subject refers to the object through some other subject's file

---

[4] This form of linking (between a regular file and an indexed file) is significantly different from linking as it operates between regular files. Linking between regular files makes it possible for information to flow freely between the linked files; but when an indexed file is linked to a regular file (*vertical* linking), that does not allow information to flow freely between them. See Chapter 15, §1. See also Kamp 1990: 71–8 for a similar idea ('internal linking').

[5] In a couple of papers Perner and colleagues use a notion very similar to that of an indexed file, and they acknowledge that a regular file and an indexed file may be 'linked' through what they call an 'asserted identity'. But they make a claim which I reject: that an indexed file can refer to some external object through some direct 'anchoring' mechanism, independently of any link between that file and some regular file in the subject's mind. See Perner and Brandl (2005), and especially Perner, Rendl, and Garnham (2007). In contrast to them, I hold that an indexed file cannot be directly anchored to a real object, but only via a regular file to which the indexed file is linked.

about it, he takes that object to exist since he himself has a regular file about it. In this way a singular thought is genuinely expressed.

2

In light of the distinction between regular files and indexed files, let us consider the possible interpretations of an attitude report of the form 'x believes that a is F'. We shall restrict ourselves to the cases where 'a' is a genuine singular term (a name or an indexical) rather than a definite description.[6]

The first type of case is the case I mentioned at the end of Chapter 13. If the singular term in the embedded clause is mutually known not to refer (as in 'Leverrier believed that the discovery of Vulcan would make him famous' or 'My son believes that Santa Claus is coming tonight'), the ascribed belief is pseudo-singular: the ascription portrays the ascribee as having a singular mental sentence tokened in her belief box, but one that fails to express any proposition. In such a case, the sense-providing file associated with the singular term in the embedded clause is a free-wheeling (unloaded) indexed file.

Next, there are the cases in which the ascription is understood transparently. In transparent attitude ascriptions, the sense-providing file associated with the singular term in the embedded clause is the speaker's regular file—his way of thinking of the object about which a belief is ascribed to some other subject. The ascribee's own way of thinking is not specified at all (or so the usual story goes): there is implicit existential quantification over the modes of presentation (mental files) in the ascribee's mind. The utterance is 'notionally open' (Crimmins 1998: 10–11) in that it only specifies the object the ascribed belief is about, not the 'notion' the ascribee deploys in thinking about it.

---

[6] As I pointed out in *Direct Reference* (chapter 20), there are three times more interpretations for such a sentence if definite descriptions are allowed as substituends for the schematic letter 'a', because with definite descriptions the relevant modes of presentation may be descriptive as well as non-descriptive.

Next there are the standard opaque attributions, where a (more or less specific) mode of presentation is part and parcel of the ascribed thought-content. In contrast to the pseudo-singular case, the mode of presentation in question is an indexed file that is 'loaded', that is, linked to a regular file in the speaker's mind. It follows that two files are potentially relevant to the interpretation of the utterance: one provides the speaker's own way of thinking of the referent, and the other the ascribee's way of thinking. In *Direct Reference* I distinguished these two modes of presentation by calling them the 'exercised' mode of presentation and the 'ascribed' mode of presentation respectively.

To see how the two modes of presentation come into play, consider the following example of an opaque attribution of attitude. I borrow it from Daniel Morgan's dissertation on first-person thinking (chapter 5).

> *The Roll-Call Game*
> A new substitute teacher comes to class. One game the class always enjoys playing with a new substitute teacher is the roll-call game. The only rule of the roll-call game is that when teacher calls out a given name, someone other than the bearer of that name calls back 'here'. When teacher calls out 'Daniel', Mark says 'here'. When teacher calls out 'Mark', Daniel says 'here'. When teacher calls out 'Susie', Tracy says 'here'. When teacher calls out 'Tracy', Susie says 'here'. Unfortunately, the principal knows about the roll-call game and has armed the substitute teacher with a chart linking all the pupils' names and photos. I, who have found this out, tell the other pupils that the game is off. 'The principal gave her a chart with our names and photos, so she already knows who everybody is. She knows that you are Mark, that Tracy is Tracy, and that I am Daniel.' (Morgan 2011: 176–7)

As Morgan rightly points out, 'She knows that I am Daniel' in the last sentence is an opaque attitude ascription, because a specific visual mode of presentation of Daniel (the referent of 'I') is ascribed to the teacher:

> Suppose...that the teacher hasn't bothered to look at her chart. Does the teacher have the knowledge I said she had? No, she doesn't.

She doesn't have the knowledge I said she had even if, for example, she has also become my new neighbor, and has been told my name, so that she does know, of the boy she has seen next door, that he is Daniel (although this *would* be enough to make my knowledge ascription true if it were just a transparent ascription). The reason what I said is false is, roughly, that the teacher cannot recognize me in class as someone whose name she knows to be 'Daniel'. Such knowledge—perhaps we might think of it as knowledge that involves deploying a recognitional concept—is precisely the kind of knowledge she would need to have to frustrate our purposes in playing the roll-call game, and the point of my remark was to indicate… that those purposes had been frustrated. So the knowledge-ascription expressed by this first-person-pronoun involving sentence does imply *something* about how the object of the attitude is being thought about—it is not to be interpreted transparently. But it does not imply that that object is being thought about using the first-person concept. (Morgan 2011: 177)

Still, I would say, the first-person concept does play a role in this example. The speaker says 'I', and this constrains the file (or one of the files) associated with the singular term: the relevant file is bound to contain the piece of information 'is uttering this token'. The file thus constrained is not the indexed file about Daniel which the utterance ascribes to the teacher, however; for the teacher is not aware of Daniel's uttering this token of 'She knows I am Daniel.' In such cases, the character of 'I' does not constrain the ascribed mode of presentation (the indexed file), it can only constrain the exercised mode of presentation (the speaker's regular file). The speaker knows that he himself is uttering this token, and as the use of 'I' indicates, it is his first-person file which the speaker deploys in thinking about himself as the object the teacher's attitude is about. So two files are involved in the interpretation of that utterance: one is the regular file which the speaker exercises in thinking/speaking about himself (a first-person file), the other is the vicarious file indexed to the teacher (a recognitional file).

Are both files relevant to the semantic content of the utterance? I think the answer has to be positive, though for different reasons.[7] The ascribed mode of presentation pertains to semantic content because it is truth-conditionally relevant. As Morgan emphasizes, the utterance 'She knows I am Daniel' is not intuitively true in the context of the Roll-Call Game unless the teacher is able to *visually recognize* the referent as Daniel. As for the exercised mode of presentation, we may take it also to be semantically relevant because (in Morgan's example at least) the referring expression, in virtue of its linguistic meaning, constrains it. As we shall see in Part VIII, the linguistic meaning of a referring expression sets a constraint on the mental file through which the reference of the expression is determined: that file has to contain the piece of information conventionally encoded by the referring expression (the information that the referent is the speaker, in the case of 'I'; that the referent is the addressee, in the case of 'you'; that the referent is named *Smith*, in the case of the proper name 'Smith'; that the referent is the *F*, in the case of a referential use of the description 'the *F*'…). In many cases, especially when indexicals are used, the constraint applies to the mode of presentation exercised by the speaker, rather than to the ascribed mode of presentation.[8] The fact that the conventional meaning of

---

[7] By saying that the answer is positive, I do not mean to endorse the presupposition that there is a well-defined, non-disjunctive notion of 'semantic content'. Actually, I think the notion is disjunctive (Recanati 2004). Thanks to Daniel Morgan for urging me to make this explicit.

[8] The reason for this is that, as I said in *Direct Reference*, 'the mode of presentation associated with an indexical is tied to the particular context in which that indexical is used. Only someone in that context can think of the referent under that mode of presentation. So the mode of presentation associated with an indexical can hardly occur outside the thoughts of the speaker and his addressee, who are both in the right context; in particular, there is no reason to suppose that the mode of presentation in question is also a constituent of the *believer's* thought, since the believer is generally not one of the participants of the speech episode' (Recanati 1993: 400). In this passage, 'the mode of presentation associated with an indexical' refers to the mode of presentation linguistically constrained by the meaning of the indexical.

the expression constrains the speaker's file is enough, I think, to make the latter relevant to the semantic interpretation of the utterance.

3

With respect to transparent cases, the important question is: Do they exist? It may be doubted that there are fully transparent uses, that is, uses where nothing whatsoever is contextually suggested regarding the way the ascribee thinks of the object his belief is about.[9] If this is right, then, with the exception of the free-wheeling cases, attitude ascriptions generally involve two modes of presentation of the object the ascribed attitude is about: the speaker's mode of presentation and the ascribee's.

Consider one of the examples from Pinillos mentioned in Chapter 9:

(2) He$_1$ was in drag, and (as a result) Sally thought that Smith$_1$ wasn't Smith.

Pinillos claims that in this example the two occurrences of the name 'Smith' are not *de jure* co-referential (as they would have to be if they were associated with the same mental file), for the following reason:

If they were *de jure* coreferential, then it should follow that Sally thought that there is an x such that x is not x (an absurd belief). (Pinillos 2009)

In response, I denied that, if the two occurrences of 'Smith' in (2) are *de jure* co-referential, it follows from (2) that what Sally thought is absurd. The only thing that follows is that, for some x, Sally thought that x wasn't x. But that is not absurd, on the transparent reading. This is like Russell's example: 'I thought your ship was longer than it is' (Russell 1905: 169–70). There are two readings: one reading on which the ascribed thought is irrational, and a transparent reading in which it is not.

---

[9] See Crimmins 1995 for discussion of this point.

On the transparent reading the two occurrences of 'Smith' in (2) are associated with the *same* mental file, namely *the speaker's mental file about Smith* (i.e. his encyclopedia entry labelled with that name); so they are *de jure* co-referential.[10] The belief ascribed to Sally is not irrational, however, but merely under-specified: the utterance says that for a certain x (namely Smith), Sally believes of x that he is not x. For that belief to be rational it is sufficient for Sally to deploy two distinct modes of presentation of x in her thought, and to think of Smith (represented under one mode of presentation) that he is not Smith (represented under the other mode of presentation). Even if Sally's modes of presentation are not specified in the speaker's utterance, their distinctness can be inferred from the presumption that Sally is rational.[11]

But is it true that the ascribee's mode of presentation is left totally unspecified in that example? This is far from obvious. In the context of (2) it is strongly suggested that one of the modes of presentation under which the ascribee thinks of Smith has something to do with his being in drag. Here too, therefore, we find that there are two files simultaneously in use in the interpretation of the grammatical subject of the embedded clause: one is the speaker's regular file about Smith, which is associated with both occurrences of the name 'Smith' in the utterance and makes them *de jure* co-referential; the other is the ascribee's demonstrative file about the man in drag (who happens to

---

[10] Indeed, anyone who understands (2) knows that the two occurrences of 'Smith' co-refer if they refer at all.

[11] The interpretation of (apparently) trivial identity statements such as 'Smith is Smith' works in the same way. The two occurrences of 'Smith' are associated with the *same* mental file, namely *the speaker's mental file about Smith* (i.e. his encyclopedia entry labelled with that name); so they are *de jure* co-referential. At the same time, as Schroeter puts it, such a claim 'is best understood as responding to a doubt about the identity' of the two Smiths (Schroeter 2007: 614 n.). That means that, in addition to being associated with the speaker's file about Smith, the two occurrences of 'Smith' are also associated with *two separate vicarious files* indexed to some (contextually determined) subject unaware of the identity.

be Smith). The speaker represents Smith directly under his regular SMITH file, and at the same time he represents him vicariously through a demonstrative file indexed to the ascribee. The indexed file in question (THAT MAN IN DRAG) is vertically linked to the speaker's regular file about Smith. So (2) is not a fully transparent belief ascription. It is a hybrid, like most belief ascriptions. Still, the contrast between that example and the other example from Pinillos holds good. In the other example ('We were debating whether to investigate both Hesperus and Phosphorus'), the constraint linguistically conveyed by the names 'Hesperus' and 'Phosphorus' is naturally construed as applying to *the ascribee's* files. The speaker entertains two vicarious files HESPERUS and PHOSPHORUS linked to his VENUS file. Here it is the speaker's VENUS file which is not linguistically specified, in the sense that it is not constrained by the lexical material in the sentence. In both cases, however, two files are at play (the speaker's file and the ascribee's file), only one of them being constrained by the linguistic meaning of the referring expression.[12]

To sum up, fully transparent uses, if they exist, are marginal. With the exception of the free-wheeling cases, attitude ascriptions typically involve two modes of presentation: the speaker's (a regular file) and the ascribee's (an indexed file). The only significant distinction which can be drawn between two classes of case is the distinction

---

[12] When there are two files (an indexed file and a regular file) associated with each of a pair of terms occurring in a sentence, what counts for the establishment of the *de jure* co-reference relation between the terms seems to be the file that is linguistically constrained—typically the speaker's regular file. This is a tentative generalization, and further investigations are needed. To remain neutral one should perhaps speak of the 'foregrounded' file(s) as being relevant to the establishment of *de jure* co-reference. In the Hesperus example, the indexed files HESPERUS and PHOSPHORUS are foregrounded, and there is no co-reference *de jure* between the terms 'Hesperus' and 'Phosphorus' despite the fact that there is a single [inclusive] file in the background which the speaker also associates with each of the terms. (The situation is further complicated by the fact that in some cases, as pointed out in Recanati 1993: 390, *both* the speaker's and the ascribee's files are constrained by the linguistic meaning of the referring expression.) I am indebted to Elizabeth Coppock for discussion of this issue.

between cases in which the linguistic meaning of the referring expression constrains the ascribee's file, and cases in which it only constrains the speaker's file. The latter might be called the 'transparent' cases, but they are not really transparent in the usual sense: even if the linguistic material only constrains the speaker's file, this does not prevent the ascribee's file from being contextually recoverable to some extent,[13] and to affect the truth-conditions of the report. Thus, in Morgan's example ('She knows that I am Daniel'), the meaning of 'I' only constrains the speaker's file, but the ascription is still opaque in the sense that it is true only if the teacher thinks of the referent under a particular (visual-demonstrative) mode of presentation.

[13] Likewise, when the linguistic meaning of the referring expression pertains to the ascribee's files rather than the speaker's, that does not prevent the speaker's file from being contextually recoverable. Example (1) is a case in point: it is contextually clear how the speaker currently thinks of the referent even though he refers to it through vicarious files indexed to his earlier self. The only cases in which no file is recoverable on the speaker's side seem to be the cases in which the indexed file that is used remains unloaded (free-wheeling cases).

15

Indexed Files at Work

1

There is an important difference between linking as it operates between regular files (horizontal linking), and linking as it operates between regular files and indexed files, or between indexed files of different degrees of embedding (vertical linking). Linking between regular files makes it possible for information to flow freely between the linked files. But indexed files are used to stand for some other subject's body of information about some object, and that function could not be served if, through linking with the subject's regular files, the indexed file was contaminated by the subject's own information about that object. Information can flow only after undergoing upward or downward conversion (for example, a predicate λxGx in an indexed file $<f, S_2>$ can be transferred into the subject's regular file to which it is vertically linked only after upward conversion into λxS_2 believes that x is G).[1] So vertical linking between regular files and indexed files (or between indexed files with different degrees of embedding) preserves the informational encapsulation of files, which standard (horizontal) linking has the effect of suppressing (Chapter 4).

---

[1] Likewise, the process of downward conversion necessary to transfer information in the other direction—from the regular file to the indexed file—involves putting the predicate in the scope of some actuality operator.

In addition to these two forms of linking—horizontal linking between regular files, and vertical linking between regular files and indexed files—we should make room also for other forms of linking involving indexed files.

Suppose Paul has been fooled into thinking that there are two distinct persons, Bert and Tom, while in fact there is a single individual; and suppose he has discovered the truth. He now believes that Bert is Tom, and we (who are agnostic about the background situation) report his doxastic state by saying, 'Paul believes that Bert is Tom.' The files respectively associated with the names 'Bert' and 'Tom' in the that-clause are indexed to Paul, and they are presented as *linked in Paul's mind* (since Paul now believes the identity 'Bert = Tom'). This is like horizontal linking, except that horizontal linking links two regular files, while the files that are linked in that example are indexed files: files which the thinker/speaker ascribes to Paul. We need a name to cover both horizontal linking in the strict sense and that kind of linking between indexed files. I propose to use 'internal linking' for that purpose.[2] Internal linking reflects *the subject's belief in some identity*, whether the subject is the speaker/thinker or some other subject whose point of view the speaker/thinker is representing.

It is only in the case of internal linking that is it possible to represent linking by entering identity information into the linked files (see §4.4), e.g. by entering the piece of information '= Bert' in the TOM file and the piece of information '= Tom' in the BERT file. Vertical linking cannot be represented in this way, for if we enter '= Bert' in the TOM file (indexed to Paul) to represent the fact that that file in Paul's mind co-refers with the speaker's regular BERT file, the result will be that we wrongly ascribe to Paul belief in that identity. The information that occurs within a file is information available to the subject who owns the file, and in the case of vertical linking the linking information is not available to the 'owner' of the indexed file

---

[2] NB: This not the same thing as what Kamp (1990) calls 'internal linking'.

(i.e. the person to whom the file is indexed), but only to the subject (the speaker/thinker) who uses the indexed file to represent the owner's point of view.

Another type of case in which linking is external and cannot be represented by storing identity information within the file is the case of *indirect linking*, illustrated by another possible interpretation for the sentence 'Paul believes that Bert is Tom.' Imagine that Paul is confused and thinks there is a single individual who is indifferently called 'Bert' or 'Tom', while the speaker knows that he mixes up two distinct persons. In that situation Paul does not deploy two distinct files but a single one. In the speaker's mind, however, there are two regular files BERT and TOM. These files are not internally linked, for the speaker does not believe that Bert is Tom, while the ascribee, Paul, does not have two files in the first place. Still, we can analyse the statement 'Paul believes that Bert is Tom' as establishing an *indirect* link between the two regular files deployed by the speaker, via a vicarious file indexed to Paul: the two regular files, BERT and TOM, are both vertically linked to that indexed file.

Clearly, storing information into the files themselves would not be appropriate for representing that indirect form of linking. From the speaker's point of view, Bert isn't Tom, so it would be wrong to store '= Tom' in the BERT file and '= Bert' in the TOM file. From the ascribee's point of view (Paul's), there is a single file, so that type of relational information can't even be formulated within Paul's filing system. Like vertical linking in general, indirect linking is external linking, and that can't be represented by entering identity information into the file(s).

2

The availability of indexed files, in addition to the thinker's regular files, provides a solution to the Forbes–Bach puzzle about merging, which Bach spells out as follows in the postscript to the second edition of *Thought and Reference*:

> Forbes mentions an interesting phenomenon that I overlooked. He suggests…that when one comes to believe an identity, two files…come to be merged, but he also points out that after the merging one can, at least for a while, distinguish what one believed about the individual in question under each of the two modes of presentation. That is, the merging does not immediately obliterate the two original files. (Bach 1994: 305)

The situation which gives rise to the puzzle is one of *partial merging*—one opens an inclusive file, but instead of deleting the initial files one retains them qua files indexed to one's earlier self. That is the sort of situation illustrated by the example I discussed in Chapter 14:

(1) We were debating whether to investigate both Hesperus and Phosphorus; but when we got evidence of their true identity, we immediately sent probes there.

According to the analysis I presented, the speaker uses two vicarious files indexed to his earlier self, namely a HESPERUS file and a PHOSPHORUS file, both of which are linked to his current VENUS file and therefore carry ontological commitment.

Another puzzle worth discussing in connection with indexed files is Schiffer's mode of presentation puzzle (Schiffer 1990: 258–65). Schiffer gives the following example. Floyd, who knows that Clark Kent is Superman, believes (2) and (3):

(2) Lois believes that Superman can fly
(3) Lois does not believe that Clark Kent can fly

How is this possible? The following principle seems to be non-negotiable:

Rationality principle
If x rationally accepts both [S(a)] and [¬S(b)], then x accepts [a ≠ b].
(Schiffer 1990: 260–1)

Indeed, as I stressed on several occasions, if a rational subject ascribes contradictory properties to some object, he must be thinking of that object through distinct mental files referring to that object, and the files in question must not be internally linked. Now in the Floyd example it seems that the principle is violated. Floyd believes both [S(a)] ('Lois believes that Superman can fly') and [¬S(b)] ('Lois does not believe that Clark Kent can fly'), yet he does *not* believe that [a ≠ b] (since he believes 'Clark Kent = Superman'). From the existence of such cases, Schiffer draws all sorts of conclusions that I will not discuss; what I want to do is explain away the apparent violation of the Rationality principle in this example.

In the example there is an individual—Clark Kent/Superman—to whom Floyd refers twice through two distinct indexed files: a CLARK KENT file and a SUPERMAN file, both indexed to Lois and vertically linked to the speaker's inclusive file CLARK KENT/SUPERMAN.[3] To that individual Floyd ascribes seemingly contradictory properties: the property of being believed by Lois to be an x such that x can fly, and the property of not being believed by Lois to be an x such that x can fly. The seemingly contradictory properties in question are *metarepresentational properties involving the mental states of the person to whom the files are indexed*, and more specifically the mental files under which that person (Lois) thinks of the object her attitudes are about. Because of that involvement of the ascribee's mental files, the seemingly contradictory metarepresentational properties are not really contradictory. Or so I will argue.

As Schiffer describes the example, the metarepresentational properties Floyd ascribes to Superman/Clark Kent are, at bottom, the

---

[3] On 'inclusive files' and 'slash-terms', see Chapter 9, §3.

following: the property of being believed by Lois *under the SUPER-MAN mode of presentation* to be an *x* such that *x* can fly, and the property of not being believed by Lois *under the CLARK KENT mode of presentation* to be an *x* such that *x* can fly. The indexed files CLARK KENT and SUPERMAN through which Floyd refers twice to Clark Kent/Superman do double duty here (Loar 1972: 51): through them reference is made to Clark Kent/Superman, but at the same time, they are tacitly ascribed to Lois (Crimmins and Perry 1989; Recanati 1993: 326, 348–63, 2000: 132–3, 151–60). There is, evidently, no contradiction when the ascribee's modes of presentation are thus factored in (as they should be): there is no contradiction between ascribing to Clark Kent/Superman the property of being believed by Lois *under the SUPERMAN mode of presentation* to be an *x* such that *x* can fly, and ascribing him the property of not being believed by Lois *under the CLARK KENT mode of presentation* to be an *x* such that *x* can fly. Nor does any contradiction arise if, through existential generalization, we abstract from the specific modes of presentation at stake. Existential generalization yields:

> (4) (∃*m*) (∃*m′*) (Lois believes of Clark Kent/Superman under *m* that he can fly and she does not believe of Clark Kent/Superman under *m′* that he can fly)

To get something that looks like a contradiction, we need to use the equivalence between 'believes of *x* that *F(x)*' and 'believes of *x* under some mode of presentation *m* that *F(x)*' (Schiffer 1977; Salmon 1986). That equivalence holds universally, just as the equivalence between 'John is dancing' and 'John is dancing somewhere' (Strawson 1997: 75, Recanati 2010b: 89–91). The absolute form 'John is dancing' is equivalent to the existentially quantified form 'John is dancing somewhere' because a dancing event is bound to have a location: there is no dancing which is not a dancing at a place. Similarly, one cannot have a thought about an object without the object being thought of under some mode of presentation or other.[4] Thus the following equivalences hold:

($\exists m$) (Lois believes of Clark Kent/Superman under m that he can fly) $\approx$ Lois believes of Clark Kent/Superman that he can fly
($\exists m'$) (Lois does not believe of Clark Kent/Superman under m' that he can fly) $\approx$ Lois does not believe of Clark Kent/Superman that he can fly

Thanks to these equivalences, (4) can be rephrased as follows:

(5) Lois believes of Clark Kent/Superman that he can fly, and she does not believe of Clark Kent/Superman that he can fly.

Now we have an apparent contradiction: (5) seems to be of the form $[S(a)\ \&\ \neg S(b)]$ with $a = b$!

But the contradiction is *only* apparent. To make (5) a real contradiction, we need to interpret negation as taking scope over the implicitly quantified mode of presentation in the second conjunct ('she does not believe of Clark Kent/Superman that he can fly'). Thus interpreted the conjunct means that it is not the case that, for some mode of presentation m, Lois thinks of Clark Kent/Superman under m that he can fly. This denies the existence of any mode of presentation under which Lois thinks of Clark Kent/Superman that he can fly, and therefore contradicts what the first conjunct says. But the second conjunct was not meant to be interpreted that way. It was introduced via the equivalence

($\exists m'$) (Lois does not believe of Clark Kent/Superman under m' that he can fly) $\approx$ Lois does not believe of Clark Kent/Superman that he can fly

[4] 'I submit that, necessarily, to have a belief about a thing is to have a belief about it under a mode of presentation, and that one may believe a thing to be such and such under one mode of presentation while disbelieving it to be such and such under another, and neither believing nor disbelieving it to be such and such under yet another' (Schiffer 1977: 32).

In other words, the second conjunct of (5) must be equivalent to the second conjunct of (4). But if it is so interpreted, then negation must be given *narrow* scope. On that interpretation, what the second conjunct of (5) says is that, for some mode of presentation m, Lois does not believe of Clark Kent/Superman under m that he can fly. And that is perfectly compatible with the first conjunct of (5). So (5) turns out not to be a contradiction (on the proper interpretation). The puzzle thus evaporates: the Floyd example does *not* violate the Rationality principle.

3

In conclusion, I would like to emphasize an important characteristics of the notion of indexed file I have introduced. Indexed files, I take it, have an *iconic* dimension. To represent the file deployed by the person to whom a singular attitude is ascribed, we deploy a similar file, indexed to that person. Or perhaps we should say that indexed files are a *simulative* device: by deploying a mental file just like the file in the mind of the indexed person, one simulates the mental state one is attempting to describe; one puts oneself in the other person's shoes (or frame of mind), by looking at things her way. As Quine says, 'we project ourselves into what...we imagine the [ascribee]'s state of mind to [be]' (Quine 1960: 218).

One way of capturing the iconic/simulative dimension of indexed files would be to treat them as quotational devices. In quotation, one refers to a linguistic expression by actually using it or, more cautiously, displaying it. Similarly, there is a sense in which an indexed file stands for itself, that is, for the file in the mind of the person one is simulating by deploying that very file.

The analogy with quotation is tricky, however. Standardly, quotations are opaque: the expression in quotes refers to itself, rather than to its ordinary referent. This, at least, is true of the central class of quotations which I dubbed closed quotations (Recanati 2001, 2010b: chapter 7).

Indexed files behave differently. While indexed, the file *still refers to its ordinary referent,* that is, it still refers to the object the simulated file is about. In standard instances of opaque attitude attribution, a singular term in the embedded clause evokes a file in the ascribee's mind and *refers to the referent of that file* (not to the file itself). This is, as Quine might put it, a mixture of use and mention. Indexed files can still be treated as a quotational device, but the type of quotation at issue has to be open quotation, not closed quotation. Open quotations have an echoic character but, typically, the quoted words keep their ordinary meaning and reference while evoking or echoing the words of some other person or persons (Recanati 2008, 2010b: chapter 8).

The following example (Recanati 1987: 63, 1996: 468–9) illustrates open quotation and can easily be analysed in terms of indexed files:

(6) Hey, 'your sister' is coming over

Here the description 'your sister' refers to Ann, who is *not* the addressee's sister, but is thought to be so by James, a third party whom the speaker is ironically echoing. The reference is the reference of the relevant file (the file which contains the information: 'is the addressee's sister'), and in this case the relevant file is a file in some other subject's mind. So the file the speaker uses to refer to Ann is a file indexed to James. The indexed file is linked to the speaker's own file about Ann (or to a public file about her shared by the speaker and her addressee). Since that file about Ann does not contain the information 'addressee's sister', it is clear that in this example the linguistic materials constrain the indexed file, rather than the regular file through which the speaker thinks of the referent.

What is interesting about (6) is that it is not globally metarepresentational. (6) is not about anybody's attitudes or representations: it ascribes to Ann the property of coming over. (6) does not even mention James, the person whose way of thinking is being echoed. The metarepresentational element that is undoubtedly present is to be found at the level of sense rather than the level of reference. The sense of the description is an indexed file, and an indexed file is a file that is tacitly ascribed to some other subject; but the ascription of the file to James remains external to the utterance's truth-conditional content.

The possible occurrence of indexed files in non-metarepresentational contexts accounts for substitutivity failures in simple sentences, as in the following example from Saul (1997):

(7) Clark Kent went into the phone booth and Superman came out
(8) Superman went into the phone booth and Clark Kent came out

Sentences (7) and (8) seem to say different things, and have different truth-conditions, despite the identity of Clark Kent and Superman. Clearly this has to do with the difference in modes of presentation associated with the co-referring names 'Clark Kent' and 'Superman'. In simple sentences, normally, the modes of presentation associated with singular terms affect cognitive significance, but have no impact upon truth-value. The Saul examples are an exception: here it seems that a difference in mode of presentation can affect truth-value, as it does in attitude reports. In attitude reports such as 'Lois believes that Superman can fly', substitutivity fails because a mode of presentation associated with the name 'Superman' is tacitly ascribed to Lois, who is said to believe of the referent (Clark/Superman), *thought of as Superman*, that he can fly. Substituting 'Clark Kent' for 'Superman' affects the ascribed mode of presentation and, ultimately, the utterance's intuitive truth-value. But with respect to (7) and (8), Saul points out, the situation is different: 'These sentences do not involve agents whose mental states are under discussion, so it is difficult to see whose [modes of presentation] might be at stake in simple sentences' (Saul 2007: 24). What I suggest, however, is this. The speaker of (7) takes the perspective of the 'unenlightened' (Moore 1999), for whom

Clark Kent and Superman are different persons. The mental files through which the speaker refers to Clark Kent/Superman are vicarious files indexed to the unenlightened. Since these files are linked to the (enlightened) speaker's own file about Clark Kent/Superman, he or she refers to Kent/Superman twice in the sentence and ascribes to him both the property of going into the phone booth and the property of coming out of it. But each of the two files is differentially invoked in connection with one of the two properties ascribed to Kent/Superman in the sentence: the property of going into the phone booth, and the property of coming out of the phone book, respectively. This suggests that, when Kent/Superman went into the phone booth, he had Clark Kent appearance (i.e. satisfied some salient predicates in the vicarious 'Clark Kent' file: being mild-mannered, wearing glasses, etc.), and that when he went out of the booth, he had Superman appearance (i.e. satisfied some salient predicates in the vicarious 'Superman' file: wearing super-hero outfit, etc.). These suggestions are easy to account for on Gricean grounds, by appealing to the maxim of manner, and they explain the felt truth-conditional difference between (7) and (8).[5]

To sum up, there is something metarepresentational about indexed files—they represent some other person's way of thinking about some object—but the metarepresentational component occurs at the level of 'sense' (even if, as in the Saul examples, the evocation of the files at the level of sense can indirectly affect truth-conditions). The important thing is that, under indexing, the file still refers to its ordinary first-order referent.

---

[5] Implicatures do not normally affect truth-conditions, but they do so (through the mechanism of 'free enrichment') when certain conditions are satisfied: 'Whenever an implicature overlaps with the semantic content of the utterance ... by providing further specifications of the described event, it tends to get incorporated into the utterance's intuitive truth-conditions, instead of remaining intuitively separate as when its contribution is orthogonal to semantic content' (Recanati 2010b: 277). The overlap condition is satisfied in the present case. For an alternative pragmatic account (in terms of 'pretence') see Crimmins 1998: 19–21.

Of course, this only applies to those indexed files that are loaded and ontologically commit the speaker/thinker. Unloaded indexed files do not refer to anything. As a result, there are only two options for an utterance containing a singular term associated with a free-wheeling indexed file.

First option: the utterance does not express a genuine thought, but only a 'mock thought', as Frege puts it (1979: 30). If I say to my children: 'Santa Claus is coming tonight', I do not express a genuine singular thought. I am only pretending to refer to Santa Claus, and pretending to predicate something of him. The same thing is arguably true if, echoing my children, I tell my wife: 'Santa Claus is coming tonight.' Here the file associated with 'Santa Claus' is indexed to Santa-Claus believers and unloaded, so the whole speech act has to be seen as a form of pretence.

Second option: the utterance expresses a thought that is globally metarepresentational—it is about someone's, e.g. my children's, representations, rather than about what these representations are about. This corresponds to pseudo-singular belief ascriptions ('My children believe that Santa Claus is coming tonight'). Negative (and positive) existentials arguably work the same way: The file associated with the singular term in 'Vulcan does not exist' is a free-wheeling indexed file, and the statement is globally metarepresentational (it says that the file does not refer). Geach's 'intentional identity' sentences, e.g. (9) below, also fall into that category:

(9) Hob thinks a witch has blighted Bob's mare, and Nob wonders whether she killed Cob's sow

The file introduced by the indefinite in the first conjunct is a free-wheeling indexed file, and the pronoun in the scope of the attitude verb in the second conjunct is anaphoric on the indefinite and inherits the associated file. The second conjunct is therefore a special case of pseudo-singular attitude ascription. The specific problem raised by (9) is this: The anaphoric relation between the indefinite and the pronoun implies that *the same file* is deployed by Nob and by Hob, even though no communication takes place between Hob and Nob. What does that mean? To answer this question we need to make room for *public* or *shared files*—files shared by distinct individuals in a community.[6] This is a very interesting issue, but one that is orthogonal to the main line of argument in this book, so I will leave it aside for future research.

---

[6] A public file corresponds to what Perry describes as 'a network of notions [files], in different people's minds but linked to others by the purposeful exchange of information aimed at affecting one another's notion [file] of the same person' (Perry 2002: 241). Communication need not take place *between Hob and Nob* for them to share, and anaphorically invoke, the same public file. (See Kamp 1990: 78, 85 for the claim that 'discourse referents', including those that are internally anchored and correspond to mental files, can be shared. See also Burge's illuminating discussion of 'quasi-anaphoric chains' in Burge (1983: 92 ff.).)

Part VIII

The Communication
of Singular Thoughts

16

Frege and the Sense of 'I'

1

In a famous passage in his article 'The Thought', Frege writes:

> Every one is presented to himself in a particular and primitive way, in which he is presented to no one else. So, when Dr. Lauben thinks that he has been wounded, he will probably take as a basis this primitive way in which he is presented to himself. And only Dr. Lauben himself can grasp thoughts determined in this way. But now he may want to communicate with others. He cannot communicate a thought which he alone can grasp. Therefore, if he now says 'I have been wounded', he must use the 'I' in a sense which can be grasped by others, perhaps in the sense of 'he who is speaking to you at this moment'...(Frege 1918–19: 25–6)

From this passage, two important ideas can be extracted. The first one is commonly accepted nowadays:

> (a) First-person thoughts concerning a person A can be grasped or entertained only by A. Another person, B, can entertain thoughts about A, but not first-person thoughts about A: only A can think of himself in the first person. To be sure, B can also entertain first-person thoughts; but these thoughts will be about B, not about A. (Even if B falsely believes that he is A, that would not make his first-person thoughts thoughts about A.)

Once we accept (a), a problem arises, which I call 'the paradox of the first person'. First-person thoughts are private, hence incommunicable; yet we do communicate them, by uttering first-person sentences. How do we manage to do this? Note that this is not just a paradox about the first person. The problem is very general. According to the view put forward in this book, non-descriptive thoughts are thoughts we can entertain in virtue of standing in certain *contextual relations* to the objects the thoughts are about. If that is so, how can we communicate such thoughts to subjects who are in a different context, that is, subjects who do not stand in those relations to the objects in question? These subjects cannot entertain the non-descriptive thoughts we express, so how is it possible to communicate such thoughts? As has been widely noted in the literature (see e.g. Davies 1982, Egan 2007, Ninan 2010), the standard model of communication as the sharing/replication/transmission of thought yields unacceptable results when the thoughts in question are indexical, perspective-bound thoughts.[1] We need a different model, or so it seems. As I will argue, the mental file framework provides one.

Frege's second idea is meant to solve the paradox in the first-person case:

> (b) There are two sorts of senses or modes of presentation associated with the first person. Let us call the 'special and primitive' mode of presentation which occurs in first person thoughts 'SELF' or rather 'SELF$_x$,' where 'x' stands for the name of the person thinking the thought (for example 'SELF$_{Lauben}$,' in the case of first-person thoughts about Lauben).[2] This mode of presentation must be distinguished from the mode of presentation associated with the word 'I' in communication ('he who is speaking to you at this moment'). The latter can be grasped by others, the former cannot.

---

[1] 'The doctrine that in successful communication the hearer (audience) comes to have a thought with the same content as the thought expressed by the speaker obviously needs to be complicated in the case of communication using [indexicals]' (Davies 1982: 293).

[2] This notation is Peacocke's. See Peacocke 1981, 1983.

The paradox is solved because, according to Frege, we do *not* communicate the original, incommunicable first-person thought involving the mode of presentation SELF$_x$, but a different thought involving the other sort of mode of presentation.

One might think that the distinction between the two modes of presentation is ad hoc and designed only to solve a particular problem. I disagree. In earlier writings (Recanati 1990, 1993) I have drawn a similar distinction on quite independent grounds. The mode of presentation 'he who is speaking to you at this moment'—technically, 'the utterer of this token'—closely corresponds to the *conventional meaning* of 'I', yet it is clearly distinct from the mode of presentation that occurs in our first-person *thoughts*, namely, the special and primitive way in which every one is presented to himself. This is demonstrated, *inter alia*, by the fact that the utterer of a token might not realize that *he* (he himself*, as Castañeda would say) is the utterer of this token. (To be sure, such a situation would be quite extraordinary, but it is by no means impossible.) This distinction between what I called 'linguistic' and 'psychological' modes of presentation is general (it affects every indexical, not merely 'I') and it holds whether or not we like Frege's solution to the paradox of the first person. Linguistic modes of presentation correspond to *the reference rule encoded by the indexical* ('I' refers to the speaker, 'you' to the addressee, etc.); in contrast, psychological modes of presentation are answerable to Frege's cognitive constraint on rational subjects: if a rational subject can think of an object a both that it is F and that it is not F, this shows that there are two distinct modes of presentation m and m' under which the subject in question thinks of a when he thinks that it is F and when he thinks it is not F (Schiffer 1978: 180; McDowell 2005: 48–9). That the two types of mode of presentation can come apart is easily seen in the case of indexicals. The linguistic mode of presentation is fixed by convention, hence it is the same for the speaker and his audience. For both of them the reference of 'I' is presented as the speaker, the person who utters the current token of 'I'.

But the speaker and the hearer don't think of that person in the same way. The speaker thinks of that person as being himself (or herself), i.e. by exercising the first-person concept, while the hearer thinks of the person talking to him or her under a very different mode of presentation.[3] Or think of an utterance like 'That ship is longer than that ship' and suppose that, unbeknown to the speaker, the same ship is demonstrated twice. By Frege's constraint, two distinct psychological modes of presentation must be involved, but the linguistic meaning of the phrase 'that ship' stays constant across occurrences, hence the linguistic mode of presentation also stays constant. This example shows that the linguistic mode of presentation may not be determinate enough to fix the reference. Often it only 'contrains' the reference.[4]

Even though it is far from ad hoc, Frege's solution is not altogether satisfactory, for it is sketchy and incomplete. What is the relation between the two sorts of mode of presentation mentioned in (b)?

---

[3] 'To put it in Lewis's terms, the person who uses "I" uses it to express self-attribution. But what an utterance containing "I" conveys to the hearer is not a self-attribution... There is an intimate connection between the meaning of "I" and the special access we have to ourselves, but this connection is restricted to the context of language production. For the interpreter the word "I" is much like a third person demonstrative such as "that man" or a deictic use of "him"' (Kamp 1990: 69).

[4] A third argument for the distinction between linguistic and psychological modes of presentation involves Campbell's 'trading-upon-identity' criterion for identity of sense (Campbell 1987: 275–6). In the following piece of reasoning the reasoner trades upon the coreference of the anaphoric description 'the bastard' and its antecedent 'the president':

I saw the President$_i$ the other day.
The bastard$_i$ wants to resign.
[So: The other day I saw someone who wants to resign]

By Campbell's criterion (§4.3, p. 49), this characteristic pattern shows that 'the President' and 'the bastard' have the same sense in this context. But clearly these descriptions have different linguistic meanings and present the referent differently. It follows that we need two types of modes of presentation. (In my framework, the two descriptions are associated with the same mental file. The file plays the role of psychological mode of presentation, while the linguistic modes of presentation which differentiate the two descriptions correspond to distinct informational elements in the file: the file contains the two predicates which the descriptions 'the President' and 'the bastard' respectively encode. See Chapter 17 for an analysis of definite descriptions in the mental file framework.)

What makes it possible for the intersubjective sense associated with 'I' in communication to *stand for* the private sense SELF$_x$ which cannot be directly communicated? These are important questions which Frege does not address, let alone answer. To do so is the main aim of this chapter. Before embarking upon this task, however, I will discuss another solution to the paradox, put forward by Michael Dummett.

2

Dummett's solution does not rely on the distinction between the two sorts of mode of presentation but on another distinction, between two forms of communication (Dummett 1981: 122–3). As we have seen, the speaker's first-person thought is not, and cannot be, communicated because the hearer does not, and could not, come to *entertain* that very thought as a result of the communication process. Still, it may be argued, the speaker's first-person thought which is expressed by the utterance 'I have been wounded' can be *recognized* as such by the hearer. Even if the speaker's thought is unavailable to the hearer, the utterance may inform the hearer *that* the speaker entertains a certain type of thought, which he himself (the hearer) is unable to entertain. The speaker who says 'I have been wounded' expresses a first-person thought, to the effect that he himself has been wounded. The hearer, upon understanding the utterance, can only form a different thought: '*He* has been wounded.' Unlike the speaker, the hearer does not think of the referent (i.e. the speaker) in a first-person way. So the speaker's thought has not been 'communicated' in the strong sense of the term. Yet it has been communicated in a weaker sense: Leo Peter knows which thought Lauben has expressed in saying 'I have been wounded.' Along these lines, it may be found unnecessary to distinguish between two sorts of thought, that which Lauben privately entertains and that which he communicates. To account for the communication of first-person thoughts despite their 'incommunicability' one needs only to draw a distinction between two forms of communication: an utterance can 'express' a thought (weak communication) even if that thought is not thereby made available to the hearer (strong communication).[5]

Even though it departs from Frege's, Dummett's solution has, from a Fregean point of view, the merit of allowing one to maintain the equation of 'thought' and 'semantic content'. Indexicals are traditionally thought to threaten that equation. The semantic content of an utterance—that which the utterance expresses and which must be grasped for it to be correctly understood—is by definition an 'objective' property of that utterance which can be recognized by both speaker and hearer and which remains stable in the process of communication; but the required stability cannot be found at the level of indexical thoughts, or so it seems. As I have already pointed out, the first-person thought which the speaker expresses by saying 'I have been wounded' differs from the hearer's thought formed upon understanding the utterance—they involve different modes of presentation of Lauben. The sentence means the same thing for speaker and hearer, and the statement that is made—to the effect that Lauben has been wounded—is also the same for both, but the associated thoughts change as communication proceeds from speaker to hearer.[6] This is what makes the Russellian notion of a (singular) 'proposition' an arguably better candidate for the status of semantic content than the Fregean notion of a thought. For the proposition ('what is said', the 'statement' that is made) remains constant from one person to the next, in contrast to the full-bodied thought.

---

[5] Bezuidenhout similarly rejects as too strong the notion of communication as involving 'the recovery of some content shared by speaker and listener' (Bezuidenhout 1997: 212).

[6] This can be denied. Thus Evans argued that there are 'dynamic Fregean thoughts' that transcend narrow contextual boundaries (Evans 1981, 1982). In Chapter 7 I have tried to show that, *pace* Evans (and Papineau), we can retain a fine-grained individuation of indexical thoughts and still account for their dynamics. The communication of indexical thoughts, dealt with in this chapter and the next, is another (inter-individual) aspect of the same dynamics. (For an account of referential communication that focuses on the dynamics, see Perini-Santos 2006.)

As John Perry says, 'one reason we need singular propositions is to get at what we seek to preserve when we communicate with those who are in different contexts' (Perry 1988: 4).

Dummett's account disposes of this objection to Frege's equation of thought and semantic content. Even though the speaker's thought is tied to his own point of view and cannot be *entertained* by someone else (e.g. the hearer), still, it is this thought which is expressed by the utterance and can be *recognized* as such by the hearer. Its being publicly recognizable confers a sufficient objectivity on the speaker's thought, despite its essential subjectivity, to make it a plausible candidate for the status of semantic content.

Let us analyse the theoretical move at work here. Two points of view are involved in the communication process: that of the speaker and that of the hearer. In Frege's example the speaker's thought includes the mode of presentation SELF$_x$, while the hearer's thought, formed upon understanding the utterance, is a demonstrative, third-person thought: '*He* has been wounded.' As long as the speaker's thought is seen as on the same footing as the hearer's, it is tied to a particular point of view and lacks the sort of objectivity needed to equate it with the utterance's semantic content. The move consists in *privileging* the speaker's thought and giving primacy to his point of view over the hearer's. On Dummett's account, it is the speaker's first-person thought rather than the hearer's which is objectively 'expressed' by the utterance and recognized as such by all participants in the speech episode.

One possible objection to this move is that it is arbitrary. How do we choose the particular point of view to be privileged? On intuitive grounds it seems natural to select the point of view of the speaker, since it is the speaker who expresses her thoughts in speaking; yet there are *also* reasons to select the hearer's point of view. As Evans emphasized (following Dummett himself), what matters, when we want to individuate semantic content, is what would count as a proper *understanding* of an utterance (Evans 1982: 92, 143 n., 171, etc.); but 'understanding' defines the task of the hearer.

To overcome the difficulty, one may try a slightly different route which (I will argue) takes us back to the Fregean solution. Instead of *privileging* a particular point of view (that of the speaker or that of the hearer), we may decide to focus on what is *common* to both points of view. As Martin Davies writes,

> We should take as the content of the assertion what is, as a matter of linguistic convention, in common between the thought that *a* expressed and the thought that *b* was intended to arrive at ultimately. (Davies 1982: 294)

This more or less corresponds to the Russellian strategy. According to the Russellian, what is common to the speaker's thought that he himself has been wounded and to the hearer's thought that that man, Lauben, has been wounded, is the singular proposition: <Lauben, the property of having been wounded>, that is, the state of affairs which both thoughts represent. Now this strategy can also be embraced by a Fregean, for there is more in common to the speaker's thought and the hearer's thought than merely the state of affairs they represent. Not only are Lauben and his addressee thinking about the same person, namely Lauben; the modes of presentation under which they respectively think of that person themselves have something in common, over and above their common reference. It is this idea which I am now going to spell out.

3

In earlier chapters I described the concept SELF as a mental file in which one stores information about oneself. What is 'special and primitive' about this sort of file is that the subject, e.g. Lauben, has a particular way of acquiring information about himself, such that (i) only Lauben can acquire information about Lauben in this way, and (ii) Lauben can acquire information in this way only about Lauben. A SELF file serves as repository for information gained in this particular way (the first-person way).

Qua mental file, a non-descriptive mode of presentation *contains* information about whatever the file concerns. This allows for the following possibility: two mental files which differ by their global content and/or by the sort of file they are may nevertheless have something in common, namely *part* of their content—some particular piece of information which they both contain. This is what happens in Frege's example. Both the speaker's thought and the hearer's thought feature a mode of presentation which corresponds to their file concerning Lauben. The modes of presentation in question are quite different from each other: the speaker's is a first-person mode of presentation (i.e. it corresponds to a mental file based on the special way of acquiring information mentioned above) while the hearer's is a third-person mode of presentation. Nor do they contain the same information: there are things which Lauben knows about Lauben which his hearer does not know, and the other way round. But there are also pieces of information which both files contain— there are things which both Lauben and his hearer know about Lauben. They provide *identificatory facts* which Lauben and his hearer can appeal to in order to secure reference when communicating about Lauben. In particular, both Lauben's and his hearer's file concerning Lauben contain the information that Lauben is the utterer of this token of 'I have been wounded.' That is part of Lauben's current notion of himself as much as it is part of his hearer's current notion of Lauben: Lauben is conscious of being the utterer, and the hearer also knows that Lauben is the utterer, the man speaking to him at this moment. That information is part of both files, even though one is a first-person file and the other a third-person file. Now that specific aspect common to both the speaker's and the hearer's notion of the reference is, I suggest, what is expressed by the linguistic expression 'I'. The reference of 'I' is presented as being the utterer of this token (linguistic mode of presentation). That linguistic mode of presentation is intersubjective, unlike the psychological mode of presentation which is subjective (i.e. the notion of *himself*, on the speaker's side, or the notion of *that man*, on the hearer's side); but the former may be construed as an *aspect* or *part* of the latter, an aspect (or part) which is *common* to the speaker's and the hearer's point of view.

Note that the identificatory fact which Lauben appeals to in order to secure reference to himself in communication belongs to a special category of identificatory facts: the category of *communication-specific* identificatory facts. Those facts do not exist independently of communication but are created in the very process of communication (Benveniste 1956). They are aspects of the speech situation, and as such they are automatically (and mutually) known to both speaker and hearer qua participants in that situation. Thus both the speaker and the hearer (in a normal conversational setting) know that the speaker—say Lauben—is the speaker, that the hearer—say, Leo Peter—is the hearer, and so forth. This enables the speaker to use these mutually manifest facts in referring to the speaker, the hearer, and other aspects of the speech situation. Indexicals are conventional means of doing so: the linguistic modes of presentation conventionally expressed by indexicals such as 'I' or 'you' ('the utterer', 'the addressee') correspond to facts about their referents which are created by the speech situation itself and are therefore mutually manifest to participants in the speech situation.

Since the identificatory fact appealed to in virtue of the linguistic sense of the indexical is mutually known to the speaker and his hearer, it belongs to their respective files concerning the reference—the speaker's first-person file and the hearer's third-person file. The linguistic sense of the indexical can therefore stand for both files through a cognitive mechanism I have described in *Direct reference* (Recanati 1993: 293–8). The linguistic sense of 'I' ('the utterer of this token') stands for the speaker's notion of himself because it corresponds to an aspect of that notion, to some information which the speaker's SELF file contains (the information that he is the utterer of this token). Interpreting the utterance—the hearer's task—consists in going back from the piece of information to the file where it belongs; but it is not the same file at both ends of the communicative process. In interpreting the utterance, the hearer contributes his own file concerning the reference. That file, just like the speaker's, contains the identificatory piece of information exploited by the indexical, so the indexical effectively mediates between the speaker's file and the hearer's file and serves to coordinate them.

The fact that the speaker who says 'I' (or 'you') and his hearer think of the referent differently is compatible with Kaplan's claim that 'An utterance of "I" can have the same cognitive significance as an utterance of "you"' (Kaplan 2012 : 137). Appearances notwithstanding, this claim does *not* support Evans's approach in terms of 'dynamic Fregean thoughts'. What Kaplan means is simply this: the hearer understands the speaker's utterance of 'you' (addressed to him) by thinking of the referent in the first-person way, that is, in the same way as he (the hearer) thinks of the referent when *he himself* says 'I'. That is exactly what I am saying: the interpretation of an indexical is the file which it evokes in the mind of the interpreter, so, for any given interpreter *x*, 'you' addressed to *x* evokes for *x* his own SELF file, and is therefore associated with the same file in *x*'s mind as 'I' when *x* himself says 'I'. This is compatible with the fact that the psychological interpretation of 'I' (or 'you') is different for the speaker and for the hearer. [7]

---

[7] Here is Kaplan's passage in full (with emphasis added by me to stress the relativization to the point of view of a *single* interpreter):

> When Donnellan says, 'Mont Blanc is older than I' and I reiterate by saying to him, 'Mont Blanc is older than you', the cognitive significance of his utterance of 'I' and my utterance of 'you' will likely be the same *for Donnellan*. And they will likely be the same *for me*. Here is why: I expect my utterance of 'you' to evoke, 'He means *me*' in Donnellan. When someone addresses me and uses 'you', I take it personally. (This presupposes that I realize that I am the person being addressed.)...I never understand the remark as saying, 'the person being addressed is...', or as saying, 'David Kaplan is...', or as saying, 'this body is...'. I always take it personally. I always understand it as saying, 'I...'. And I expect others to react the same way. So when I say, 'I am not!' and you assert, 'you are too!', *my* understanding of my utterance directly contradicts *my* understanding

On this view Frege was right: that which is communicated and comes to be shared by Gustav Lauben and Leo Peter is not Lauben's original thought, involving his own way of thinking of himself. What is shared goes beyond the reference—it involves a mode of presentation ('the utterer of this token')—but that 'linguistic' mode of presentation, closely related to the meaning of 'I', differs from the 'psychological' mode of presentation SELF$_{Lauben}$ which occurs in Lauben's thought that he himself has been wounded. In contrast to the linguistic mode of presentation, which goes proxy for it, the psychological mode of presentation is context-bound and defies communication.

of your utterance. The cognitive significance (*for me*) of the two utterances are contradictory (it is not just the two objective contents that are contradictory). This is why I say that the cognitive significance of Donnellan's utterance of 'I' and my utterance of 'you' will likely be the same *for Donnellan* (Kaplan 2012 : 137; see also Kamp 1990: 64–70 for similar remarks).

17

Reference through Mental Files: Indexicals and Definite Descriptions

1

Let us take stock. To entertain a singular thought about an object *a* is to activate a mental file based upon some acquaintance relation with *a*. The 'mode of presentation' under which *a* is thought of is not constituted by the properties which the thinker takes the referent to have (i.e. the properties represented in the file) but, rather, by the file itself. The file is what plays the role which Fregean theory assigns to modes of presentation.

In the Fregean framework, modes of presentation are meant to provide a solution to the following puzzle: A rational subject can think of a given object *a* both that it is and that it is not *F*—how can that be? Frege solved the problem by appealing to modes of presentation over and above the objects thought about. A rational subject can believe of *a*, thought of under a mode of presentation *m*, that it is *F*, and at the same time believe of the same object *a*, thought of under a different mode of presentation *m'*, that it is not *F*. Insofar as the modes of presentation are distinct, there is no irrationality. On the present understanding, modes of presentation are mental files: in all the relevant instances (e.g. Quine's 'Ortcutt' example, or Kripke's puzzle about belief), the subject has two distinct files about one and the same object, and that is what enables him or her to ascribe contrary predicates to that object without (internal) contradiction.

Among the predicates in a file, some have the distinguishing property that they are 'singular', i.e. they are supposed to be satisfied by a unique object. 'Tallest mountain in Europe' is a case in point. That is a predicate which my MONT BLANC file contains, along with other predicates such as 'called Mont Blanc' or '4,000 metres high', but it differs from these predicates in being singular. Descriptivism holds that, in singular thought, we exercise such predicates, which play the role of individual concepts: we think of the object the thought is about as 'the *F*'—e.g. the tallest peak in Europe.[1] Following many others, I have argued that we do not think of objects in this manner when we entertain a singular thought: we think of them under *non-descriptive* modes of presentation, that is, mental files. Still, singular predicates have a role to play in the communication of singular thoughts. Singular predicates may occur as part of the content of files, and, like any piece of information in a file, they can, if expressed, trigger the activation of the file to the content of which they belong.

On the story I presented in Chapter 16, indexicals have descriptive meanings in virtue of which they present their referent as having certain identificatory properties—being the speaker in the case of 'I', being the hearer in the case of 'you', and so forth. These 'linguistic modes of presentation' conventionally associated with the indexicals are singular predicates ('speaker of *u*', 'hearer of *u*', where '*u*' is the utterance in which the indexical occurs), but the predicates in question are not what the indexicals contribute to the expressed thought. What the indexicals contribute, rather, are mental files to

---

[1] Individual concepts correspond to (partial) functions from situations to individuals. With respect to any situation in which there is a unique *F*, the function returns that object as value. The function is undefined for all situations in which there is no *F* or more than one. NB. Following Kaplan (1978), Abbott (2011) introduces another kind of individual concepts which are 'constant' rather than 'variable', that is, which return the same object irrespective of the situation talked about. Abbott's constant individual concepts are non-satisfactional (non-descriptional, as she says), so mental files would count as constant individual concepts by her characterization.

the content of which the predicates belong. Thus the singular predicate associated with the word 'I' is contained in the speaker's SELF file (since the speaker is conscious of being the speaker) and it stands for the whole file to the content of which it belongs. The speaker expresses a thought with his own SELF file as a constituent, when he says 'I'. When the hearer processes the speaker's utterance, the same singular predicate associated with the word 'I' evokes, in the hearer's mind, the hearer's mental file containing that predicate, and that file is the hearer's file about the person speaking to him. So, in understanding the speaker's utterance, the hearer forms a singular thought about the speaker that matches the thought expressed by the speaker since both thoughts have the same singular truth-conditions, but differs from that thought in that the (non-descriptive) modes of presentation they involve are distinct for the speaker and for the hearer: the speaker thinks of the referent of 'I' as being himself—he exercises his SELF concept— while the hearer thinks of the referent of 'I' in a third-person way. On this picture, the singular predicate associated with an indexical *stands for some mental file to which it belongs*: what the thought contains is the mental file (a non-descriptive mode of presentation) rather than the singular predicate whose role is merely to stand for the file and trigger its activation. If the thought contained the singular predicate, the referent would be thought of descriptively rather than non-descriptively.

The same sort of story applies to the referential use of definite descriptions (Recanati 1993: 294–6). The singular predicate encoded by a description may be what the description contributes to the thought expressed by the speaker (attributive use), but it may also stand for some file to which it belongs (referential use). In Donnellan's example,[2] the singular predicate 'man drinking a martini' stands for a demonstrative file based upon the speaker's ER relation to the

---

[2] See Chapter 2, §2 (p. 20).

interesting-looking person holding a martini glass. In that demonstrative file, the speaker stores information gained through the acquaintance relation, such as the information that the referent (the man he is watching) holds a martini glass and, presumably, drinks a martini. By using the description 'the man drinking a martini' referentially, the speaker expresses a demonstrative thought about that man—a thought involving his demonstrative file as a constituent. On the hearer's side, the same mechanism is at work: the predicate 'man drinking a martini' readily evokes for the hearer her own file about the presumed martini-drinker. If there is no pre-existing file containing the singular predicate in the mind of the hearer, but she takes the speaker to express a singular thought, she will put herself in the right epistemic position by looking in the same direction as the speaker and *acquiring* a demonstrative file about the man holding the martini glass, which file will make it possible for her to entertain a singular thought about the man in question in order to understand what the speaker is saying.

The main difference between indexicals and definite descriptions is that the role of the singular predicate encoded by an indexical is purely instrumental: it is to evoke the file to which the predicate belongs. The singular predicate itself *cannot* be what the indexical contributes to the thought (with the exception of so-called 'descriptive indexicals', which are somewhat marginal and which I leave aside in this book).[3] In the case of definite descriptions, in contrast, there are two options on the same footing. The description may contribute either the singular predicate it encodes (attributive use) or the mental file to which that predicate belongs (referential use). The mode of presentation of the reference is descriptive in the former case, non-descriptive in the latter. Just as in the case of indexicals, the mental files will not remain stable across subjects, but each conversational protagonist will have to entertain a thought involving a

---

[3] On descriptive uses of indexicals, see *Direct Reference* (Recanati 1993: chapter 16).

similar mental file, based upon some relation to the referent and including the singular predicate in question.[4]

How do we account for the fact that the step from the singular predicate to the mental file to which it belongs is mandatory in the case of indexicals? In *Direct Reference* I offered an account based on the following premises:

1. In addition to encoding a singular predicate, indexicals carry a lexical feature, REF, which indicates that the truth-condition of the utterance where the indexical occurs is singular. (The truth-condition of an utterance $G(t)$ is singular just in case there is an object x such that the utterance is true if and only if x satisfies $G()$.)

2. A general 'principle of congruence' requires the thoughts entertained by an interpreter upon understanding an utterance to match the truth-conditional content of that utterance. This entails that, if the utterance (because of REF) is bound to have singular truth-conditions, the interpreter's thought should have singular truth-conditions too.

3. Only thoughts featuring non-descriptive modes of presentation (mental files) are truth-conditionally singular: thoughts involving descriptive modes of presentation are truth-conditionally general.[5]

Together, the three premises entail that the thought entertained by an interpreter upon understanding an utterance with an indexical will have to feature a non-descriptive mode of presentation, that is, a mental file. The singular mode of presentation encoded by the index-ical will not be a possible constituent of the thought. Its (purely instrumental) role is to raise the salience of some mental file to the

---

[4] This justifies Bezuidenhout's claim that 'we need recognize only speaker-relative utterance content and listener-relative utterance content and a relation of similarity holding between these two contents' (Bezuidenhout 1997: 212).

[5] This premise can be doubted, on the grounds that actuality operators can make a descriptive thought truth-conditionally singular. But this issue has more complexity than meets the eye. To actualize a description in thought, we need to open a mental file, and mental files are primarily a tool for non-descriptive thinking. See Chapter 13 (§3) on the (derived) 'actualizing function' of files.

content of which it belongs, thus making that mental file available as a constituent of the thought through which the utterance is interpreted.

2

The issue arises whether the mechanism I have described—the linguistic evocation of mental files via elements of their content—should be considered as semantically relevant, or relegated to 'pragmatics'. I will frame the issue in terms of Donnellan's distinction between 'denotation' and 'reference'. A description may be used referentially or attributively, but even when a description does not 'refer' in Donnellan's sense, it 'denotes':

> Russell's definition of denoting (a definite description denotes an entity if that entity fits the description uniquely) is clearly applicable to either use of descriptions. Thus whether or not a description is used referentially…it may have a denotation. Hence, denoting and referring, as I have explicated the latter notion, are distinct…If one tried to maintain that they are the same notion, one result would be that a speaker might be referring to something without knowing it. If someone said, for example, in 1960, before he had any idea that Mr Goldwater would be the Republican nominee in 1964, 'The Republican candidate for president in 1964 will be a conservative,' (perhaps on the basis of an analysis of the views of party leaders) the definite description here would *denote* Mr Goldwater. But would we wish to say that the speaker had referred to, mentioned, or talked about Mr Goldwater? I feel these terms would be out of place. (Donnellan 1966: 54–5)

The denotation is fixed satisfactionally: a description 'the F' denotes whatever is F if a unique object is, and nothing otherwise. Reference is an entirely different matter, according to Donnellan. Reference involves 'having in mind', something that requires some relation to the object thought about.[6] In the present framework, this is

---

[6] On Donnellan's notion of 'having in mind', see Kaplan 2012.

interpreted by saying that the reference of an expression is always the reference of some mental file containing the predicate associated with the expression. The reference of a file, as we have seen, is determined relationally.

Note that the denotation/reference distinction applies to indexicals as well as to definite descriptions. An indexical 'denotes' whatever satisfies the linguistic mode of presentation (assuming a single object does), but the *denotatum* need not be what the speaker who uses the indexical refers to. Consider Rip van Winkle. He goes to bed one evening (on day d) and wakes up twenty years later. He does not know that he has slept for more than one night, so he thinks of d as 'yesterday'. Now which day does he refer to when he says 'Yesterday was a nice day'? This is a tricky question. In virtue of the reference rule associated with the word 'yesterday', it seems that it must refer to the day preceding the day of utterance. But that is not the day *Rip* is referring to and characterizing as a nice day. Rip refers to the day he remembers, namely d, of which he wrongly believes that it is the previous day (so that his memory file contains the predicate 'previous day' which the indexical exploits). Donnellan's distinction between denotation and reference comes in handy here: we can say that the *denotation* of Rip's use of 'yesterday' is the day before his utterance, while the *reference*—what Rip himself refers to and describes as a nice day—is d, the last waking day he remembers.

We see that for indexicals too, the reference, understood à la Donnellan, is the reference of some mental file containing the encoded predicate. Just as for definite descriptions, whether the reference actually satisfies the singular predicate is irrelevant since the reference is determined relationally. Thus Rip refers to day d by saying 'Yesterday was a nice day', even though d is not actually the previous day. He can do so because d is the referent of his memory file, a file that contains both the predicates 'previous day' and 'nice day'. Likewise, the subject in Donnellan's example refers to the man she is looking at when she says 'the man drinking a martini is a famous philosopher', even though the man in question is not drinking a martini, but water. This is possible because that man is the reference of the speaker's demonstrative file based on the perception of the man in question, and the file contains the predicate 'man drinking a martini' (and also the predicate 'famous philosopher').

But is reference, thus understood, relevant to semantics? Many philosophers think that it is not. As far as definite descriptions are concerned, there is a well-known position according to which the referential/attributive distinction is a matter of speaker's meaning and does not affect truth-conditional content.[7] Whether or not the speaker 'refers', and to what, by using a description that denotes a certain object, is irrelevant to semantics. Only denotation matters to semantic content. The same thing holds for indexicals. Even if Rip refers to *d* by his use of 'yesterday', this is *speaker's* reference, not semantic reference. The semantic reference is what the word itself refers to—its 'denotation'. In general, the use of *improper* descriptions or *improper* indexicals to refer to some object the speaker has in mind has no direct relevance to semantics. Such use is like the improper use of names, as Kripke pointed out. In Kripke's example, the speaker refers to Smith (the man he sees raking the leaves) but, under the misapprehension that the man he sees raking the leaves is Jones, he uses the name 'Jones' to refer to him (Kripke 1977: 263). As Kripke says, the name 'Jones' refers to Jones (semantic referent) even if the speaker who uses the name has someone else in mind, namely Smith (speaker's referent). Indeed the speaker's utterance 'Jones is raking the leaves' is intuitively false in that sort of case, if the man seen raking the leaves happens to be Smith (and Jones does not happen to be raking the leaves at the same time).

---

[7] The pragmatic account goes back to Peter Geach (1962) and Paul Grice (1969); see also Kripke (1977), Sainsbury (1979), Davies (1981) and Evans (1982), to mention some of the early advocates. For a review and a sustained defence of the account, see Neale (1990: chapter 3).

How does the denotation/reference distinction relate to the semantic reference/speaker's reference distinction? One option—corresponding to the pragmatic account I have just presented—is to say that they are just the same distinction: the denotation of an expression *is* its semantic reference. So, in the case of Rip van Winkle, the day *d* is the speaker's reference, and the semantic reference is the day before the day of utterance, i.e. the denotation. Similarly, when the speaker in Kripke's example uses the name 'Jones' to refer to Smith, Smith is only the speaker's reference; the semantic reference is Jones, the bearer of the name (and the satisfier of the metalinguistic predicate 'called Jones'). But the view that the semantic reference just is the denotation ought to be resisted if one takes the referential use of descriptions to be semantically relevant. For, as Donnellan points out, descriptions denote *whether they are used referentially or attributively*. If denotation equals semantic reference, there can be no semantic difference between the referential use and the attributive use: the description will have the same 'semantic reference' in both cases (namely the denotation). It follows that the equation of denotation and semantic reference can be maintained only by someone who holds that the referential use of definite descriptions is *always* a matter of speaker's meaning or speaker's reference.

There are philosophers who take the referential use of descriptions to be semantically relevant, however. They stress the analogy between indexicals and definite descriptions (on their referential use).[8] According to their account, the descriptive meaning of a referential description has a purely instrumental role—it serves to fix the reference. The semantic content of the utterance is a singular proposition, just as it is when an indexical is used instead of a description.[9]

---

[8] See Stalnaker (1970), Peacocke (1975), and Kaplan (1978) for early statements of the semantic view, and Recanati (1989) for a defence of the view against the 'ambiguity' objection raised by Kripke and many others.

[9] On the analogy between referential descriptions and demonstrative pronouns, see Schiffer 1997: 263.

In contrast, when descriptions are used attributively, the semantic content of the utterance is a general proposition. Now, if one treats the referential use of descriptions as semantically relevant in this way, as I think one should if one wants to capture the striking analogy with indexicals, one needs a *threefold* distinction between denotation, semantic reference, and speaker's reference. When a description is used attributively, as in Donnellan's 'Goldwater' example, it does not refer (though it denotes). When a description is used referentially, it refers, but sometimes its reference is mere 'speaker's reference', while in other cases it is 'semantic reference'. The reference will be (mere) speaker's reference in all the cases in which it does not satisfy the singular predicate encoded by the expression. But that does not prevent us from acknowledging a genuine semantic contrast between attributive and referential uses. On the referential use, if the description is proper, that is, if what the speaker refers to satisfies the description, then the truth-condition of the utterance is singular, in contrast to what happens when the description is used attributively.

Note that for indexicals we don't need the threefold distinction between denotation, semantic reference, and speaker reference, because indexicals are bound to be used referentially (again, leaving aside the descriptive uses which are somewhat marginal). We only need a distinction between the cases in which an indexical is used to refer to its denotation, and the cases like Rip van Winkle in which an indexical is used to refer to something other than its denotation (speaker's reference).

3

In the previous section I have introduced the two main approaches to the referential/attributive distinction. According to the pragmatic account, all referential uses of definite descriptions, whether proper or improper, are, indeed, *uses* and, as such, they are of concern to pragmatics, which deals with uses, but not to semantics, which deals with meanings. According to the semantic account, proper referential uses make a distinctive (singular) contribution to semantic content, but improper uses, that is, cases in which the speaker refers to something which does not satisfy the description, are to be ignored as irrelevant to semantic content. The implicit premise here is that a necessary condition for an object to be the semantic referent is that it satisfy the encoded predicate. Now there is a third type of position, less familiar but closer to Donnellan's original inspiration, which rejects that premise, on the grounds that reference is determined relationally, not satisfactionally. It is that position which I would like to explore in this section.

The semantic account takes seriously the idea that descriptions can be used a devices of direct reference. But there are two notions of direct reference on the market: the strong, Millian notion, and the weaker, Kaplanian notion. The semantic account is based on the Kaplanian notion, while the less familiar account I am about to present is based on the Millian notion.

According to the Millian notion, a directly referential expression is like a 'tag' to which an object is directly assigned without going through a satisfactional mechanism. Proper names are directly referential in that strong sense—they are 'tags'—but personal pronouns like 'I' and 'you' are not because they carry a descriptive meaning and present their referent as, respectively, the speaker or the addressee. On the Kaplanian picture, direct reference *is* compatible with the possession of such meaning: what matters for direct reference in the weaker, Kaplanian sense is only the *truth-conditional irrelevance* of the mode of presentation (Recanati 1993). The mode of presentation (or 'character') only plays an instrumental role: it provides a way of identifying the referent in context, but it is the referent, not the mode of presentation, which contributes to the possible worlds truth-conditions of the utterance.

Definite descriptions, on their referential use, can be understood on either model. The standard semantic approach, defended by

Kaplan and Stalnaker, takes referential descriptions to be directly referential in the weak sense, just like indexicals. A referentially used description 'the F' presents its referent as being the F, but what is truth-conditionally relevant, on that use, is only the *referent* contextually picked out through the property of being the F. The descriptive meaning of the description only serves to 'fix the reference', just as the character of an indexical only serves to 'fix the reference' of the expression in context. According to the Millians, however, (i) the mere truth-conditional irrelevance of the mode of presentation is not sufficient for direct reference in the *strong* sense, and (ii) Donnellan's comparison of referential descriptions with 'logically proper names' (Donnellan 1966: 43, 64–5) clearly indicates that he took referential descriptions to be directly referential in just that sense.

Genoveva Martì has eloquently expressed the Millian point of view and its rejection of the standard semantic approach à la Kaplan/Stalnaker:

> What defines a referential use of a definite description, or of any device, is...the absence of a semantic mechanism to search for and determine the referent...If a definite description can be used as a device of direct reference in this sense, *the attributes associated with it should not play a role in the determination of reference*. Therefore, if a definite description 'the F' can be used referentially, in the strong sense, it must be possible to use it to refer to an object independently of whether that object satisfies the attributes associated with 'the F'. And that's the characteristic mark of referential uses of descriptions according to Donnellan. (Martì 2008: 49; emphasis mine)

What Martì objects to is the idea that definite descriptions can only be directly referential in the weak sense. She thinks this misses the thrust of Donnellan's original observations. Indeed, Donnellan has much insisted on the fact that a referentially used definite description need not be 'satisfied' by its referent. In the martini example, the man referred to by means of the description 'the man drinking a martini' may actually be drinking water, not martini. Such 'improper' uses of definite descriptions have been ignored by proponents of the standard semantic account, or explicitly put aside as semantically irrelevant (Recanati 1993: 281–4). But the Millian thinks a directly referential expression is like a tag, so if a definite description can be a device of direct reference, it must be possible for it to target a referent and get assigned to it in context, *whether or not the referent possesses the property encoded by the description*. The property in question, though semantically encoded, becomes irrelevant when the description is used referentially because the mechanism through which the referent is determined is no longer the satisfactional mechanism but a different, relational mechanism.

I think Martì is right: the anti-descriptivist thrust of early theories of direct reference such as Donnellan's is lost if we say that the singular predicate encoded by a referentially used description or an indexical 'fixes the reference' of the expression. Two-dimensional Descriptivism is still Descriptivism. The mental file account preserves the original, Millian inspiration of direct reference theories in giving pride of place to acquaintance relations and downplaying satisfactional factors. According to the account, a referentially used description refers to what the mental file containing the encoded predicate is about, and the file is about the entity to which it is appropriately related. That entity may or may not satisfy the singular predicate which occurs in the file and which the referential description exploits (to activate in the hearer's mind the appropriate counterpart of the mental file in the speaker's mind). In Donnellan's example, 'the man drinking a martini', the singular predicate does not even 'fix the reference' since the reference does not satisfy the predicate.

To say that the referent of a referential expression is the referent of the appropriate file is to say that linguistic meaning does not determine reference directly, as it does on 'satisfactional' approaches. The linguistic meaning of a referential expression (whether a description, an indexical, or a name)[10] takes us to an intermediary entity, namely the relevant mental file, and the reference of the expression just is the reference of the file. As Chastain puts it,

> A theory of singular reference will have to be combined with a systematic account of certain internal states of the speaker—his thoughts, beliefs, perceptions, memories, and so on—which are, so to speak, the intermediate links connecting the singular terms he utters with their referents out in the world. These intermediaries can themselves be understood only if we treat them as being quasi-linguistic in structure and content...and as containing elements analogous to singular terms which can be referentially connected with things in the world... (Chastain 1975: 197)

What about the semantic reference/speaker's reference distinction? From Donnellan and Chastain to Martì, the Millians tend to ignore it, but that is a mistake. As far as I am concerned, I am in sympathy with the non-satisfactional approach to reference determination put forward by the Millians—an approach I try to implement in this book—but I take it as obvious that the use of *improper* descriptions to trigger the relevant mental file in the hearer's mind has no direct relevance to semantics. Such use is like the improper use of names, as Kripke pointed out.

Let us assume, with the Millians, that the reference of a description is determined non-satisfactionally: it always is the reference of some file containing the predicate encoded by the description. We can *still* distinguish between the case in which the description is proper and the case in which it is improper. The reference of the file, on the improper use, will not count as semantic reference for

---

[10] In the case of proper names the mode of presentation contributed by the expression type is arguably metalinguistic. The referent of a name NN is presented as *bearing the name NN*. In addition proper names carry the feature REF. The utterance of a name NN therefore triggers the search for a mental file containing the information 'called NN'. The referent of a file containing that information may not actually be called by that name (improper uses).

obvious reasons; it will be mere 'speaker's reference'. But when the reference of the file satisfies the descriptive material, the speaker's reference becomes semantic reference. On that view, which we may call the 'moderate Millian view' (MM view for short), neither the denotation nor the reference of the file count as 'semantic reference' when they diverge. There is semantic reference only when they converge.

One consequence of this view is that the day before the utterance (a day which Rip slept through and had no acquaintance with) *cannot be* the semantic reference in the Rip van Winkle case. It cannot be the reference (but only the denotation) because the epistemological constraints on reference are not met. But the day Rip was referring to—the day *d* he remembers and mistakes for the previous day—cannot be the semantic reference either. It cannot be the semantic reference (but only the speaker's reference) because the correctness conditions imposed by the linguistic material are not met.

4

On the MM view the reference (vs denotation) of a description always is the reference of some mental file or dossier to which the description belongs (Grice 1969), but there are two sorts of case to consider. The reference of a file counts as 'semantic reference' when, and only when, the predicate used to activate the file is a predicate which the reference actually satisfies.

What exactly is the difference between the MM view and the standard semantic account? If Martì is right, the problem with the standard semantic account is that the semantic reference is said to be determined satisfactionally: it is what fits the singular predicate encoded by the referring expression. To be sure, the speaker's referential intention is acknowledged and ascribed semantic significance: when a description is used referentially the referent goes into truth-conditional content in lieu of the reference-fixing condition. But the descriptive condition encoded by the expression is what determines the reference, and that is what the Millian is objecting to. On the MM view, in contrast, the reference is determined relationally—it is the reference of the file—even if satisfaction of the encoded predicate comes into play to distinguish semantic reference from speaker's reference.

Is there an argument in support of the MM view as opposed to what I will henceforth call the satisfactional view? I think there is. It has been pointed out that, just like definite descriptions, *indefinite* descriptions can be used referentially to activate a file.[11] George Wilson (1978) gives the following example:

(1) A convicted embezzler is trying to seduce your sister

The non-singular predicate 'convicted embezzler' encoded by the indefinite description in (1) does not determine a unique object, so the reference cannot be determined satisfactionally here—it is bound to be determined relationally (the speaker is referring to the man he is looking at). To be sure, this is not much of a problem for the satisfactional approach because, on standard accounts, indefinite descriptions are not semantically referential, so they should not be expected to carry 'semantic reference' anyway: whatever reference occurs with them is bound to be speaker's reference. The satisfactional view need not deny that speaker's reference is determined relationally. Its claim only concerns semantic reference.

But the same sort of problem arises with so-called 'incomplete' definite descriptions, e.g. 'the man', 'the car', or 'the table'. Incomplete descriptions are like indefinite descriptions in that they fail to determine a singular denotation. They can only achieve singular reference

---

[11] On the referential use of indefinite descriptions, see Chastain (1975), Wilson (1978), and Fodor and Sag (1982).

via the file to which they belong. But, qua *definite* descriptions, they are supposed to carry semantic reference.[12] So they raise a dilemma for the satisfactional theorist: she or he must either give up the claim that incomplete descriptions have semantic referents, or give up the claim that semantic reference is determined satisfactionally. Since the latter claim defines the view as opposed to the MM view, the first option is the only one that can be seriously considered. So the satis-factional theorist must say that an incomplete description can only carry speaker's reference, not semantic reference. From a semantic point of view, incomplete descriptions are defective.

The problem is that almost all the definite descriptions we use in referential communication are incomplete, so an account which treats them as special in this way (and passes them down to another branch of the theory—the pragmatics—for special treatment) is less attractive than an account which straightforwardly makes room for them. This suggests that we should rather start from incomplete descriptions, and acknowledge the fact that they don't 'denote' (in Donnellan's sense). Given that they don't denote, if they are still granted a semantic referent, *that referent will not be determined satisfactionally, but via the files to which the non singular predicate belongs.* As Donnellan writes,

> In these examples some particular [objects] are being talked about, and the definite descriptions...seem surely to have particular semantic referents. If the descriptive content of the uttered descriptions even augmented by background assumptions, etc., is insufficient to determine the referents, how is this possible? My answer will not be unexpected. The person having some [object] in mind to talk about can provide the needed definiteness. (1978: 60–1)[13]

---

[12] Or at least, that is so *unless* one accepts Russell's claim that definite descriptions are just as non-referential semantically as indefinite descriptions. See Neale 1990 for a defence of that view.

[13] See Strawson 1950/1971: 14–15 for a similar argument using incomplete descriptions. Kripke himself suggests that incomplete descriptions are the best argument in favour of Donnellan's picture (Kripke 1977: 255–6, 271).

At this point, to unify the theory of descriptions, the best strategy is to generalize this relational account to all definite descriptions. On the resulting account (the MM view), the reference of a referentially used description is the reference of some file containing the encoded predicate, and it counts as 'semantic reference' only if it actually satisfies the predicate. (The predicate in question may, but need not, be singular.)

The MM view is similar to the view held by some linguists regarding pronouns, including indexical pronouns such as 'I' and 'you'. Pronouns are treated as variables which (unless they are bound) must be assigned values in context, and which also carry presuppositions, corresponding to the 'features' of the pronoun (gender, number, etc.). The semantic reference of a pronoun is the value contextually assigned to it, *provided* the value in question satisfies the presuppositions. There is no semantic reference if the value assigned to the pronoun does not satisfy the presuppositions—for example if I point to a male person and say 'She is a philosopher.' The analysis extends to indexical pronouns such as 'I' and 'you': in this case what is presupposed is that the individual the speaker contextually refers to possesses the property of being the speaker or the hearer. If the presupposition is satisfied, the speaker's referent becomes the semantic reference of the pronoun; otherwise the pronoun fails to semantically refer. Schlenker gives the following example:

> Suppose that I am pointing towards one person (say, to my right) while talking to another person (to my left). If I then utter *You are nice* with emphasis on *you* and a correlative pointing gesture, the result is decidedly odd—in the same way as if, pointing towards John, I were to say: *She is nice*. This is a welcome result: a presupposition failure is predicted because the person that is pointed to is not an addressee of the speech act (similarly, *she is nice* is odd when pointing to John because *she* carries a presupposition that it denotes a female individual). (Schlenker 2005: 162)

I suggest generalizing this view: in all the cases I have discussed (descriptions, names, indexicals) the predicate carried by the expression acts like a presupposition which the speaker's reference (namely the reference of the associated mental file) must satisfy. The speaker's reference becomes the semantic reference only if the presupposition is satisfied.[14]

[14] The idea that what fixes the reference of a referential expression always is some associated mental file may seem incompatible with the view that some referential expressions, e.g. proper names, have a reference of their own, independent of what users of the expression use it to refer to. But the two ideas can be reconciled by appealing to the notion of *public file* mentioned at the very end of Chapter 15 (in connection with Geach's intentional identity sentences): we can say that the reference of a name—i.e. the name's *semantic* reference—is the reference of the public file associated with it. In the Smith/Jones case, the public file associated with the name 'Jones' refers to Jones (and does so in virtue of relational factors), while the demonstrative file deployed by the speaker who mistakenly thinks he sees Jones refers to Smith.

Part IX

Conclusion

18

The Mental File Framework
and its Competitors

1

The view I have argued for in this book inherits from Frege a commitment to 'modes of presentation' or ways of thinking of objects. Reference is not enough: without a level of sense or mode of presentation in addition to the objects thought about, one cannot account for the Fregean data regarding cognitive significance. Or rather: one cannot account for cognitive significance phenomena within a purely referential (= monostratal) semantics à la Russell *unless*, like Russell, one is prepared to buy Descriptivism.[1] To be sure, Frege himself was a descriptivist, but the strongest argument I can find in favour of his distinction between sense and reference is (paradoxically) the need to account for cognitive significance without buying Descriptivism.

The key, then, is to make room for *non-descriptive* modes of presentation. Such modes of presentation, I have argued following Perry and others, are mental files. Linguistic expressions refer via the mental files with which they come to be associated. Mental files themselves refer, and linguistic expressions inherit their reference. (What is non-descriptive about mental files is the fact that the mechanism of reference determination is relational, not satisfactional.)

---

[1] See Chapter 1.

Some theorists, most prominently Jerry Fodor, reject the Fregean distinction between sense and reference on the grounds that what plays the mode of presentation role is not anything semantic—not anything having to do with the content of the representation—but something *syntactic*: the representational vehicle itself. Indeed, as I have said several times in the book, mental files can be construed as 'singular terms in the language of thought'. My view is therefore very much like Fodor's, so it is worth spelling out his objection to the very idea of a two-level semantics to see whether the (apparent) disagreement is terminological or substantial.

From the Fodorian point of view, what may give the impression that we need a two-level semantics is the focus on language. In the case of language, there are three things: the expression, its reference, and the mode of presentation (= the associated mental file, through which the expression refers). This appears rather Fregean. But if, like Fodor, we are interested in thought rather than language, then it is clear that we need only *two* things: the representational vehicle (= the mental file) and its referential content. It is the representational vehicle, Fodor argues, that plays the role of mode of presentation, so we do *not* need Fregean senses as an extra level of meaning in addition to referential content. As far as meaning is concerned, referential content is all there is. Cognitive significance phenomena are to be accounted for in terms of the vehicles through which the meanings are apprehended. Such vehicles are concepts, which Fodor himself is willing to construe as mental files (Fodor 2008: 92–100). But mental files are not an extra level of content. They are syntactic through and through. (See Millikan 2000: 129–32 for a similar rejection of the Fregean framework.)

In recent work, Sainsbury and Tye (2011, 2012) also argue against the Fregean sense/reference distinction:

> A Fregean datum is that it's one thing to think that Hesperus is Hesperus, and another to think that Hesperus is Phosphorus; one thing to think that Hesperus is visible, another to think that Phosphorus is visible.

We agree. Different thoughts are involved, that is, different structures of concepts, since the concept HESPERUS is distinct from the concept PHOSPHORUS. We disagree with Fregeans that the difference requires postulating any additional semantic layer....The differences can be fully and satisfyingly explained using just concepts (and their combination into thoughts) and their contents (conceived just as referents). (Sainsbury and Tye 2012: 53)

The nature of cognition depends, unsurprisingly, not only on contents but also on the vehicles which serve to represent contents: concepts and thoughts. These are metaphysically real elements of our mental life, involved in reasoning and related cognitive activities. Concepts and thoughts can differ, and thereby differentially affect cognition and action, even when they have the same content. (Sainsbury and Tye 2011: 118)

Fregeans are right to think that something more than reference is needed in a complete account, but wrong to think that this something more needs to be epistemically or semantically individuated. Millians are right to think that content is referential, but wrong to think that nothing else is needed to explain cognition. Cognitive processing depends on the vehicles of content, concepts and thoughts, not just on their content. (Sainsbury and Tye 2012: 57)

So what is the difference between the view I have expounded and the view, argued for by Fodor and by Sainsbury and Tye, that modes of presentation are syntactic? Not much, since I accept that mental files are representational vehicles. The difference is primarily terminological. Fodor endorses the claim that concepts/files are 'modes of presentation' because (like me) he takes modes of presentation to be whatever plays the mode of presentation role and accounts for cognitive significance phenomena. But he does not want to use the word 'sense' which (to him) suggests the non-syntactic nature of such modes of presentation. As far as I am concerned, I take 'sense' and 'mode of presentation' to be more or less interchangeable. No substantial disagreement here.

To be sure, mental files are not purely syntactic entities, in my framework; they have a function or a role which determines their cognitive significance. The significance they owe to their function is distinct from the referential content they acquire in context. This distinction is very much like the Kaplanian distinction between content and character, or Perry's analogous distinction between two aspects of attitudinal states—the content of the state and the state itself with its characteristic role (Kaplan; Perry 1993). Indeed, the mental file framework is a descendant of the two-tiered framework put forward by Kaplan and Perry.

The Kaplan–Perry framework was introduced to deal with indexicals in language and thought. To understand indexicals we need two notions of content (in the intuitive sense of 'content').[2] If you and I both think 'I am tired', there is a sense in which we think the same thing, and another sense in which we think different things. It would be misleading to say that the first level (the level at which we think the same thing) is 'purely syntactic'; for what characterizes that level is the function or role of the files we deploy in our respective thoughts. The function or role stays constant: we both deploy a SELF file. But the proper characterization of the relevant (type of) file is functional; it is not purely syntactic.

There is nothing here with which Fodor should disagree, however; for he too holds that modes of presentation are functionally distinguished (Fodor 1998: 19). Indeed, he provides an argument to the effect that, because senses must be transparent in order to play their role in accounting for rational thought and behaviour, they must be *mental objects*, that is, vehicles individuated by their functional roles. That is exactly what mental files are.

The postulation of a primary layer of content akin to character answers Tim Crane's objection to my use of the vehicle/content distinction:

> Recanati describes thought episodes as 'vehicles' and his view of
> singular thought content means that when Le Verrier says to himself

---

[2] In the case of mental files, we arguably need *three* notions (Chapter 3, n. 10). We need to distinguish the role/function of the file (that which makes it the type of file it is), the reference of the file, and the informational content of the file at a given time, that is, the set of predicates in the file.

'The discovery of Vulcan will make me famous', the thought has no content. Yet the content of someone's thought is what they are thinking, and how can it be that Le Verrier was not thinking anything, merely airing an empty 'vehicle'? (Crane 2011: 39)

Note that Crane, by using the definite description 'the content of someone's thought', presupposes that there is a single notion of content and thereby begs the question against his opponent. In contrast to Crane, I hold that there are two distinct notions: what someone is thinking in the sense of the mental representation that is tokened in one's mind (which representation is endowed with a primary content akin to a Kaplanian character), and the semantic (truth-conditional, secondary) content of that representation. When I say that Leverrier's thought has no content, I mean, of course, that it fails to determine the singular truth-conditions that (qua singular vehicle) it is its function to determine; but the vehicle retains its function even when it malfunctions, and insofar as that function counts as a (primary) content, the thought *has* a content. So I cannot be accused of crediting Leverrier with no thought at all (in the non-technical sense of 'thought').

The Kaplan–Perry framework is two-dimensional, and I have introduced the mental file framework in contrast to two-dimensionalism; so the idea that the mental file framework is a version of the Kaplan–Perry framework may seem strange. But what I objected to in Chapter 2 and elsewhere was not two-dimensionalism per se, but the *descriptivist* construal: the idea that the acquaintance relations which determine what a given thought is about are represented in the content of the thought in question.[3] Kaplanian

---

[3] See Chalmers 2002: 169 ff. for a non-descriptivist construal of two-dimensionalism. See also Gertler 2002, who advocates a non-descriptivist form of internalism. (According to Gertler, the subject's dispositions to apply a term in actual or imaginary circumstances are sufficient to endow him or her with an 'implicit grasp of how the term's reference is fixed' (2002: 29). Such grasp constitutes mastery of the term's 'primary' content in the two-dimensional framework, and is not very different from what Perry calls 'attunement'—see next footnote.)

characters (and Perry's 'roles') have a *procedural* nature. They correspond to certain functions which words or mental vehicles have. The functions in question are not represented.[4] The vehicles simply *have* those functions, and they operate in context according to these functions. The referential content of the vehicle depends upon that operation.

The Kaplan–Perry framework is no longer as influential as it used to be—many linguists and philosophers prefer Lewis's centred worlds framework (Lewis 1979), or some variant of it, for dealing with indexical thought. Perry himself has put forward yet another framework, the token-reflexive framework, independently elaborated by people as diverse as Higginbotham, Searle, and Garcia-Carpintero. It is worth comparing the mental file framework to these influential alternatives; for if they work, why bother to articulate an another position? But, I will argue, they do not work, or not satisfactorily—they carry a descriptivist commitment, which the mental file framework allows us to dispense with.

Both the centred worlds account and the token-reflexive account are, it seems to me, attempts to deal with mental indexicality purely at the level of truth-conditional content, without appealing to the notion of sense or mode of presentation.[5] According to Lewis, the problem with truth-conditional contents, standardly construed, is

---

[4] As Perry says, 'there is a difference between being able to think of a thing or person in virtue of some role it plays in one's life, and being able to articulate that role in thought or speech and think of it as the thing or person playing that role in one's life' (Perry 1997/2000: 363; see also Perry 2001a : 132 and 2006: 218). And also: 'Attunement to the relation that our self-notions have to ourselves, or our perceptions have to the object they are of, does not require belief or thought about the relation; it requires know-how, not knowledge that' (Perry 2012: 99).

[5] As Stalnaker points out, 'one worry about any such notion [i.e. the notion of sense or mode of presentation] is that it may blur the line between the content of a representation and the relation between the representation and its content' (Stalnaker 2008: 28). For that reason, it would be good to dispense with senses/modes of presentation and do everything in terms of truth-conditional content. The problem (I take it) is that we can't do that, without going descriptivist.

that they are too coarse-grained. Instead of introducing the vehicles into the picture and endowing them with functional significance (so that they can play the role of mode of presentation), he proposes to make the contents themselves more fine-grained by characterizing them as sets of centred possible worlds rather than as sets of possible worlds *tout court*. Centring the possible worlds on an individual at a time gives us the subjective perspective which is the hallmark of indexical thought.

The token-reflexive framework also appeals to a special sort of truth-conditional content, in order to deal with indexical thought. Indexical thoughts are thoughts with *reflexive contents*, that is, thoughts that are about themselves and ascribe properties to themselves. As I will try to show, the token-reflexive framework is best construed as a variant of the centred worlds framework, whose main weakness it inherits. Remedying the weakness is possible, I will argue, but the resulting account leads us back to the mental file framework.

2

Like the Kaplan–Perry framework, the centred worlds framework is two-dimensional. The content of an attitude, for Lewis, determines a truth-value only when evaluated with respect to a contextual index, containing the thinking subject and the time of thought in addition to the world in which the thinker thinks the thought. The content is therefore not a classical proposition (which only requires a possible world to determine a truth-value), but a relativized proposition or, as Lewis puts it, a *property* of thinker-time pairs.[6] Yet the relativized proposition is meant to apply to the contextual index (the subject of thought at the time of thought), and when it does, it determines a classical content, to the effect that the subject in question has, at

---

[6] Chisholm has independently put forward an analogous theory (Chisholm 1979, 1981). See also Loar 1976 for the seminal idea which inspired Lewis.

the time in question, the property that is the content of the attitude. The distinction between the relativized proposition and the classical proposition it contextually determines parallels the Kaplan–Perry distinction between the character/role of the state and the content it contextually determines (Stalnaker 2003: 255 n.).[7]

One of the things that distinguish the Lewis framework from the Kaplan–Perry framework is the fact that those objects of thought that belong to the contextual index are treated completely differently from the objects of thought that are represented in the content of the thought. The objects of thought in the content are represented descriptively: they are described as *bearing such and such relations to the subject of thought (at the time of thinking)*. So the acquaintance relations are 'internalized' and reflected into the content of one's thought. On this picture, if I see something, I primarily think of it as 'what I see'—the object that bears a certain perceptual relation to me. In Chapter 2 I criticized this view as unduly intellectualistic. But note that, in 'what I see', there is an occurrence of the first person. It corresponds to the subject in the contextual index, and the subject is *not* represented in the content: it is externalized and directly provided by the context. The subject is not represented but, qua subject of the thought episode, it is involved pragmatically in the process of 'self-ascription' through which Lewis characterizes the attitudinal mode. To believe something, for Lewis, *is* to self-ascribe a

---

[7] One way of representing the distinction between the relativized proposition and the classical proposition is by appealing to 'Austinian propositions' consisting of a centred worlds content à la Lewis *and* an index of evaluation (Recanati 2007). In contrast to the centred worlds proposition, which only has relative, 'truth-at'-conditions, the Austinian proposition is classical: it is true iff the centred world proposition that features in it (what I call the 'lekton') is true at the index that features in it (the 'situation of evaluation'). In this framework, reminiscent of Barwise (1989, see also Barwise and Etchemendy 1987) and McCarthy (1993), there are two levels of content, not one. All the objections which Stalnaker (2008: 50–1) levels against Lewis's centred worlds account of belief content can be addressed and met by thus appealing to the Austinian proposition in addition to the centred worlds content. As Ninan (2008: 63 n.) notes, Stalnaker's own account in terms of a systematic 'link' between the centred worlds in the relativized proposition and the 'base world' serving as index of evaluation is (in spirit at least) similar to my account in terms of Austinian propositions.

certain content (a property). So Lewis offers an externalist treatment of reference to oneself (and the present time) in thought, a treatment that is reminiscent of Arthur Prior's;[8] but at the same time he defends a thoroughgoing Descriptivism for the other objects of thought, which are presented descriptively as bearing certain acquaintance relations to the 'centre' (i.e. the subject–time pair in the contextual index).

I applaud Lewis's externalization of the subject of thought and whatever occurs in the contextual index; but I deplore the descriptivist construal of the content of thought and the internalization of acquaintance relations. The theory I have presented is thoroughly anti-descriptivist: objects are thought of under modes of presentation which are mental files. Mental files are based on acquaintance relations, but to think of an object through a mental file you don't have to think of the relation on which the file is based.

The other alternative framework, the token-reflexive framework, is very similar to Lewis's. Objects are thought of as bearing certain relations not to the subject at the time of thinking but to the occurrence of the thought in which they are represented. Each thought or utterance is therefore ascribed a *reflexive content* that is about that thought or utterance itself. For example, an occurrence u of 'I am tired' in speech or thought means something like 'the utterer/thinker of u is tired at the time of u in the world of u'. In this framework as in Lewis's, acquaintance relations are internalized: relational descriptions provide the modes of presentation under which objects are thought of. As in Lewis's framework, there is an exception: the occurrence in terms of which everything is descriptively characterized is not itself descriptively characterized, as we shall see.

If I say or think 'I am tired', and this is analysed as 'the utterer/thinker of u is tired at the time of u in the world of u', then I have referred to myself under the descriptive-relational mode of presentation 'the

---

[8] See *Perspectival Thought* (Recanati 2007) for an elaboration of this sort of approach, with historical references.

utterer/thinker of u'. In the token-reflexive framework, every object of thought is referred to under such a descriptive-relational mode of presentation which exploits the object's relation to u. But what about u itself? Under which mode of presentation is it referred to?

One possible option for the reflexivist is to say that u is thought of as 'this occurrence', where 'this' is understood *reflexively*. Such a reflexive mode of presentation cannot be understood descriptively, however. If 'this occurrence' were analysed as 'the occurrence that is identical to this', we would be using the *analysandum*, namely the reflexive 'this', in the *analysans*. If it were analysed as 'the occurrence that is identical to u', we would be back to where we started and would still be in need of a mode of presentation for u. I conclude that, if one goes for reflexive modes of presentation, they must be treated as non-descriptive. At this point, clearly, we need a theory of non-descriptive modes of presentation—the sort of theory I have tried to provide—and the token-reflexive framework is of no help in this endeavour. So the reflexivist is in a rather bad situation: her account does not stand on its own feet and needs support from the account it is supposed to be an alternative to.

There is another option for the reflexivist, however. Instead of appealing to reflexive modes of presentation, he or she may appeal to *super-direct reference*, the sort of thing that Russell was after. In super-direct reference, there is no mode of presentation: the referent itself serves as its own vehicle, as it were. No mental file is needed to stand for the object in such a case, because the object itself is directly recruited as a thought constituent. This of course cannot be done with many objects, but with mental occurrences arguably it can. Super-direct reference is reminiscent of Russell's strong notion of acquaintance (the sort of acquaintance we have only with ourselves and our sense-data), and indeed super-direct reference is supposed to be 'transparent', in contrast to ordinary direct reference.[9]

---

[9] Perry notes the similarity between the token-reflexive framework and Russell's brand of relational Descriptivism according to which 'I' means 'the person with *this*

This idea can be couched in Lewis's framework, by externalizing the occurrence *u* and letting it be directly provided by the context. Everything is then described relative to *u*, but *u* itself is *given*, it is not represented. On this mixture of the two frameworks (centred worlds and reflexivism), the content of a mental occurrence is a *property of occurrences*, and that content is evaluated with respect to a contextual index containing the occurrence itself. On this Lewis-inspired view, to judge something by assertively tokening a certain representation is to ascribe to the token the property that is its content. Here reflexivity is guaranteed by the pragmatic architecture of the act of judgement. So when you think 'I am tired', the content of the thought is the property an occurrence has just in case the thinker of that occurrence is tired at the time of the occurrence in the world of the occurrence. To think the thought (or to think it assertively) is to ascribe that property to the current occurrence *u* you are producing.

Again, the main problem I see with that theory is the asymmetry between different objects of thought. Everything is thought of descriptively, except for a single element which is externalized and serves as *universal anchor* for all the content. Although I have no knock-down argument against this approach, I find it insufficiently motivated and too much in the grip of a rather extreme Cartesian picture. Why not appeal instead to *multiple* anchors, corresponding to all the acquaintance relations in which we stand to objects of thought? Multiple anchors are precisely what the mental file framework gives us.

---

sensation' (Perry 2002: 234). Moreover, I think I remember a conversation during which he (Perry) embraced the idea of super-direct reference to mental occurrences in defending the token-reflexive framework. I also seem to remember Martine Nida-Rümelin advocating super-direct reference. (In general, the idea of super-direct reference tends to surface in discussions of phenomenal concepts and related matters. See e.g. Chalmers's statement that, in the phenomenal case, 'the referent of the concept is somehow present inside the concept's sense in a way that is much stronger than in the usual case of direct reference' (Chalmers 2003: 233).)

3

Recently, several authors have put forward versions of the Lewis story which incorporate the idea of multiple anchors and give up the asymmetry which characterizes both the Lewis framework and the reflexivist framework. These authors enlarge the contextual index so as to include in it the various *objects of thought* in addition to the world, the time, and the subject of thought. The property that is the content of the thought changes accordingly: it is now a property of a sequence of objects (at a world and a time), and as such it is no longer representable as a set of 'centred worlds' (where the centre is a single individual—the subject—at a time) but as a set of 'multi-centered worlds' (Torre 2010) or 'sequenced-worlds' (Ninan forthcoming).[10]

The multi-centred view is in the spirit of my own approach, so I am sympathetic; but I do not think it allows one to dispense with mental files. There is, indeed, a dilemma for the multi-centred theorist. In the multi-centred framework, the content is a property of a sequence of objects. But are the acquaintance relations in which the objects participate themselves represented as part of that content, or are they not? If they are, we internalize the acquaintance relations once again. But if they are not—if, following Ninan, we explicitly refrain from internalizing the acquaintance relations[11]—then we face the *mode of presentation problem*.

The starting point of the whole enquiry is the possibility of thinking of an object in different ways, with various behavioural and cognitive consequences. If the objects of thought are fed into the contextual index, and it is stipulated that the thought is about these

[10] As Torre notes, Stalnaker himself considered the possibility of using 'centered worlds with multiple individuals at their centers' to model the beliefs of a community (Stalnaker 2008: 73 ff.).

[11] Ninan has a special reason for resisting Descriptivism: 'centred Descriptivism', as he aptly calls Lewis's framework, is unable to account for the counterfactual attitudes (e.g. imagining), so it is empirically and not merely philosophically flawed. See Ninan 2008 and forthcoming.

objects, what will determine *how* the objects in question are thought of? The descriptivist packs the modes of presentation into the content, but if we don't do that, we need some other way of pairing the objects with the right modes of presentation.

In Lewis's original framework, there is a (non-descriptivist) way of pairing the subject in the contextual index with the right mode of presentation (the SELF mode of presentation). An attitudinal state is analysed into content and mode. The content, for Lewis, is a property. The belief mode itself is analysed by saying that to believe a content (analysed as a property) is for the subject of thought to 'self-ascribe' that property. Now what is it to 'self-ascribe' a property, in the relevant sense? It is not just to ascribe that property to oneself (Stanley 2011: 89). There are different ways in which one can ascribe a given property to oneself, corresponding to different modes of presentation of oneself. The thinker can think of himself that he is tired, when seeing himself, looking tired, in the mirror (but without realizing that he is looking at himself). Or the thinker can think that he is tired on the grounds that he *feels* tired. Only in the latter case does Lewis analyse the content of the thought as the property of being tired, which the subject 'self-ascribes'. When the subject, looking at himself in the mirror (but failing to realize that he is looking at himself), thinks 'That man is tired', he does not 'self-ascribe' the property of being tired, though he ascribes that property to himself (under a demonstrative mode of presentation). This suggests that it is the attitudinal act of 'self-ascription' itself—a primitive of the theory—which determines a particular mode of presentation of the subject to whom a property is ascribed. There is no possibility of 'self-ascribing' a property under a different mode of presentation of oneself (say, as the man seen in the mirror).[12] In other words, the first-personal mode of presentation is built into the self-ascriptive relation.

---

[12] In the mirror case, the subject simultaneously ascribes to himself the property of being tired (under a demonstrative mode of presentation), and 'self-ascribes' a different property (the property of *looking at a man who is tired*).

Now consider what happens when we enrich the contextual index by feeding it a sequence of objects. Each object in the sequence can be thought of under a number of distinct modes of presentation. We need a way of pairing the objects with the appropriate modes of presentation. But we can't use the Lewis trick. There is a *single* self-ascriptive mode. On that mode we can base a special mode of presentation in Lewis's original framework because a single individual occupies the centre, and it is that individual that we need to pair with the right mode of presentation to avoid mirror-type counter-examples. By determining the right mode of presentation, the self-ascriptive mode effects the pairing. But when we multiply the individuals in the contextual index, what we need is not a single mode of presentation, but a sequence of modes of presentation corresponding to the sequence of objects. Appealing to the attitudinal mode is of no use here.

So, should we give up multi-centred worlds? Not necessarily. Another option would be to bring, as I have just suggested, a sequence of modes of presentation into the picture. Modes of presentation, I have argued at length, are mental files, so what we need to bring into the picture are *sequences of files*. In this regard, the simplest solution would be to substitute a sequence of files for the sequence of objects used by the multi-centred theorists. Let us see how this replacement might proceed.

Ninan presents a sequenced world as a triple consisting of a world w, a time t, and a sequence g of n objects, where (on a first approximation) n is the number of objects the subject is acquainted with. Following Stalnaker (2008), Ninan distinguishes the 'base world', which corresponds to the contextual index in the Lewis framework, and the set of 'belief worlds' which represent the subject's doxastic alternatives. Both the base world and the belief worlds are sequenced worlds consisting of a possible world, a time, and a sequence of n objects (the *res*-sequence), in Ninan's framework. The n-th object in the *res*-sequence of a given belief world represents the n-th object the subject is acquainted with in the base world.

But there is a problem with this account. It will not do to have the sequence in the base world be *the sequence of objects the subject is acquainted with*. The subject may bear distinct acquaintance relations to the same object—e.g. Ortcutt. If the subject is confused, in some of the belief worlds there will be two distinct objects x_i and x_j corresponding to what is in fact one and the same object. It follows that the number of objects in the belief worlds must not be the number of objects the subject is acquainted with, but, rather, the number of (token) acquaintance relations the subject actually bears to objects in the base world. If the subject bears several acquaintance relations to the same object—e.g. Ortcutt—that object will occur as many times as needed in the sequence of objects in the base world, and there will be, in some of the subject's doxastic alternatives, distinct objects x_i and x_j (e.g. the man on the beach and the suspicious looking man with a brown hat) corresponding to one and the same individual in reality. In a nutshell: objects in the belief worlds should represent actual individuals only 'relative to acquaintance relations'. To achieve that result, Ninan suggests making the *res*-sequence in the base world a sequence of < object, acquaintance relation > pairs:

> Since we now think of d and f [the two distinct objects that represent Ortcutt for the confused subject] as representing individuals relative to acquaintance relations, it would be natural to replace our sequence of individuals with a sequence of pairs of individuals and acquaintance relations. (Ninan forthcoming)

When the subject is acquainted with the same object twice, as in the Ortcutt case, there will be two separate elements $< y_1, R_1 >$ and $< y_2, R_2 >$ in the subject's *res*-sequence such that $y_1 = y_2$, but $R_1 \neq R_2$.

By making this move, Ninan, in effect, introduces modes of presentation into the sequenced world framework; but he does not go far enough. It will not do to have the sequence in the base world be the sequence of acquaintance relations the subject actually bears to objects, or, equivalently, a sequence of < object, acquaintance relation > pairs. Suppose the subject has an empty singular term in his repertoire, e.g. he thinks he has been followed all day long by someone (whom he thinks of as 'that guy who keeps following me') while actually there is no such person—nobody has been following him. In such a case, intuitively, there is one more object in the belief worlds than the subject is actually acquainted with in the base world. Ninan's revised framework does not allow him to represent that situation, for the number of objects in the *res*-sequence for every belief world has to match the number of acquaintance relations the subject actually bears to objects. Instead, the number of objects in the *res*-sequences in the belief worlds should correspond to the number of *files* in the subject's mind (based on *putative* acquaintance relations).

To get what we want we could, simply, replace the sequence of < object, acquaintance relation > pairs in the base world with a sequence of files. Given the files and the world, we can retrieve the objects (namely the referents of the files in the world in question). But the world already gives us the files, so we don't even have to introduce them into the base world—they are already there. That means that we can take the base world to be *an ordinary centred world* < w, t, x > (as Stalnaker suggests). The files we need can be extracted from that centred world: they are the files which the subject x uses in w at t to think about the objects in w (including herself). Ninan's system should therefore be amended as follows:

1. A base world now is a *proper centred world* < w, t, x >, i.e. a centred world < w, t, x > such that the individual x exists in world w at time t and there exists also (in w at t) a sequence $f = < f_1 ... f_n >$ of files through which x thinks of objects (including herself) in w. That sequence is called the *file-sequence*.

2. A belief world is a sequenced world < w', t', g' >, where $g' = < g'_1 ... g'_n >$ is a sequence of objects (the *res*-sequence, in Ninan's terminology).

3. The subject's belief state is represented by a pair of a base world and a set of belief worlds. The set of belief worlds represents the subject's doxastic alternatives relative to the base world, via the following stipulation: In any belief world $< w', t', g' >$, the nth element of the res-sequence g', namely g'_n, will represent the object which is the reference of f_n, the nth file in the subject's file-sequence. If f_n does not refer, g'_n does not represent any actual individual; it is a pure 'intentional object'.

We have, in effect, substituted a sequence of n files for the sequence of n objects used by the multi-centred theorist. In this way we achieve more fine-grainedness. Given the files and the world, we can retrieve the objects (namely the referents of the files in the world in question), but the files give us something more: the modes of presentation.

REFERENCES

Abath, A. (2008) Possessing Demonstrative Concepts. *Facta Philosophica* 10: 231–45.

Abbott, B. (2011) Support for Individual Concepts. *Linguistic and Philosophical Investigations* 10: 1–23.

Anderson, J. (1977) Memory for Information about Individuals. *Memory and Cognition* 5: 430–42.

Anderson, J. and Hastie, R. (1974) Individuation and Reference in Memory: Proper Names and Definite Descriptions. *Cognitive Psychology* 6: 495–514.

Austin, J. L. (1971) *Philosophical Papers*, 2nd edn. Oxford: Clarendon Press.

Azzouni, J. (2011) Singular Thoughts (Objects-Directed Thoughts). *Proceedings of the Aristotelian Society*, Supp. Vol. 85: 45–61.

Bach, K. (1986) Thought and Object: *De Re* Representations and Relations. In M. Brand and R. M. Harnish (eds.) *The Representation of Knowledge and Belief*, pp. 187–218. Tucson, Ariz.: The University of Arizona Press.

Bach, K. (1987) *Thought and Reference*. Oxford: Clarendon Press.

Bach, K. (1994) *Thought and Reference*, 2nd edn. (with a postscript). Oxford: Clarendon Press.

Barwise, J. (1989) *The Situation in Logic*. Stanford, Calif.: CSLI.

Barwise, J. and Etchemendy, J. (1987) *The Liar: An Essay on Truth and Circularity*. New York: Oxford University Press.

Beaney, M. (1997) *The Frege Reader*. Oxford: Blackwell.

Benveniste, E. (1956) La Nature des pronoms. Reprinted in his *Problèmes de linguistique générale*, pp. 251–7. Paris: Gallimard, 1966.

Beyer, C. (2008) Noematic Sinn: General Meaning-Function or Propositional Content? In F. Mattens (ed.), *Meaning and Language: Phenomenological Perspectives*, pp. 75–88. Dordrecht: Springer.

Bezuidenhout, A. (1997) The Communication of De Re Thoughts. *Noûs* 31: 197–225.

Bochner, G. (2010) Cognitive Significance and Non-Descriptive Senses. MS.

Boghossian, P. (1994) The Transparency of Mental Content. *Philosophical Perspectives* 8: 33–50.

Borg, E. (2004) *Minimal Semantics*. Oxford: Clarendon Press.

Breckenridge, W. and Magidor, O. (2012) Arbitrary Reference. *Philosophical Studies*, 158: 377–400. DOI: 10.1007/s11098-010-9676-z.

Brown, J. (2004) *Anti-Individualism and Knowledge*. Cambridge, Mass.: MIT Press/ Bradford Books.

Burge, T. (1977) Belief *De Re*. *Journal of Philosophy* 74: 338–62.

Burge, T. (1983) Russell's Problem and Intentional Identity. In J. Tomberlin (ed.), *Agent, Language, and the Structure of the World: Essays Presented to Hector-Neri Castañeda, with His Replies*, pp. 79–110. Indianapolis: Hackett Publishing Company.

Burge, T. (1988) Individualism and Self-Knowledge. *Journal of Philosophy* 85: 649–65.

Burge, T. (1998) Memory and Self Knowledge. In P. Ludlow and N. Martin (eds.) *Externalism and Self Knowledge*, pp. 351–70. Stanford: CSLI.

Burge, T. (2010) *Origins of Objectivity*. Oxford: Clarendon Press.

Camp, J. (2002) *Confusion: A Study in the Theory of Knowledge*. Cambridge, Mass.: Harvard University Press.

Campbell, J. (1987) Is Sense Transparent? *Proceedings of the Aristotelian Society* 88: 273–92.

Campbell, J. (1994) *Past, Space and Self*. Cambridge, Mass.: MIT Press.

Campbell, J. (2002) *Reference and Consciousness*. Oxford: Oxford University Press.

Campbell, J. (2006) Sortals and the Binding Problem. In F. McBride (ed.) *Identity and Modality*, pp. 203–18. Oxford: Clarendon Press.

Cappelen, H. and Lepore, E. (2005) *Insensitive Semantics*. Oxford: Blackwell.

Cappelen, H. and Hawthorne, J. (2009) *Relativism and Monadic Truth*. Oxford: Oxford University Press.

Castañeda, H.-N. (1999) *The Phenomeno-Logic of the I: Essays on Self-Consciousness*, ed. J. Hart and T. Kapitan. Bloomington, Ind.: Indiana University Press.

Chafe, W. (1976) Givenness, Contrastiveness, Definiteness, Subjects, Topics, and Points of View. In C. Li (ed.) *Subject and Topic*, pp. 25–55. New York: Academic Press.

Chalmers, D. (2002) On Sense and Intension. *Philosophical Perspectives* 16: 135–82.

Chalmers, D. (2003) The Content and Epistemology of Phenomenal Belief. In Q. Smith and A. Jokic (eds.) *Consciousness: New Philosophical Perspectives*, pp. 220–72. Oxford: Oxford University Press.

Chastain, C. (1975) Reference and Context. In K. Gunderson (ed.) *Language, Mind, and Knowledge*, pp. 194–269. Minneapolis: University of Minnesota Press.

Chisholm, R. (1979) Objects and Persons: Revisions and Replies. In E. Sosa (ed.) *Essays on the Philosophy of Roderick M. Chisholm*, pp. 317–88. Amsterdam: Rodopi.

Chisholm, R. (1981) *The First Person*. Minneapolis: University of Minnesota Press.

Crane, T. (2011) The Singularity of Singular Thought. *Proceedings of the Aristotelian Society*, Supp. Vol. 85: 21–44.

Crimmins, M. (1989) Having Ideas and Having the Concept. *Mind and Language* 4: 280–94.

Crimmins, M. (1992) *Talk about Beliefs*. Cambridge, Mass.: MIT Press/Bradford Books.

Crimmins, M. (1995) Notional Specificity. *Mind and Language* 10: 464–77.

Crimmins, M. (1998) Hesperus and Phosphorus: Sense, Pretence, and Reference. *Philosophical Review* 107: 1–47.

Crimmins, M. and Perry, J. (1989) The Prince and the Phone Booth: Reporting Puzzling Beliefs. Reprinted in Perry 1993: 249–78.

Cumming, S. (2011) Creatures of Darkness. Unpublished MS, UCLA.

Davies, M. (1981) *Meaning, Quantification, Necessity*. London: Routledge and Kegan Paul.

Davies, M. (1982) Individuation and the Semantics of Demonstratives. *Journal of Philosophical Logic* 11: 287–310.

Devitt, M. (1989) Against Direct Reference. *Midwest Studies in Philosophy* 14: 206–40.

Dickie, I. (2010) We are Acquainted with Ordinary Things. In R. Jeshion (ed.) *New Essays on Singular Thought*, pp. 213–45. Oxford: Clarendon Press.

Dickie, I. (2011) Visual Attention Fixes Demonstrative Reference by Eliminating Referential Luck. In C. Mole, D. Smithies, and W. Wu (eds.) *Attention: Philosophical & Psychological Essays*, pp. 292–322. New York: Oxford University Press.

Dickie, I. and Rattan, G. (2010) Sense, Communication, and Rational Engagement. *Dialectica* 64: 131–51.

Donnellan, K. (1966) Reference and Definite Descriptions. Reprinted in S. Schwartz (ed.) *Naming, Necessity, and Natural Kinds*, pp. 42–65. Ithaca, NY: Cornell University Press, 1977.

Donnellan, K. (1970) Proper Names and Identifying Descriptions. *Synthese* 21: 335–58.

Donnellan, K. (1977) The Contingent A Priori and Rigid Designators. *Midwest Studies in Philosophy* 2: 12–27.

Donnellan, K. (1978) Speaker Reference, Descriptions and Anaphora. *Syntax and Semantics* 9: 47–68.

Dretske, F. (1988) *Explaining Behavior*. Cambridge, Mass.: MIT Press.

Du Bois, J. (1980) Beyond Definiteness: The Trace of Identity in Discourse. In W. Chafe (ed.) *The Pear Stories: Cognitive, Cultural and Linguistic Aspects of Narrative Production*, pp. 203–74. Norwood, NJ: Ablex.

Dummett, M. (1978) *Truth and Other Enigmas*. London: Duckworth.

Dummett, M. (1981) *The Interpretation of Frege's Philosophy*. London: Duckworth.

Edelberg, W. (1992) Intentional Identity and the Attitudes. *Linguistics and Philosophy* 15: 561–96.

Edelberg, W. (1995) A Perspectivalist Semantics for the Attitudes. *Noûs* 29: 316–42.

Egan, A. (2007) Epistemic Modals, Relativism and Assertion. *Philosophical Studies* 133: 1–22.

Erteschik-Shir, N. (1997) *The Dynamics of Focus Structure*. Cambridge: Cambridge University Press.

Evans, G. (1973) The Causal Theory of Names. *Proceedings of the Aristotelian Society*, Supp. Vol. 47: 187–208.

Evans, G. (1981) Understanding Demonstratives. In H. Parret and J. Bouveresse (eds.) *Meaning and Understanding*, pp. 280–303. Berlin: De Gruyter.

Evans, G. (1982) *The Varieties of Reference*, ed. J. McDowell. Oxford: Clarendon Press.

Evans, G. (1985) *Collected Papers*. Oxford: Clarendon Press.

Fine, K. (2007) *Semantic Relationism*. Oxford: Blackwell.

Fodor, J. (1998) *Concepts: Where Cognitive Science Went Wrong*. Oxford: Clarendon Press.

Fodor, J. (2008) *LOT 2: The Language of Thought Revisited*. Oxford: Clarendon Press.

Fodor, J. D. and Sag, I. (1982) Referential and Quantificational Indefinites. *Linguistics and Philosophy* 5: 355–98.

Forbes, G. (1989) Cognitive Architecture and the Semantics of Belief. *Midwest Studies in Philosophy* 14: 84–100.

Forbes, G. (1990) The Indispensability of *Sinn*. *Philosophical Review* 99: 535–63.

Frege, G. (1918–19) The Thought: A Logical Enquiry. English trans. by A. and M. Quinton in P. Strawson (ed.) *Philosophical Logic*, pp. 17–38. Oxford: Oxford University Press, 1967.

Frege, G. (1979) *Posthumous Writings*. Oxford: Blackwell.

Frege, G. (1980) *Philosophical and Mathematical Correspondence*. Chicago: University of Chicago Press.

Frege, G. (1984) *Collected Papers on Mathematics, Logic, and Philosophy*. Oxford: Blackwell.

Gale, R. (1968) *The Language of Time*. London: Routledge and Kegan Paul.

Gale, R. and I. Thalberg (1965) The Generality of Predictions. *Journal of Philosophy* 62: 195–210.

Geach, P. (1962) *Reference and Generality*. Ithaca, NY: Cornell University Press.

Geach, P. (1967) Intentional Identity. *Journal of Philosophy* 74: 627–32.

Geach, P. (1972) *Logic Matters*. Oxford: Blackwell.

Genabith, J., Kamp, H., and Reyle, U. (2011) Discourse Representation Theory. In D. Gabbay and F. Guenthner (eds.) *Handbook of Philosophical Logic*, vol. 15, pp. 125–394. Berlin: Springer.

Gerken, M. (2009) Conceptual Equivocation and Epistemic Relevance. *Dialectica* 63: 117–32.

Gerken, M. (2011) Conceptual Equivocation and Warrant by Reasoning. *Australasian Journal of Philosophy* 89: 381–400.

Gertler, B. (2002) Explanatory Reduction, Conceptual Analysis, and Conceivability Arguments about the Mind. *Noûs* 36: 22–49.

Goodsell, T. (2011) Mental File Explanations. MS.

Grice, P. (1969) Vacuous Names. In D. Davidson and J. Hintikka (eds.) *Words and Objections*, pp. 118–45. Dordrecht: Reidel.

Harman, G. (1973) *Thought*. Princeton: Princeton University Press.

Harman, G. (1977) How to Use Propositions. *American Philosophical Quarterly* 14: 173–6.

Hawkins, J. (1978) *Definiteness and Indefiniteness: A Study in Reference and Grammaticality Prediction*. London: Croom Helm.

Hawthorne, J. and Manley, D. (forthcoming) *The Reference Book*. Oxford: Oxford University Press.

Heim, I. (1983) File Change Semantics and the Familiarity Theory of Definiteness. Reprinted in P. Portner and B. Partee (eds.) *Formal Semantics: The Essential Readings*, pp. 223–48. Oxford: Blackwell, 2002.

Heim, I. (1988) *The Semantics of Definite and Indefinite Noun Phrases*. New York: Garland.

Hendriks, H. (2002) Information Packaging: From Cards to Boxes. In K. van Deemter and R. Kibble (eds.) *Information Sharing: Reference and Presupposition in Language Generation and Interpretation*, pp. 1–33. Stanford, Calif.: CSLI.

Higginbotham, J. (2009) *Tense, Aspect, and Indexicality*. Oxford: Oxford University Press.

Humberstone, L. and Townsend, A. (1994) Co-Instantiation and Identity. *Philosophical Studies* 74: 243–72.

Hylton, P. (2005) *Propositions, Functions, and Analysis: Selected Essays on Russell's Philosophy.* Oxford: Clarendon Press.

Jackson, F. (1998a) Reference and Description Revisited. *Philosophical Perspectives* 12: 201–18.

Jackson, F. (1998b) *From Metaphysics to Ethics.* Oxford: Clarendon Press.

James, W. (1890) *Principles of Psychology.* New York: Holt.

Jeshion, R. (2002) Acquaintanceless *De Re* Belief. In J. Campbell, M. O'Rourke, and D. Shier (eds.) *Meaning and Truth,* pp. 53–78. New York: Seven Bridges Press.

Jeshion, R. (2004) Descriptive Descriptive Names. In M. Reimer and A. Bezuidenhout (eds.) *Descriptions and Beyond,* pp. 591–612. Oxford: Oxford University Press.

Jeshion, R. (2010) Singular Thought: Acquaintance, Semantic Instrumentalism, and Cognitivism. In R. Jeshion (ed.) *New Essays on Singular Thought,* pp. 105–40. Oxford: Clarendon Press.

Kadmon, N. (2001) *Formal Pragmatics.* Oxford: Blackwell.

Kahneman, D. and Treisman, A. (1984) Changing Views of Attention and Automaticity. In R. Parasumaran et al. (eds.) *Varieties of Attention,* pp. 29–62. New York: Academic Press.

Kahneman, D., Treisman, A., and Gibbs, B. (1992) The Reviewing of Object Files: Object-Specific Integration of Information. *Cognitive Psychology* 24: 175–219.

Kamp, H. (1981) A Theory of Truth and Semantic Representation. Reprinted in P. Portner and B. Partee (eds.) *Formal Semantics: The Essential Readings,* pp. 189–222. Oxford: Blackwell, 2002.

Kamp, H. (1990) Prolegomena to a Structural Theory of Belief and Other Attitudes. In A. Anderson and J. Owens (eds) *Propositional Attitudes,* pp. 27–90. Stanford, Calif.: CSLI.

Kamp, H. and Bende-Farkas, A. (2006) Epistemic Specificity from a Communication-Theoretic Perspective. MS.

Kaplan, D. (1978) Dthat. *Syntax and Semantics* 9: 221–43.

Kaplan D. (1989a) Demonstratives. In J. Almog, H. Wettstein, and J. Perry (eds.) *Themes from Kaplan,* pp. 481–563. New York: Oxford University Press.

Kaplan, D. (1989b) Afterthoughts. In J. Almog, H. Wettstein, and J. Perry (eds.) *Themes from Kaplan,* pp. 565–614. New York: Oxford University Press.

Kaplan, D. (1990) Words. *Proceedings of the Aristotelian Society,* Supp. Vol. 64: 93–119.

Kaplan, D. (2012) An Idea of Donnellan. In J. Almog and P. Leonardi (eds.) *Having in Mind: The Philosophy of Keith Donnellan,* pp. 122–75. New York: Oxford University Press.

Karttunen, L. (1976) Discourse Referents. *Syntax and Semantics* 7: 363–85.

Kelly, S. (2001) Demonstrative Concepts and Experience. *Philosophical Review* 110: 397–420.

Kim, J. (1977) Perception and Reference without Causality. *Journal of Philosophy* 74: 606–20.

Kripke, S. (1977) Semantic Reference and Speaker's Reference. *Midwest Studies in Philosophy* 2: 255–76.

Kripke, S. (1979) A Puzzle about Belief. In A. Margalit (ed.) *Meaning and Use*, pp. 239–83. Dordrecht: Reidel.

Kripke, S. (1980) *Naming and Necessity*. Oxford: Blackwell.

Landman, F. (1990) Partial Information, Modality, and Intentionality. In P. Hanson (ed.) *Information, Language, and Cognition*, pp. 247–84. New York: Oxford University Press.

Lawlor, K. (2001) *New Thoughts about Old Things*. New York: Garland.

Levine, J. (1998) Conceivability and the Metaphysics of Mind. *Noûs* 32: 449–80.

Lewis, D. (1979) Attitudes *De Dicto* and *De Se*. *Philosophical Review* 88: 513–43.

Lewis, D. (1983) *Philosophical Papers*, vol. i. New York: Oxford University Press.

Lewis, D. (1999) *Papers in Metaphysics and Epistemology*. Cambridge: Cambridge University Press.

Loar, B. (1972) Reference and Propositional Attitudes. *Philosophical Review* 81: 43–62.

Loar, B. (1976) The Semantics of Singular Terms. *Philosophical Studies* 30: 353–77.

Lockwood, M. (1971) Identity and Reference. In M. Munitz (ed.) *Identity and Individuation*, pp. 199–211. New York: New York University Press.

Lowe, J. (2007) Sortals and the Individuation of Objects. *Mind and Language* 22: 514–33.

Ludlow, P. (1995) Externalism, Self-Knowledge and the Prevalence of Slow-Switching. *Analysis* 55: 45–9.

Ludlow, P., and Martin. N. (eds.) *Externalism and Self Knowledge*. Stanford, Calif.: CSLI.

MacFarlane, J. (2007) The Logic of Confusion: Remarks on Joseph Camp's *Confusion: A Study in the Theory of Knowledge*. *Philosophy and Phenomenological Research* 74: 700–8.

McCarthy, J. (1993) Notes on Formalizing Contexts. *Proceedings of the Thirteenth International Joint Conference on Artificial Intelligence*, vol. i, pp. 555–60. San Mateo, Calif.: Morgan Kaufmann Publisher.

McDowell, J. (1977) On the Sense and Reference of a Proper Name. *Mind* 86: 159–85.

McDowell, J. (1984) *De Re* Senses. In C. Wright (ed.) *Frege: Tradition & Influence*, pp. 98–109. Oxford: Blackwell.

McDowell, J. (2005) Evans's Frege. In J. L. Bermudez (ed.) *Thought, Reference, and Experience: Themes from the Philosophy of Gareth Evans*, pp. 42–65. Oxford: Clarendon Press.

Markman, E. (1989) *Categorization and Naming in Children: Problems of Induction.* Cambridge, Mass.: MIT Press/Bradford Books.

Markman, E. and Wachtel, G. (1988) Children's Use of Mutual Exclusivity to Constrain the Meanings of Words. *Cognitive Psychology* 20: 121–57.

Martì, G. (2008) Direct Reference and Definite Descriptions. *Dialectica* 62: 43–57.

Millican, P. (1990) Contents, Thoughts and Definite Descriptions. *Proceedings of the Aristotelian Society*, Supp. Vol. 64: 167–203.

Millikan, R. (1990) The Myth of the Essential Indexical. *Noûs* 24: 723–34.

Millikan, R. (1993) *White Queen Psychology and Other Essays for Alice.* Cambridge, Mass.: MIT Press/Bradford Books.

Millikan, R. (1997) Images of Identity. *Mind* 106: 499–519.

Millikan, R. (1998) A Common Structure for Concepts for Individuals, Stuffs, and Basic Kinds: More Mama, More Milk, and More Mouse. *Behavioral and Brain Sciences* 22: 55–65.

Millikan, R. (2000) *On Clear and Confused Ideas.* Cambridge: Cambridge University Press.

Moore, J. (1999) Saving Substitutivity in Simple Sentences. *Analysis* 59: 91–105.

Morgan, D. (2011) *First Person Thinking.* Ph.D. dissertation, University of Oxford.

Murez, M. (2009) Mental Files and Coreference. Part 2 of his *Self-Location without Mental Files*, pp. 47–78. Paris: Institut Jean-Nicod.

Murez, M. (2011) Mental Files and the Dynamics of Identity. MS.

Neale, S. (1990) *Descriptions.* Cambridge, Mass.: MIT Press/Bradford Books.

Ninan, D. (2008) *Imagination, Content, and the Self.* Ph.D. dissertation, MIT.

Ninan, D. (2010) *De Se* Attitudes: Ascription and Communication. *Philosophy Compass* 4: 1–16.

Ninan, D. (forthcoming) Self-Location and Other-Location.

Nuccetelli, S. (ed.) (2003) *New Essays on Semantic Externalism and Self-Knowledge.* Cambridge, Mass.: MIT Press/Bradford Books.

Owens, J. (1990) Cognitive Access and Semantic Puzzle. In C. A. Anderson and J. Owens (eds.) *Propositional Attitudes*, pp. 147–73. Stanford, Calif.: CSLI.

Papineau, D. (2006) Phenomenal and Perceptual Concepts. In T. Alter and S. Walter (eds.) *Phenomenal Concepts and Phenomenal Knowledge: New Essays on Consciousness and Physicalism*, pp. 111–44. New York: Oxford University Press.

Peacocke, C. (1975) Proper Names, Reference, and Rigid Designation. In S. Blackburn (ed.) *Meaning, Reference and Necessity*, pp. 109–32. Cambridge: Cambridge University Press.

Peacocke, C. (1981) Demonstrative Thoughts and Psychological Explanation. *Synthese* 49: 187–217.

Peacocke, C. (1983) *Sense and Content*. Oxford: Clarendon Press.

Peacocke, C. (2012) Subjects and Consciousness. In A. Coliva (ed.) *The Self and Self-Knowledge*, pp. 74–101. Oxford: Oxford University Press.

Peirce, C. S. (1967a) *Exact Logic: Collected Papers*, vol. iii. Third printing, Cambridge, Mass.: The Belknap Press of Harvard University Press.

Peirce, C. S. (1967b) *The Simplest Mathematics: Collected Papers*, vol. iv. Third printing, Cambridge, Mass.: The Belknap Press of Harvard University Press.

Pérez Otero, M. (2006) *Esbozo de la filosofía de Kripke*. Barcelona: Editorial Montesinos.

Perini-Santos, E. (2006) Perceptual Modes of Presentation and the Communication of *De Re* Thoughts. *Facta Philosophica* 8: 23–40.

Perner, J. and Brandl, J. (2005) File Change Semantics for Preschoolers: Alternative Naming and Belief Understanding. *Interaction Studies* 6: 483–501.

Perner, J., Rendl, B., and Garnham, A. (2007) Objects of Desire, Thought, and Reality: Problems of Anchoring Discourse Referents in Development. *Mind and Language* 22: 475–513.

Perry, J. (1980) A Problem about Continued Belief. *Pacific Philosophical Quarterly* 61: 317–32.

Perry, J. (1988) Cognitive Significance and New Theories of Reference. *Noûs* 22: 1–18.

Perry, J. (1993) *The Problem of the Essential Indexical and Other Essays*. New York: Oxford University Press.

Perry, J. (1997) Rip Van Winkle and Other Characters. *European Review of Philosophy* 2: 13–39. Reprinted in Perry 2000: 355–76.

Perry, J. (2000) *The Problem of the Essential Indexical and Other Essays*, expanded edn. Stanford, Calif.: CSLI.

Perry, J. (2001a) *Knowledge, Possibility and Consciousness*. Cambridge, Mass.: MIT Press.

Perry, J. (2001b) *Reference and Reflexivity*. Stanford, Calif.: CSLI Publications.

Perry, J. (2002) *Identity, Personal Identity, and the Self*. Indianapolis: Hackett.

Perry, J. (2006) Stalnaker and Indexical Belief. In J. Thomson and A. Byrne (eds.) *Content and Modality: Themes from the Philosophy of Robert Stalnaker*, pp. 204–21. Oxford: Clarendon Press.

Perry, J. (2012) Thinking about the Self. In J. Liu and J. Perry (eds.) *Consciousness and the Self: New Essays*, pp. 76–100. Cambridge: Cambridge University Press.

Pinillos, A. (2009) *De jure* Coreference and Transitivity. MS.

Pinillos, A. (2011) Coreference and Meaning. *Philosophical Studies* 154: 301–24.

Pollock, J. (2008) Defeasible Reasoning. In J. Adler and L. Rips (eds.) *Reasoning: Studies of Human Inference and its Foundations*, pp. 451–70. Cambridge: Cambridge University Press.

Prior, A. (1959) Identifiable Individuals. *Review of Metaphysics* 12: 521–39. Reprinted in his *Papers on Time and Tense*, pp. 66–77. Oxford: Clarendon Press, 1968.

Prosser, S. (2005) Cognitive Dynamics and Indexicals. *Mind & Language* 20: 369–91.

Putnam, H. (1975) The Meaning of Meaning. In his *Philosophical Papers 2: Mind, Language and Reality*, pp. 215–71. Cambridge: Cambridge University Press.

Pylyshyn, Z. (2003) *Seeing and Visualising*. Cambridge, Mass.: MIT Press/Bradford Books.

Pylyshyn, Z. (2007) *Things and Places: How the Mind Connects to the World*. Cambridge, Mass.: MIT Press/Bradford Books.

Quine, W. v. O. (1960) *Word and Object*. Cambridge, Mass.: The Technology Press of MIT.

Quine, W. v. O. (2000) Response to Recanati. In A. Orenstein and P. Kotatko (eds.) *Knowledge, Language and Logic: Questions for Quine*, pp. 428–30. Dordrecht: Kluwer.

Recanati, F. (1987) Contextual Dependence and Definite Descriptions. *Proceedings of the Aristotelian Society* 87: 57–73.

Recanati, F. (1988) Rigidity and Direct Reference. *Philosophical Studies* 53: 103–17.

Recanati, F. (1989) Referential/Attributive: A Contextualist Proposal. *Philosophical Studies* 56: 217–49.

Recanati, F. (1990) Direct Reference, Meaning, and Thought. *Noûs* 24: 697–722.

Recanati, F. (1993) *Direct Reference: From Language to Thought*. Oxford: Blackwell.

Recanati, F. (1995) The Communication of First-Person Thoughts. In J. Biro and P. Kotatko (eds.) *Frege: Sense and Reference One Hundred Years Later*, pp. 95–102. Dordrecht: Kluwer.

Recanati, F. (1996) Domains of Discourse. *Linguistics and Philosophy* 19: 445–75.

Recanati, F. (1998) Talk about Fiction. *Lingua e Stile* 33: 547–58.

Recanati, F. (2000) *Oratio Obliqua, Oratio Recta*. Cambridge, Mass.: MIT Press/ Bradford Books.

Recanati, F. (2001) Open Quotation. *Mind* 110: 637–87. (Revised version in Recanati 2010b: chapter 7.)

Recanati, F. (2004) *Literal Meaning*. Cambridge: Cambridge University Press.

Recanati, F. (2006a) Indexical Concepts and Compositionality. In M. Garcia-Carpintero and J. Macia (eds.) *Two-Dimensional Semantics*, pp. 249–57. Oxford: Clarendon Press.

Recanati, F. (2006b) Loana dans le métro: Remarques sur l'indexicalité mentale. In S. Bourgois-Gironde (ed.) *Les Formes de l'indexicalité: Langage et pensée en contexte*, pp. 19–34. Paris: Éditions Rue d'Ulm.

Recanati, F. (2007) *Perspectival Thought*. Oxford: Oxford University Press.

Recanati, F. (2008) Open Quotation Revisited. *Philosophical Perspectives* 22: 443–71. (Revised version in Recanati 2010b: chapter 8.)

Recanati, F. (2010a) Singular Thought: In Defence of Acquaintance. In R. Jeshion (ed.) *New Essays on Singular Thought*, pp. 141–89. Oxford: Clarendon Press.

Recanati, F. (2010b) *Truth-Conditional Pragmatics*. Oxford: Oxford University Press.

Recanati, F. (2011) Mental Files and Identity. In A. Reboul (ed.) *Philosophical Papers Dedicated to Kevin Mulligan*. Electronic publication, University of Geneva, Philosophy Department (http://www.philosophie.ch/kevin/festschrift/).

Recanati, F. (2012a) Immunity to Error through Misidentification: What it is and Where it Comes From. In S. Prosser and F. Recanati (eds.) *Immunity to Error through Misidentification: New Essays*, pp. 180–201. Cambridge: Cambridge University Press.

Recanati, F. (2012b) Empty Singular Terms in the Mental-File Framework. In M. Garcia-Carpintero and G. Martì (eds.) *Thinking and Speaking about Nothing*. Oxford: Oxford University Press.

Recanati, F. (forthcoming a) Reference through Mental Files. To appear in C. Penco and F. Domaneschi (eds.) *What Have You Said?* Stanford, Calif.: CSLI.

Recanati, F. (forthcoming b) Perceptual Concepts: In Defence of the Indexical Model. To appear in *Synthese* (special issue edited by J. Åkerman, P. Pagin, and R. van Rooij).

Reichenbach, H. (1947) *Elements of Symbolic Logic*. London: Macmillan.

Reinhart, T. (1981) Pragmatics and Linguistics: An Analysis of Sentence Topics. *Philosophica* 27: 53–94.

Russell, B. (1903) *The Principles of Mathematics*. London: George Allen & Unwin.

Russell, B. (1905) On Denoting. Reprinted in R.M. Harnish (ed.) *Basic Topics in the Philosophy of Language*, pp. 161–73. New York: Harvester Wheatsheaf, 1974.

Russell, B. (1910–11) Knowledge by Acquaintance and Knowledge by Description. *Proceedings of the Aristotelian Society* 11: 108–28.

Russell, B. (1912) *The Principles of Philosophy*. London: Williams and Norgate.

Russell, B. (1956) *Logic and Knowledge: Essays 1901–1950*, ed. R. C. Marsh. London: George Allen & Unwin.

Ryle, G. (1954) *Dilemmas*. Cambridge: Cambridge University Press.

Sainsbury, M. (1979) *Russell*. London: Routledge and Kegan Paul.

Sainsbury, M. (2002) *Departing from Frege*. London: Routledge.

Sainsbury, M. (2005) *Reference without Referents*. Oxford: Clarendon Press.

Sainsbury, M. and Tye, M. (2011) An Originalist Theory of Concepts. *Proceedings of the Aristotelian Society*, Supp. Vol. 85: 101–24.

Sainsbury, M. and Tye, M. (2012) *Seven Puzzles of Thought*. Oxford: Oxford University Press.

Salmon, N. (1986) *Frege's Puzzle*. Cambridge, Mass.: MIT Press/Bradford Books.

Saul, J. (1997) Substitution and Simple Sentences. *Analysis* 57: 102–8.

Saul, J. (2007) *Simple Sentences, Substitution, and Intuitions*. Oxford: Oxford University Press.

Schiffer, S. (1977) Naming and Knowing. *Midwest Studies in Philosophy* 2: 28–41.

Schiffer, S. (1978) The Basis of Reference. *Erkenntnis* 13: 171–206.

Schiffer, S. (1981) Indexicals and the Theory of Reference. *Synthese* 49: 43–100.

Schiffer, S. (1990) The Mode-of-Presentation Problem. In C. A. Anderson and J. Owens (eds.) *Propositional Attitudes*, pp. 249–68. Stanford, Calif.: CSLI.

Schiffer, S. (1995) Review of *Direct Reference*. *Linguistics and Philosophy* 19: 91–102.

Schiffer, S. (1997) Descriptions, Indexicals and Belief Reports: Some Dilemmas. In W. Künne, A. Newen, and M. Anduschus (eds.) *Direct Reference, Indexicality and Propositional Attitudes*, pp. 247–75. Stanford, Calif.: CSLI.

Schlenker, P. (2005) Person and Binding: A Partial Survey. *Italian Journal of Linguistics/Rivista di Linguistica* 16: 155–218.

Schroeter, L. (2007) The Illusion of Transparency. *Australasian Journal of Philosophy* 85: 597–618.

Schroeter, L. (2008) Why Be an Anti-Individualist? *Philosophy and Phenomenological Research* 77: 105–41.

Searle, J. (1983) *Intentionality*. Cambridge: Cambridge University Press.

Segal, G. (2002) Two Theories of Names. In A. O'Hear (ed.) *Logic, Thought and Language*, pp. 75–93. Cambridge: Cambridge University Press.

Stalnaker R. (1970) Pragmatics. *Synthese* 22: 272–89.

Stalnaker, R. (2003) *Ways a World Might Be*. Oxford: Clarendon Press.

Stalnaker, R. (2008) *Our Knowledge of the Internal World*. Oxford: Clarendon Press.

Stanley, J. (2011) *Know How*. Oxford: Oxford University Press.

Strawson, P. (1950) On Referring. *Mind* 59: 320–44. Reprinted in Strawson 1971: 1–27.

Strawson, P. (1952) *Introduction to Logical Theory*. London: Methuen.

Strawson, P. (1961) Singular Terms and Predication. *Journal of Philosophy* 58: 393–412. Reprinted in Strawson 1971: 53–74.

Strawson, P. (1964) Identifying Reference and Truth-Values. *Theoria* 30: 96–118. Reprinted in Strawson 1971: 75–95.

Strawson, P. (1971) *Logico-Linguistic Papers*. London: Methuen.

Strawson P. (1974) *Subject and Predicate in Logic and Grammar*. London: Methuen.

Strawson, P. (1997) *Entity and Identity*. Oxford: Clarendon Press.

Taylor, K. (2003) *Reference and the Rational Mind*. Stanford, Calif.: CSLI.

Torre, S. (2010) Centered Assertion. *Philosophical Studies* 150: 97–114.

Treisman, A. (1988) Features and Objects. *Quarterly Journal of Experimental Psychology* 40: 201–37.

Treisman A. (1992) L'Attention, les traits, et la perception des objets. In D. Andler (ed.) *Introduction aux sciences cognitives*, pp. 153–91. Paris: Gallimard.

Treisman, A. and Schmidt, H. (1982) Illusory Conjunctions in the Perception of Objects. *Cognitive Psychology* 14: 107–42.

Tye, M. (1998) Externalism and Memory. *Proceedings of the Aristotelian Society*, Supp. Vol. 72: 77–94.

Vallduvì, E. (1992) *The Informational Component*. New York: Garland.

Vallduvì, E. (1994) The Dynamics of Information Packaging. In E. Engdahl (ed.) *Integrating Information Structure into Constraint-Based and Categorial Approaches*, pp. 1–27. ESPRIT Basic Research Project 'DYNA', Amsterdam: ILLC.

Vendler, Z. (1967) *Linguistics in Philosophy*. Ithaca, NY: Cornell University Press.

Wikforss, Å. (forthcoming) The Insignificance of Transparency.

Wilson, G. (1978) On Definite and Indefinite Descriptions. *Philosophical Review* 87: 48–76.

Woodfield, A. (1991) Conceptions. *Mind* 100: 547–72.

Wright, C. (2012) Reflections on François Recanati's 'Immunity to Error through Misidentification: What it is and Where it Comes From'. In S. Prosser and F. Recanati (eds.) *Immunity to Error through Misidentification: New Essays*, pp. 247–80. Cambridge: Cambridge University Press.

INDEX